Landscape Protection in International Law

AMY STRECKER

OXFORD
UNIVERSITY PRESS

OXFORD
UNIVERSITY PRESS

Great Clarendon Street, Oxford, OX2 6DP,
United Kingdom

Oxford University Press is a department of the University of Oxford.
It furthers the University's objective of excellence in research, scholarship,
and education by publishing worldwide. Oxford is a registered trade mark of
Oxford University Press in the UK and in certain other countries

First Edition published in 2018

Published in the United States of America by Oxford University Press
198 Madison Avenue, New York, NY 10016, United States of America

British Library Cataloguing in Publication Data
Data available

Library of Congress Control Number: 2018952417

ISBN 978–0–19–882624–8

In memory of my father Charlie, who loved and lived the Irish landscape.

Series Editor's Preface

A fascinating aspect of international cultural heritage law is its ability constantly to expand its scope and pervade other fields of international law. This is especially evident with regard to the topic so well addressed by Amy Strecker in this book on the role of international law in the protection of cultural landscapes. Although this subject is a latecomer in the field of cultural heritage law, it has already influenced the normative action and the judicial practice in other fields of international law: human rights, environmental law, international economic law, just to mention the areas most directly affected. And yet, in spite of this growing relevance and influence, the adoption of a specific normative instrument of universal application on landscape has so far eluded the international community. The only legally binding instruments dealing with cultural landscape protection are the 1972 World Heritage Convention—which covers cultural landscapes as part of cultural heritage by way of expansive interpretation of its original text—and the 2000 Council of Europe Convention on European Landscape. Both these instruments are limited in scope since the first deals only with landscapes of 'outstanding universal value' and the second is confined only to the geographic area of Europe.

This book contributes to filling this gap in the international legal framework for landscape protection in international law. It provides a compelling argument in support of a progressive approach to the international protection of landscape at a time when the consumption of the land and the incessant deterioration of the environment caused by industrialisation, construction, and desertification have profound impacts, not only on the physical elements of the territory, but also on the socio-cultural fabric of national societies and local communities, often with the effect of adulterating the sense of place and belonging of people. The evolving legal framework for the protection of landscape—rural and urban—is carefully reconstructed by the author, pointing out the positive normative developments, the emerging judicial and arbitral practice that, especially in the field of human rights and investment law, now consider respect and protection of cultural landscape as legitimate aims that may limit the economic freedoms and property rights otherwise protected under national and international law. The implication of the approach is the idea that in the context of globalisation state sovereignty should not be understood any longer as unfettered dominion of every state over the physical space included in the national boundaries: rather, like property in domestic law, territorial sovereignty should be conceived in a functional perspective as a bundle of powers to be exercised in view of the attainment of the general interest of the international community, which includes the respect of human rights, the protection of the environment and the respect for the most significant manifestations of the cultural heritage of peoples. It is in this perspective of 'responsible' sovereignty that the thesis brings an innovative message that landscape must be protected not only because of its natural and aesthetic value, but also because it is the public space indispensable for the performance of associated life, the unifying element for people of different origin and social status, and thus a guarantee of equality and of continuity between present and future generations.

Francesco Francioni and Ana F. Vrdoljak

Acknowledgements

Many people have contributed consciously or unconsciously to this book. First and foremost, I thank Francesco Francioni, who supervised the PhD thesis on which it is based. For his continued support and masterful guidance from my time as a PhD researcher at the EUI in Florence until now, I am most grateful. I am also extremely grateful to Ana Vrdoljak for her wonderful encouragement over the years, as well as her contagious sense of humour.

Thank you to the other people who gave their time in reading parts, or all, of this book, or who contributed in other ways through discussion and inspiration: Michael Jones, Federico Lenzerini, Bruno de Witte, Jimmy Dunne (†), Riccardo Priore, Bas Pedroli, Conor Newman, my colleagues at Leiden University: Willem Willems (†), Ian Lilley, Maarten Jansen, Mara de Groot, Mariana Françozo, Jimmy Mans, and Manuel May Castillo, as well as the former members of the EUI Working Group on Cultural Heritage: Alessandro Chechi, Andrzej Jakubowski, Lucas Lixinski, Adriana Bessa, Jeanne-Marie Panayoutoupolos, and Robert Peters.

A special thanks to the team at Oxford University Press and to the anonymous reviewers of my book manuscript, whose time and feedback are much appreciated.

Lastly, and most importantly, I thank my family in Ireland: my father Charlie, who sadly died in October 2017 after a short but tough battle with cancer, was very much looking forward to seeing this in print, and this book is dedicated to his memory. I thank my mother Claire, my aunt Bernie, Jenny, Martin, and my own family in Leiden, Irial and Laragh, for their infinite support and sustenance.

Contents

Table of Cases

INTERNATIONAL AND EUROPEAN

African Commission on Human and Peoples' Rights

European Commission on Human Rights

European Court of Human Rights

European Court of Justice

Table of Legislation

ORGANIZATION OF AMERICAN STATES

SECRETARIAT OF THE ANTARCTIC TREATY

SECRETARIAT OF THE CONVENTION ON BIOLOGICAL DIVERSITY

UNITED NATIONS

UNITED NATIONS ECONOMIC COMMISSION FOR EUROPE

UNITED NATIONS ENVIRONMENTAL PROGRAMME

UNITED NATIONS EDUCATIONAL SCIENTIFIC AND CULTURAL ORGANISATION

WORLD TRADE ORGANIZATION

List of Abbreviations

ACHR	American Convention on Human Rights
ACmHPR	African Commission on Human and Peoples' Rights
BIT	Bilateral Investment Treaty
CAHMIN	Committee for the Protection of National Minorities of the Council of Europe
CBD	Convention on Biological Diversity
CDPATEP	Steering Committee for Cultural Heritage and Landscape
CEMAT	Council of Europe Congress of Ministers for Spatial/Regional Planning
CLRAE	Congress of Local and Regional Authorities of Europe
CoE	Council of Europe
EC	European Communities
ECHR	European Convention on Human Rights
ECJ	European Court of Justice
ECtHR	European Court of Human Rights
EIA	Environmental Impact Assessment
EIS	Environmental Impact Statement
ELC	European Landscape Convention
ESCR	Economic, Social, and Cultural Rights
EU	European Union
GATT	General Agreement on Tariffs and Trade
IACtHR	Inter-American Court of Human Rights
IACHR	Inter-American Commission on Human Rights
ICCPR	International Covenant on Civil and Political Rights
ICCROM	International Council for the Conservation and Restoration of Monuments
ICESCR	International Covenant on Economic, Social, and Cultural Rights
ICJ	International Court of Justice
ICOMOS	International Council of Monuments and Sites
ICSID	International Centre for the Settlement of Investment Disputes

IFLA	International Federation of Landscape Architects
IUCN	International Union for the Conservation of Nature
MAB	Man and Biosphere Programme
NAFTA	North American Free Trade Agreement
NGO	Non-Governmental Organization
OECD	Organization for Economic Co-operation and Development
RECEP/ENELC	European Network of Local and Regional Authorities for the Implementation of the European Landscape Convention
TFEU	Treaty Establishing the European Community
UDHR	United Nations Declaration of Human Rights
UN	United Nations
UNCLOS	United Nations Convention on the Law of the Sea
UNCTAD	United Nations Conference on Trade and Development
UNEP	United Nations Environment Programme
UNESCO	United Nations Educational, Scientific, and Cultural Organization
UNISCAPE	European Network of Universities for the Implementation of the European Landscape Convention
WHC	World Heritage Convention
WTO	World Trade Organization

Ill fares the land, to hast'ning ills a prey
Where wealth accumulates, and men decay

—Oliver Goldsmith, 'The Deserted Village', 1769

Abraham Bosse

frontispiece to Thomas Hobbes' *Leviathan*, 1651

1
Introduction

[T]he word landscape was, historically, a thoroughly humanized word[1]

The above epigraph refers to a time, long before the Industrial Revolution, when 'landscape' stood as much for a people—their customs, laws, and institutions—as for a natural unit.[2] Kenneth Olwig has shown how 'the identification of country as polity characterised by a socially constituted political landscape became subordinated, in many ways, to the idea of country as scenic physical landscape'.[3] This scenic conceptualization of landscape extended beyond the domain of nation-state imagery into law-making. Many early national laws focused on the 'beauty' and 'character' of landscapes and sites.[4] This was also the case in the first international instruments dealing with landscape protection.[5] Landscape was often conceived as a static or bucolic entity, not as something socially and culturally dynamic. However, the legal conception of landscape in international law began to change towards the end of the twentieth century, particularly since the 1990s, when World Heritage categories were broadened to include the listing of 'cultural landscapes' within the scope of the World Heritage Convention.[6] 'Cultural landscapes'

[1] Yi Fu Tuan, 'Foreword', in Kenneth Olwig (ed.), *Landscape, Nature and the Body Politic: From Britain's Renaissance to America's New World* (University of Wisconsin Press, 2002), xix.

[2] Ibid.

[3] Kenneth Olwig, 'Introduction', in Kenneth Olwig (ed.), *Landscape, Nature and the Body Politic: From Britain's Renaissance to America's New World* (University of Wisconsin Press, 2002), xxxii.

[4] For example, the Belgian Law of 12 August 1911 on the 'Conservation of the Beauty of Landscapes' and the 1916 Spanish *Ley de Parques Nacionales*, which refers to 'remarkable natural landscapes'. The 1947 Italian Constitution refers to the 'safeguarding of the landscape and the cultural and artistic heritage of the nation' (Article 9). The German Constitution of 1949 mentions landscape alongside nature protection, as does the 1874 Swiss Constitution (Article 24).

[5] See, for example, the UNESCO Recommendation on the Beauty and Character of Landscapes and Sites, 11 December 1962.

[6] On 27 March 1992, at its sixteenth session, the *Operational Guidelines* incorporating the categories of Cultural Landscapes were adopted by the World Heritage Committee. Decision 16COM XIII. 1–3.

were intended to give recognition to the intangible and associative values attached to certain landscapes, to sustainable agricultural practices, and to 'people and communities'—essentially, the human dimension of landscape.[7] This conceptual shift came full circle with the adoption of the European Landscape Convention in 2000.[8] The European Landscape Convention conceives of landscape above all as a people's landscape, and accordingly, provides for the active participation of the public in the formulation of landscape plans and polices.[9] It focuses not only on outstanding landscapes, but also on the everyday and degraded landscapes where most people live and work.[10] The transformation of the concept of landscape from certain areas of conservation to the territory as a whole brings landscape closer to its earlier etymological origins (in Germanic and Latin) when it corresponded to a 'close-up' perspective: the territory of a small community.[11] Olwig's work shows that early conceptions of landscape were closely tied to notions of community justice and custom.[12] At the institutional level, landscape has once again become 'humanized', which in turn has implications for human rights and democracy.

Since the adoption of the European Landscape Convention in 2000, there has been a burgeoning amount of literature relating to landscape from a variety of disciplines.[13] However, in the realm of legal analysis there has been comparatively scarce investigation.[14] This may be because the vast complexities of

[7] Mechtild Rössler has defined the opening of the World Heritage List to cultural landscapes as a shift towards 'people and communities'. Mechtild Rössler, 'World Heritage Cultural Landscapes: A UNESCO Flagship Programme 1992–2006', *Landscape Research*, 31 (4) (2006) 333–53.

[8] Council of Europe, European Landscape Convention, 20 October 2000, ETS No. 176. Since August 2016, the ELC has been officially renamed the 'Council of Europe Landscape Convention'. See the Protocol amending the European Landscape Convention, Strasbourg, 01/08/2016, CETS No. 219. As stated in the protocol, the aim of this amendment is essentially to promote European co-operation with non-European states wishing to implement the provisions of the Convention. It will be referred to for the remainder of this book as the European Landscape Convention (ELC).

[9] Arts 5(c) and 6.

[10] Article 2 states 'this Convention applies to the entire territory of the Parties and covers natural, rural, urban and peri-urban areas. [. . .] It concerns landscapes that might be considered outstanding as well as everyday or degraded areas'.

[11] For a more detailed etymology, see Chapter 2.

[12] Kenneth Olwig, 'Recovering the Substantive Nature of Landscape', *Annals of the Association of American Geographers*, 86 (1996) 630–53.

[13] A small sample includes, for example, Michael Jones and Marie Senseke (eds), *The European Landscape Convention: The Challenges of Public Participation* (Springer, 2011); Bas Pedroli and Tessa Goodman (eds), *Landscape as a Project* (Melfi, 2010); Michael Jones, 'The European Landscape Convention and Questions of Public Participation', *Landscape Research*, 32 (5) (2007) 613–33. Bas Pedroli et al. (eds), *Europe's Living Landscapes: Essays Exploring our identity in the Countryside* (KNNV, 2007); UNISCAPE, 'Living Landscape. The European Landscape Convention in Research Perspective', Proceedings of the Conference in Florence, 18–20 October 2010, 2 Volumes (Bandecchi and Vivaldi, 2010).

[14] With the exception of the research group based at the Norwegian Academy of Science and Letters, who have produced some insightful interdisciplinary work on the interplay between

landscape lie outside the remit of law in the fields of agricultural policy, urban and spatial planning, landscape architecture, ecology, or external forces such as climate change and migration. Or it may be due to the fact that landscape is problematic from a legal perspective. Of course, real changes in the landscape can only be brought about through real changes in society. However, the primary interest for the purposes of this analysis is the role of law as an instrument of landscape protection. As noted by Michael Jones, 'law and landscape are in turn both shaped by conceptions of justice, as well as by contestations over what is considered just and unjust in different societies'.[15] How does international law, which deals for the most part with universality, deal with something so region-specific and particular as landscape? What is the legal conception of landscape and what are the various roles played by international law in its protection? Given the ever-increasing assertion of a 'right to landscape', what is the exact nature of the relationship between landscape and human rights? This book aims to answer these questions.

To date, there has been no volume solely dedicated to the protection of landscape in international law and none that examines the interplay between landscape and contemporary international human rights law, which is one of the aims of the present analysis. Perhaps the most comprehensive text concerning landscape's conceptual shift and its link to human rights and social justice is Shelley Egoz, Jala Makhzoumi, and Gloria Pungetti's edited collection *The Right to Landscape: Contesting Landscape and Human Rights*.[16] However, while providing an innovative collection by some of the most eminent landscape scholars from cultural geography and other disciplines, only three chapters in the volume provide a legal perspective, including a chapter by this author on the right to landscape in international law.[17] Cultural geographers such as Kenneth Olwig and Michael Jones have produced pioneering work on the origins, meaning, and theory of landscape as it relates to law and justice,[18] and public participation in landscape

landscape, law, and justice. See, for example, Michael Jones (ed.) 'Essays on Landscape, Law and Justice', *Norwegian Journal of Geography*, 60 (1) (2016); Tina Peil and Michael Jones (eds), *Landscape, Law and Justice* (Novus, 2005). Other commentary on the European Landscape Convention includes Karsten Jorgensen et al. (eds), *Mainstreaming Landscape through the European Landscape Convention* (Routledge, 2016); Council of Europe, *Paysage et Développement Durable, les Enjeux de la Convention Européenne du Paysage* (Council of Europe Publishing, 2006).

[15] Michael Jones, 'Landscape, Law and Justice—Concepts and Issues', *Norwegian Journal of Geography*, 60 (1) (2016) Special Issue: Essays on Landscape, Law and Justice (ed.) Michael Jones.

[16] Shelley Egoz et al. (eds), *The Right to Landscape: Contesting Landscape and Human Rights* (Ashgate, 2011).

[17] Amy Strecker, 'The Right to Landscape in International Law', in ibid, 57–71.

[18] See, for example, Olwig, 'Recovering the Substantive Nature of Landscape' (n 12); Kenneth Olwig, *Landscape, Nature and the Body Politic—From Britain's Renaissance to America's New World* (University of Wisconsin Press, 2002); Kenneth Olwig, 'The Landscape of "Customary" Law Versus

policies.[19] Both authors have made erudite observations on the European Landscape Convention.[20] The European Landscape Convention has also been widely commented on by landscape architects, art historians, ecologists, and planners.[21] More recently, a number of scholars involved in the 'Right to Landscape' initiative have diverted their attention to the links between landscape and democracy, and a conference on the theme was hosted in June 2015 by the Norwegian University of Life Sciences organized by the recently established Centre for Landscape Democracy in Oslo.[22] Again, however, the contribution of legal perspectives within this volume of proceedings is minimal. While it is true that landscape requires more than strict legal approaches, the conceptual convergence of landscape, law, and justice means that law as a discipline can contribute to discussions on landscape governance in a productive way, especially given the expanding normative framework dealing with landscape protection at the international level.

This book is structured as follows: the following chapter (Chapter 2) traces the etymological origins of the term 'landscape', and discusses the theoretical and historical underpinnings of the term. In particular, it discusses how the concept of landscape has evolved from being conceptually dependent upon nature, to a much wider conception of landscape as something socially and culturally produced, and that this social interpretation of landscape brings it closer to its early etymological origins, to what Olwig terms the 'substantive nature' of landscape.[23] Here the relationship between landscape and other related concepts is briefly explored, in particular the relationship between landscape, property, and heritage. Landscape is a major theme in a variety of disciplines, including inter alia, cultural geography, ecology, archaeology,

that of "Natural" Law', *Landscape Research*, 30 (2005) 299–320; Michael Jones, 'The Elusive Reality of Landscape. Concepts and Approaches in Landscape Research', *Norsk Geografisk Tidsskrift*, 45 (1991) 229–44; and Michael Jones, Landscape, Law and Justice. Report. *Annual Report* 2003, 39–62 (Centre for Advanced Study at the Norwegian Academy of Science and Letters, 2003).

[19] Michael Jones, 'The European Landscape Convention and Questions of Public Participation', *Landscape Research*, 32 (5) (2007) 613–33; Michael Jones, et al., 'Rhetoric and Reporting of Public Participation in Landscape Policy', *Journal of Environmental Policy and Planning*, 13 (1) (2011) 23–47.

[20] See, for example, Michael Jones, Peter Howard, Kenneth Olwig, et al. (eds), 'Multiple Interfaces of the European Landscape Convention', *Norwegian Journal of Geography*, 61 (4) (2007) 207–16.

[21] See, for example, UNISCAPE, 'Living Landscape. The European Landscape Convention in Research Perspective' (n 13); Karsten Jorgensen et al. (eds), *Mainstreaming Landscape through the European Landscape Convention* (Routledge, 2016); Michael Jones and Maria Stenseke (eds), *The European Landscape Convention: Challenges of Participation* (Springer, 2011).

[22] Defining Landscape Democracy, International Conference, Centre for Landscape Democracy, Norwegian University of Life Sciences, Oslo, 3–6 June 2015.

[23] Olwig, 'Recovering the Substantive Nature of Landscape' (n 12).

heritage studies, and architecture, each of which place different emphasis on different meanings attached to landscape. Some emphasize the importance of the past (archaeology), while others place importance on the future (architecture, design, and planning); some disciplines focus on the environmental aspects of landscape (ecology) and others on social justice dimensions (cultural geography, landscape architecture). For these reasons, landscape has been termed a 'chaotic concept'.[24] Jones nevertheless notes that one person's chaotic concept might be another person's or group's 'cherished concept'.[25]

Bearing this in mind, how can public policy and law equitably deal with the issue of landscape protection, and what exactly is meant by the term 'protection'? This is an important issue and only seems overwhelming if we conceive of landscape as 'everything' for the purposes of law making. Of course, not everything can or should be 'protected'. According to Lyndel Prott and Patrick O'Keefe in reference to cultural heritage,

> selection should be based on the nature of the material in question, its rarity and significance in illustrating the development of the human condition. On the other hand, the cultural heritage does not consist solely of a few selected objects singled out by national legislation, a notion put forward by some lawyers but at complete variance with that held by cultural experts in the social sciences.[26]

Certain representative landscapes are important because they embody a way of life or a continuous relationship between people and places over a period of time, and as such should be afforded an elevated level of care. This is the first conception of landscape protection referred to in this book. 'Protection' means the protection of the integrity and accessibility of landscapes. It does not imply the 'freezing' of certain places, but could mean the refusal of planning permission for unsuitably large-scale infrastructural projects (such as motorways or hydroelectric dams) in culturally or naturally sensitive areas, or unsustainable tourist developments based on prior impact assessment which demonstrably predicts a negative outcome.

The second conception of 'landscape protection' for the purposes of this analysis is the protection of the rights associated with culture (including custom) and the environment, both substantive and procedural. 'Protection' here means protection of the rights of access, of participation in plans and policies, and of access to justice when abuse of power occurs. Both of these

[24] Jones, 'The Elusive Reality of Landscape' (n 18).

[25] Michael Jones, 'The Concept of Cultural Landscape: Discourse and Narratives', in Palang and Fry (eds), *Landscape Interfaces* (Springer, 2003).

[26] Lyndel V. Prott and Patrick J. O'Keefe, 'Cultural "Heritage" or Cultural "Property"', *International Journal of Cultural Property*, 1 (1) (1992) 309.

conceptions of landscape protection fit with the emerging global vision of landscape described by Lionella Scazzosi:

> There is a significant mainstream convergence towards a global and unitary vision of landscape, i.e. a tendency to integrate nature and culture, a shift in interest from outstanding places of excellence (natural or anthropic) to the whole territory, an assertion of the right to quality in all the living places of the populations who are invited to participate actively in such a process, to try to find adequate instruments for the sustainable management of territorial transformations, aiming at civil and political goals to preserve identity and the specificity of people and places.[27]

Jones points out that in pluralistic understanding, concepts and terms can be expected to change in meaning over time.[28] This is certainly the case with landscape. The normative developments made at the international level since the 1990s, to be discussed in following chapters, have contributed significantly to this conceptual shift. In sum, it is this unitary (but multifaceted) vision of landscape as described by Scazzosi—what I term 'landscape as public space'—that is referred to in this book. While the term 'public space' has been attached to landscape research dealing with urban areas and social justice issues (in particular in the work of Don Mitchell),[29] the term is used here to connote the public interest in landscape as understood in law, as a limiting factor on the unfettered property rights of individuals, the state, or non-state actors. It is also used to underline the socio-cultural dimension to landscape and the elements of use or custom that arise over time, but which may not be the subject of concrete rights set down in law.

Following the conceptual overview of landscape, Chapters 3 through 6 set out the international legal context relevant for the safeguarding of landscape, and the institutional framework for its protection. Indeed, the 'humanization' of landscape protection in international law can be seen as contemporaneous to the humanization of international law itself.[30] This includes the idea that the earth's resources are not 'property'—to be exclusively owned and utilized to the detriment of present and future populations—but public goods, the care of which is in the interest of every state as a member of the international

[27] Lionella Scazzosi, 'Reading and Assessing the Landscape as Cultural and Historical Heritage', *Landscape Research*, 29 (4) (2004) 335–55.

[28] Jones, 'The Concept of Cultural Landscape: Discourses and Narratives' (n 25).

[29] Don Mitchell, *The Right to the City, Social Justice and the Fight for Public Space* (The Guilford Press, 2003); Don Mitchell, 'Introduction: Public Space and the City', *Urban Geography*, 17 (2) (1996) 127–31. Special Issue: Public Space and the City (ed.) Don Mitchell.

[30] 'Humanization' is a term used by authors such as Karen Wellens in *Public Interest Rules of International Law* (Routledge, 2009); Antonio Cancado Trindade, *International Law for Humankind. Toward a New Jus Gentium* (M. Nijhoff, 2010); Antonio Cassese, *International Law* (Oxford University Press, 2005).

community. The World Heritage Convention is discussed in relation to cultural landscapes and is contrasted with the approach of the European Landscape Convention. Both instruments, while complementary to one another, have very different scope, aims, and institutional arrangements. The World Heritage Convention focuses on cultural landscapes of 'outstanding universal value', while the European Landscape Convention focuses on all landscapes, including everyday or degraded ones. Despite the emergent institutional framework for safeguarding the landscape and providing the means for public participation in the planning process, there is no shortage of conflicts between the demands of economic development on the one hand, and landscape and cultural heritage on the other. Yet the narrative of 'conservation versus development' is overly simplistic, and ultimately eschews the fundamental link between human development and the safeguarding of landscape and public space. Given the regional focus of the European Landscape Convention and its link to environmental justice, Chapter 7 of the book discusses the protection of landscapes in EU law, particularly in relation to environmental impact assessment (EIA) and procedural rights. However, while public participation in environmental decision-making (including landscape) is now an established norm, it is not matched by broad access to justice for breaches of the first and second pillars, or when abuse of power occurs.

Since there is no international court for the settlement of cultural heritage or environmental disputes, many tensions are played out in the realm of human rights jurisprudence. Chapters 8 and 9 therefore explore the interplay between human rights and landscape: first, by analysing the substantive rights associated with landscape protection, particularly cultural rights; and second, through analysing the case law of international human rights courts dealing with landscape issues. The relationship between landscape and human rights contains a number of synergies and antagonisms. These include the false dichotomies of 'Indigenous' versus 'Western' notions of landscape, the culture–nature dichotomy and the private right to property versus the public interest in the landscape (non-proprietary interests), as exemplified in a number of cases before the European Court of Human Rights.[31] The reasons for exploring a human rights approach to landscape protection are several, not least because a right to landscape is something that is increasingly being asserted, even though the extent and nature of rights envisaged in such a right are not at all clear. First, human rights mechanisms are increasingly being used as a means for indirectly protecting the natural and cultural environment. This is due, in part, to the absence of other judicial fora for challenging governmental

[31] See Chapter 9 for an in-depth analysis of the case law.

decisions affecting public spaces. In relation to cultural rights, this has been most clearly evidenced at the international level through the jurisprudence of the International Covenant on Civil and Political Rights (ICCPR) Article 27, and its application to the right of Indigenous Peoples to access their culture, as well as the right to property in some cases decided by the Inter-American Court of Human Rights.[32] Second, in relation to the environment, the right of communities and groups to take part in the decisions affecting their environment is recognized in a number of instruments,[33] and in recent years human rights courts have begun to address environmental protection when it is directly linked to the fulfilment of other human rights and freedoms. However, participation does not always have a meaningful impact on policies and decisions approved by the state, nor does it always lead to desirable outcomes. As noted by Conor Gearty, the appeal of a human rights approach lies in its emphasis on 'controlling the abuse of power and its capacity to equip social movements with a language of protest'.[34]

Landscape as a concept combines integrity for physical environments and identity for communities and individuals. In his foreword to a volume on sustainable development and international law, former International Court of Justice Judge Bruno Simma stated that 'major concerns, as well as interests, beget ideas, then concepts, principles and eventually practice of law'.[35] This truism regarding the incremental nature of the progress of ideas and principles must be borne in mind when considering landscape protection in international law.

[32] A number of such cases are discussed in detail in Chapters 8 and 9.

[33] Convention on Access to Information, Public Participation and Access to Justice in Environmental Matters (opened for signature 25 June 1998, entered into force 30 October 2001), 2161UNTS 447; European Landscape Convention (opened for signature 20 October 2000, entered into force March 2004), ETS 176; and more recently, the Framework Convention on the Value of Cultural Heritage for Society (opened for signature 27 October 2005, entered into force 1 December 2009) ETS 199.

[34] Conor Gearty, 'Do Human Rights Help or Hinder Environmental Protection?', *Journal of Human Rights and the Environment*, 1 (1) (2010) 7–22 at 7.

[35] Bruno Simma, 'Foreword', in Nico Schrijver and Freidl Weiss, *International Law and Sustainable Development* (M. Nijhoff, 2004).

2

Conceptualizing Landscape

2.1 Etymological and Epistemological Origins of 'Landscape'

The term 'landscape' has many nuances of meaning, which can be traced to its varying etymological and epistemological origins. According to Wolfgang Haber, the term 'landscape' combines 'land' with a word of ancient German origin, the verb 'scapjan' which means to work, to be busy, to do something creative—mostly with a plan in mind.[1] In this understanding, according to Barbara Bender, landscape meant a sheaf, a patch of cultivated ground, something small-scale that corresponded to a 'peasant's perception'.[2] During the evolution of the Germanic languages, 'scapjan' apparently became 'schaffen' in German. Richard Hartshorne has shown that the German term *Landschaft* was thought to relate to a restricted piece of land, but also a perceived appearance of a piece of land, and in some German contexts, 'a region'.[3] Likewise, according John B. Jackson, landscape signified a tract of land which could be seen at a glance and which could be defined as a unit or territory, often the territory of a small rural community.[4]

Kenneth Olwig has conducted extensive research on the early origins of landscape. In his seminal paper 'Recovering the Substantive Nature of Landscape',[5] Olwig argues that *Landschaft* in fact contained meanings of great significance for the construction of personal, political, and place identity at

[1] See Wolfgang Haber, 'Concept, Origin and Meaning of "Landscape"', in Bernd Von Droste et al. (eds), *Cultural Landscapes of Universal Value: Components of a Global Strategy* (Gustav Fischer Verlag with UNESCO, 1995), 38–42.

[2] Barbara Bender, 'Landscape: Meaning and Action', in Barbara Bender (ed.), *Landscape Politics and Perspectives* (Berg, 1993), 2.

[3] Richard Hartshorne, 'The Nature of Geography: A Critical Survey of Current Thought in Light of the Past', *Association of American Geographers* 29 (3) (1939), 173–412.

[4] John Brinckerhoff Jackson, 'The Vernacular Landscape', in Edmund Charles Penning-Roswell and David Lowenthal (eds), *Landscape Meaning and Values* (Allen & Unwin, 1986), 65.

[5] Kenneth Olwig, 'Recovering the Substantive Nature of Landscape', *Annals of the Association of American Geographers*, 86 (1996), 630–53.

the time it entered the English landscape. In particular, he emphasizes the elements of territory and community, community justice, body politic, and custom as inherently embedded in early landscape (or the Norse conception of *landskapr*),[6] thereby going beyond the territorial and scenic conceptualization that later emerged and illustrating that, in essence, it was customary law that lay at the root of the term. This meaning has some parallels to the Latin etymology of 'landscape' in Italian and French (*paesaggio, paysage*), which contains two parts: *pagus* and *ager*. *Pagus* is the peasant's village and *ager* is the field the peasant population of the village is cultivating. However, during the Renaissance with the rise of the territorial state, the concept of landscape as land and local custom became increasingly subverted in favour of a more scenic, territorial conception. Olwig has shown how the concept of landscape developed from its early connotation of an area belonging to and shaped by a people, to its Renaissance application, meaning such an area depicted in painting.[7] In medieval England, according to Marvin Mikesell, the word denoted a piece of land occupied by a particular group or controlled by a particular lord.[8] By the late nineteenth century, however, it was regarded as a portion of territory that the eye could comprehend in a single view. Landscape's scenic connotations developed in the immediate post-medieval period, when the Dutch *Landschap* painters were exerting their influence. The term came to be associated increasingly with the painting of natural scenery, or a painting of rural surroundings as an idealized picture of nature. At one point, notes Michael Jones, the words 'nature' and 'landscape' became almost synonymous.[9]

The modern definition of 'landscape' offered by the Oxford English Dictionary includes 'all the visible features of an area of land, often considered in terms of their aesthetic appeal' or 'a picture representing an area of countryside' both of which connote essentially a scenic conception.[10] The Cambridge English dictionary defines landscape as 'a large area of countryside, especially in relation to its appearance' as well as 'a view or picture of the countryside, or the art of making such pictures'.[11] Similar definitions of landscape are offered

[6] Ibid, 631.

[7] Kenneth Olwig, *Landscape, Nature and the Body Politic: From Britain's Renaissance to America's New World* (University of Wisconsin Press, 2002).

[8] Marvin Mikesell, 'Landscape', in D. L. Sills (ed.), *International Encyclopaedia of Social Sciences*, 8 (Collier & Macmillan, 1968), 575–80.

[9] Michael Jones, 'The Elusive Reality of Landscape. Concepts and Approaches in Landscape Research', *Norsk Geografisk Tidsskrift*, 45 (1991), 229–44.

[10] 'Landscape'<https://en.oxforddictionaries.com/definition/landscape> accessed 30 December 2017.

[11] 'Landscape' <http://dictionary.cambridge.org/dictionary/british/landscape> accessed 30 December 2017.

by authoritative Spanish, French, and Italian dictionaries. The dictionary of the Real Academia Española, for example, describes landscape as 'part of the territory that can be observed from a single place', 'a natural space admired for its artistic aspects', and also 'a painting or drawing that represents a landscape'.[12] The Académie Française defines landscape as 'the extent of a territory the eye can embrace', a 'tract of land whose appearance is unique to a place, a region that has special characteristics', a 'graphic or pictorial work as a representation or description of natural sites', and also 'a set of phenomena, a combination of elements and facts which lend themselves to observation and reflection'.[13] Only the Italian dictionary offers a physical definition—referring to biological as well as anthropic characteristics—in addition to the more pictorial ones.[14] From this cursory glance at some modern European language definitions, it appears that landscape retains a predominantly scenic, rural connotation. This is one of the reasons why the European Landscape Convention's definition of landscape is so innovative.[15]

2.2 Landscape, Representation, and Power

As evidenced by the modern definitions above, the influence of landscape painting on the development of the concept of landscape cannot be overestimated, especially in Europe. The innovations of perspective introduced by fourteenth- and fifteenth-century Florentine painters laid the foundations for the technical advancement of landscape painting during the Renaissance.[16] While considered an inferior art form during the fifteenth century, some theorists wrote enthusiastic appreciations of the pleasures afforded by landscape

[12] 'Paisaje' <http://lema.rae.es/drae/?val=paisaje> accessed 30 December 2017. 1. Parte de un territorio que puede ser observada desde un determinado lugar. 2 Espacio natural admirable por su aspecto artístico. 3. Pintura o dibujo que representa un paisaje.

[13] 'Paysage' <http://www.la-definition.fr/definition/paysage> accessed 30 December 2017. Etendue d'un territoire que l'œil peut embrasser. Étendue de terrain dont l'aspect est propre à un lieu, a une région, que présente des caractères particuliers. 2. Ouvre graphique ou picturale prenant pour sujet la représentation, la description de sites naturels. 3. Ensemble de phénomènes, combinaison d'éléments, de faits qui s'offre à l'observation, a la réflexion.

[14] 'Paesaggio' <https://www.dizionario-italiano.it/dizionario-italiano.php?parola=paesaggio> accessed 30 December 2017. 1. aspetto di un luogo che si abbraccia con lo sguardo. 2 pitture, fotografia che ha per sogetto un paesaggio. 3. Particolare fisionomia da una regione determinate dale sue characteristiche fisiche, antropiche, biologiche, etniche.

[15] See Chapter 6 for a discussion on the paradigm shift brought about by the ELC.

[16] In particular, Leon Battista Alberti's treatise, *De Pictura* (1435) containing the first scientific study of perspective, and the paintings of Piero della Francesca (c.1415–1492), which were characterized by a serene humanism and which introduced perspective and foreshortening.

scenery for solace and psychological recreation.[17] Throughout the sixteenth century, landscape artists portrayed either pastoral scenes of aristocratic leisure or Georgic landscapes enriched by agricultural activities that the aristocrat could 'observe with satisfaction'.[18] Landscape increasingly became associated with amenity, the derivative of which is the Latin adjective *amoenus*, meaning pleasant.[19] The *locus amoenus* was a phrase used in classical and Renaissance times to designate distinctively beautiful rural or garden retreats.[20] One of the first writers to discuss landscape aesthetics was Giovanni Paolo Lomazzo, who gave an account of different categories of landscape which drew distinctions of importance between 'privileged places' enriched with noble architecture, wild landscapes, forests, rocks and stones, and 'places of delight' with fountains, fields, and gardens.[21] During the eighteenth century, landscape was enriched with new ideals and a new spectrum of taste was developed along the lines of beauty, the sublime, the picturesque, and the neo-Gothic. These ideas, together with the historic-stylistic models such as the classic, the baroque, the rococo, and the romantic, closely connected the idea of landscape with the sentiment of nature. Emphasis was placed on the 'natural' state of landscape—to be discovered, preserved, and to which people were in some way external.[22] Landscape was not seen as something socially or culturally produced. The influence of this 'natural' conceptualization of landscape can be seen in the opening lines of Kenneth Clark's *Landscape into Art* (1949):

> We are surrounded with things which we have not made and which have a life and structure different from our own: trees, flowers, grasses, rivers, hills, clouds. For centuries they have inspired us with curiosity and awe. They have been objects of delight. We have recreated them in our imagination to reflect our moods. And we have come to think of them as contributing to an idea which we have called nature. Landscape painting marks the stages in our conception of nature. Its rise and development since the middle ages is part of a cycle in which the human spirit attempted once more to create harmony with its environment.[23]

[17] Much earlier, the Greeks and Romans had evolved a school of landscape painting of their own. The Greeks had no word for landscape, but used a variety of expressions and terms that revealed a love for nature and the 'spirit of place'. Examples can also be found in the '*beatus vor*' topos in Virgil's (70–19BC) *Georgics*, Horace's (65–8BC) *Epodes*, and Petrarch's meditations on a life of solitude.

[18] Jane Turner, *The Grove Dictionary of Art* (Oxford University Press, 2003) vol. 18, 700.

[19] Malcolm Andrews, *Landscape and Western Art* (Oxford University Press, 1999), 53.

[20] Ibid.

[21] Giovanni Paolo Lomazzo, *Trattato dell'arte della pittura, scoltura, et architettura*, Pietro Tini, Paolo Gottardo da Ponte, 1584.

[22] Tadhg O'Keeffe, 'Landscape and Memory: Historiography, Theory, Methodology', in Yvonne Whelan (ed.), *Heritage, Memory and the Politics of Identity: New Perspectives on the Cultural Landscape* (Ashgate, 2007), 3.

[23] Kenneth Clark, *Landscape into Art* (Murray, 1949), 1.

W. J. T. Mitchell dissects Clarke's words in his book *Landscape and Power*.[24] He points out that the idea of European landscape as being composed of purely natural factors has been made redundant by cultural geographers.[25] He observes that a historical interpretation of these lines reveals another view of the rise of landscape painting, whereby the 'different structure' of nature referred to by Clark is read as a symptom of alienation from the land; the 'rise and development' of landscape is read as a symptom of the rise and development of capitalism, and the harmony sought in landscape is read as compensation for and screening off of the actual violence perpetrated there.[26] This interpretation echoes the work of Dennis Cosgrove, who notes that 'landscape' arises increasingly as land acquires capital value and becomes itself a form of capital—a commodity with little or nothing of the personal value and social meaning it had for those who called it home—and an aesthetic value replaced a use and dependency value.[27] For Christopher Wood 'landscape in the West was itself a symptom of modern loss, a cultural form that emerged only after humanity's primal relationship to nature had been disrupted by urbanism, commerce and technology. For when mankind still "belonged" to nature in a simple way, nobody needed to paint a landscape'.[28] It can be seen from this brief overview that the etymology and representation of landscape are closely tied to the social and cultural circumstances of its development. From this perspective, the rise of landscape painting emerges in a much broader context of cultural changes, such as the growth of interest in empirical science, the pictorial representation of the natural world, and early capitalist attitudes towards the land.[29]

However, landscape is not merely raw material to be represented in paint but is already a symbolic form in its own right. Each landscape has a 'biography'.[30] It is a social construction, both the result of intentional and

[24] William John Thomas Mitchell, 'Imperial Landscape', in William John Thomas Mitchell (ed.), *Landscape and Power* (2nd edn, University of Chicago Press, 2002), 6.

[25] See, for example, Dennis Cosgrove and Stephen Daniels, *The Iconography of Landscape: Essays on the Symbolic Representation, Design, Use of Past Environments* (Cambridge University Press, 1988).

[26] This refers to the Enclosure Movement and the accompanying dispossession of the peasantry that began in the post-medieval period and came to a height across Europe in the eighteenth and nineteenth centuries. Enclosure was the process of enclosing and appropriating land—previously worked and enjoyed by a peasant community in common. Enclosed land became privately owned land; it excluded the interests and access of all but the owner, usually the individual. See, for further discussion, Nicole Graham, *Lawscape. Property, Environment and Law* (Routledge, 2011), especially 51–5.

[27] Dennis Cosgrove, *Social Formation and Symbolic Landscape* (University of Wisconsin Press, 1998), 19.

[28] Christopher Wood, *Albrecht Altdorfer and the Origins of Landscape* (Reakton Books, 1993), 25.

[29] Malcolm Andrews, *Landscape and Western Art* (Oxford University Press, 1999), vol. 10, 51.

[30] Marwyn S. Samuels, 'The Biography of Landscape', in Donald William Meinig (ed.), *The Interpretation of Ordinary Landscapes* (Oxford University Press, 1979), 51–88.

unintentional actions. It is not only as Cosgrove has described it, 'a way of seeing', it is also 'a way of thinking and a way of doing' which involves what David Harvey terms a 'process of creative destruction', sparking opposition from all sorts of different groups.[31] Such an approach to landscape requires the consideration of material and non-material motivations. The Marxist-derived approach to landscape views landscape as essentially social–cultural in its production, with power as its operating system. In this view, landscape is implicated in relations of power through ownership, control, and manipulation by social elites: the non-elite simply 'being reduced to acts of compliance or resistance'.[32]

More recently, as pointed out by Tadhg O'Keefe, landscape theory has taken a counter-Marxian and constructivist turn: landscapes are seen not as a reflection of power (and therefore external to many) but as 'spaces' or 'places' that exist in our cognitive as well as corporeal experiences.[33] For this reason, they have a democratic value, something alluded to by Ralph Waldo Emerson as far back as 1836:[34]

> This charming landscape which I saw this morning is indubitably made up of some twenty or thirty farms. Miller owns this field, Locke that, and Manning the woodland beyond. But none of them owns the landscape. There is a property on the horizon which no man has but he whose eye can integrate all the part, that is, the poet. This is the best part of all these men's farms, yet to this their land-deeds give them no title.[35]

John Barrell has argued that in eighteenth-century Britain, the capacity to read the landscape as a whole, to be able to relate particulars into a comprehensible unity, marked out the 'liberal mind'.[36] As contended by Malcolm Andrews, 'in so far as the representation of panoramic prospects serves as an instantiation of the ability of the man of "liberal mind" to abstract the general from the particular, it was also understood to be an instantiation of the ability to abstract the true interests of humanity, the public interest, from the labyrinth of private interests which were imagined to be represented by mere unorganized detail'.[37] Yet the contradiction inherent here is that Barrell is assessing the credentials of the 'man of taste', and marking out the intellectual

[31] David Harvey, *The Condition of Post-Modernity, An Enquiry into the Origins of Cultural Change* (Blackwell, 1989), 258.

[32] O'Keefe, 'Landscape and Memory: Historiography, Theory, Methodology' (n 22), 3.

[33] Ibid.

[34] Ralph Waldo Emerson, quoted in W. T. J. Mitchell, 'Imperial Landscape' (n 24), 14.

[35] Ibid.

[36] John Barrell, *The Political Theory of Painting from Reynolds to Hazlitt: The Body of the Public* (Yale University Press, 1995).

[37] Andrews, *Landscape and Western Art* (n 19), 51.

ground exclusive to this social categorization. However, he points to an inherent characteristic of landscape: its democratic value. Indeed, landscape has emerged in recent discourse as a sort of corrective to an exclusive, narrow interpretation of property rights.

2.3 Landscape and Property

In a similar way to landscape, the history of the word property illustrates the way in which modern relationships between people and place have changed over time. Indeed, while the terms would appear on the surface to diverge conceptually, on closer inspection, it can be seen that they share a similar trajectory, at least in terms of their historical evolution. Nicole Graham illustrates how the English word 'property' originated via the old French *propreté*, which comes from the Latin word *proprietas* meaning 'proper to', 'one's own', or 'special character'.[38] In *Lawscape*, her study of how property law transforms natural environments and social economies, Graham provides a thoughtful insight into the origins of the term property and how its meaning has shifted over time, from which I will borrow substantially for the purposes of presenting the term's etymological development. The French word 'propre' originally indicated the sense of something 'close or near' and 'in place'. Therefore, to say that 'this is my own' would suggest that it is connected to my identity, that it form part of who I am.[39] The immediate connection between people and things in the Western origin of the concept suggests that property and identity were mutually formative. This relationship between property and identity continued and remained an important one in medieval England and in the early common law view of land. Legal historian David Seipp wrote: '[L]and had significance greater than the sum of its economic production and use value. Land was also an important component of identity.'[40] Seipp found in his archival research that the word property in Anglo–Norman texts from the 1180s to Middle English texts from the 1380s meant an 'attribute' or 'characteristic' of a person or thing. There was a secondary and less-common usage of the word property in medieval English and this was a person's interest in having a thing, 'usually the context of this meaning was religious and the connotation was overwhelmingly negative':

> Dozens of surviving manuscripts from the fourteenth and fifteenth centuries praised monastic establishments for holding all goods in common and shunning 'property'

[38] Graham, *Lawscape. Property, Environment and Law* (n 26), 25. [39] Ibid, 26.

[40] David J. Seipp, 'The Concept of Property in the Early Common Law', *Law and History Review* 12 (1) (1994) 29–91, 49, cited in Graham, ibid.

or condemned them for doing the opposite. To have property of goods (or goods 'in proper') was a sin, and monks guilty of this vice were denounced as 'proprietaries' or 'owners'![41]

Graham rightly notes how today this second usage has become the primary definition of property.[42] In modern usage, the meaning of the word divorces property from identity. Indeed, it denotes the inalienability rather than the mutual identification of the owner and the owned. Property in today's usage refers to an object or thing whose only relationship to the owner is that it is owned. This also illustrates a shift in people–place relations. According to the original sense of property, 'the thing possesses me, I belong to it, and am identified by it'.[43] According to the modern sense of property, argues Graham, I possess the thing, it belongs to me. Graham notes that 'Where place once characterised a person, now place and person are disconnected.'[44] The particular and physical qualities of place have been erased from property relations in legal discourse and replaced with entirely social relationships using a vocabulary of rights. The legal discourse of property rights has come to dominate the cultural discourse of property more generally. (Enter the term 'landscape' as a sort of remedy to this disconnect between people and place.) Yet if one delves deeper into the legal conceptualization of property it becomes clear that property has long been understood to include ideas of trust and duties as well as rights.[45] Discussing eighteenth-century property in England, Robert Gordon wrote:

> What strikes the backward looking observer as curious is simply this: that in the midst of such a lush flowering of absolute dominion talk in theoretical and political discourse, English legal doctrines should contain so very few plausible instances of absolute dominion rights. [...] The real building blocks of eighteenth-century social and economic institutions were [...] property rights fragmented and split among many holders; property rights held and managed collectively; [...] property subject to arbitrary and discretionary direction or destruction; property surrounded by restriction on use and alienation; property qualified and regulated for communal or state purposes. [...][46]

[41] Graham, *Lawscape. Property, Environment and Law* (n 26), 26. [42] Ibid.

[43] Ibid. [44] Ibid.

[45] See Laura S. Underkuffler, *The Idea of Property: Its Meaning and Power* (Oxford University Press, 2003). Carole M. Rose, 'Property as Wealth, Property as Propriety', in John Chapman (ed.), *Nomos XXXIII: Contemporary Justice* (NYU Press, 1991), 223, 232–39. Laura S. Underkuffler, 'On Property: An Essay', *Yale Law Journal*, 100, at 127, reprinted in Elizabeth Mensh and Alan Freeman (eds), *Property Law, International Library of Essays in Law and Legal Theory* (New York University Press, 1992).

[46] Robert Gordon, 'Paradoxical Property', in John Brewer and Susan Staves (eds), *Early Modern Conceptions of Property* (Routledge, 1996), 95–6.

One could echo Gordon's observation regarding property today. As observed by some authors:

> today the concept of property in land may well denote no more than a temporarily licensed form of utility or user privilege which may be extended, varied, or withdrawn at the sole discretion of the state and on terms dictated by it. [...] so distant is this perception from the classical liberal image of property as a self-interested claim of unfettered power that some American commentators have begun to predict a wholesale reconstruction of property in terms of 'socially derived' privileges of use.[47]

Environmental laws, planning, and zoning regulations, endangered species laws, historic preservation, and cultural heritage laws have overwhelmed traditional ideas about what property is and the extent to which it should be protected. Even the right to property as conceived in human rights instruments has limitations in the general interest in a democratic society, which interestingly often takes the form of landscape protection safeguards. It is the link between landscape and identity (something no longer fulfilled by property) that lends landscape its heritage value, and which has generated an oppositional relationship between the two concepts.

2.4 Landscape, Heritage, Commons

According to Yi-Fu Tuan, landscape is a sector of reality 'out there'. 'It is made up of fields and buildings, yet it is not a bounded entity in the same way as tree or a building. Landscape, in the same way as culture, is elusive and difficult to describe in a phrase.'[48] As noted by David Lowenthal, 'landscape is all-embracing—it includes virtually everything around us—and has manifest significance for everyone'.[49] In Lowenthal's words, landscape emerges as a 'significant component of the overall heritage which endows communities and nations with their identity'.[50] Lowenthal considers that 'awareness of the past is essential to the maintenance of purpose in life. Without it we would lack all sense of continuity, all apprehension of causality, all knowledge of our own identity'.[51] In a similar line, Simon Schama in his much-cited *Landscape*

[47] Kevin Gray and Susan Francis Gray, 'The Idea of Property in Land', in Susan Bright and John Dewar (eds), *Land Law: Themes and Perspectives* (Oxford University Press, 1998), 15, 41, 43.

[48] Yi-Fu Tuan, 'Thought and Landscape', in Donald W. Meinig (ed.), *The Interpretation of Ordinary Landscapes* (n 30), 89.

[49] David Lowenthal, 'Introduction', in Penning-Roswell and Lowenthal (eds), *Landscape Meaning and Values* (n 4), 1.

[50] David Lowenthal, 'Age and Artefact. Dilemmas of Appreciation', in Meinig (ed.), *The Interpretation of Ordinary Landscapes* (n 30), 103.

[51] Ibid.

and Memory states that inherited landscape myths and memories share two common characteristics: 'their surprising endurance through the centuries and their power to shape institutions that we still live with'.[52] National identity would lose much of its potency without the mystique of a particular landscape tradition.[53] Some historians and theologians have focused on the associative and emotive significance of landscape, articulated in terms of memory, identity, and a sense of place.[54] Indeed 'place' has become a significant theme in a range of disciplines, partly reflecting the so-called 'crisis of place' in Western societies—a sense of rootlessness, dislocation, or displacement, the root of which lies in the perceived decline of values and symbols.[55]

> The acceleration of history: let us try to gauge the significance, beyond metaphor, of this phrase. An increasingly rapid slippage of the present into a historical past that is gone for good, a general perception that anything and everything may disappear—this indicates a rupture of equilibrium.[56]
>
> Pierre Nora, *Les Lieux de Mémoire*, 1989

The term *lieu de memoire* attempts to encapsulate this, as well as 'place'—that an essential ingredient of a cultural landscape must be a strong personal element, something that cannot be measured.[57] Graham Fairclough notes that such attitudes tend not to be a part of European landscape tradition in the same way as they are in indigenous contexts.[58] Yet, this does not detract from this kind of landscape. Former IUCN Chair Adrian Philips articulated this well when he stated that

> landscape is both physical and metaphysical, with social, cultural and artistic associations. While landscape is how we see the world, it is thus more than mere scenery and appearance. We take it in with all our senses. While we can experience landscape only in the present, it is the sum of all past changes to the environment; it is where past and present meet; landscape gives identity to place, and hence diversity to the setting of our lives.[59]

[52] Simon Schama, *Landscape and Memory* (HarperCollins, 1995), 15. [53] Ibid.

[54] See, for example, Phillip Sheldrake, *Spaces for the Sacred, Place, Memory and Identity* (John Hopkins, 2001), Pierre Nora, 'Between Memory and History: Les Lieux de Mémoire', *Representations*, (Spring 1989), 7–24, and Schama, *Landscape and Memory* (n 52).

[55] Sheldrake, *Spaces for the Sacred, Place, Memory and Identity* (n 54), 3.

[56] Nora, 'Between Memory and History: Les Lieux de Mémoire', (n 54), 7.

[57] Graham Fairclough, 'Archaeologists and the European Landscape Convention', in Graham Fairclough and Stephen Rippon (eds), *Europe's Cultural Landscape: Archaeologists* and *the Management of Change* (EAC Occasional Paper 2, 2003), 33.

[58] Ibid.

[59] Adrian Philips, 'Practical Considerations for the Implementation of the European Landscape Convention', in IUCN, *Landscape Conservation Law, Present Trends and Perspectives in International and Comparative Law*, Environmental Policy and Law Paper No. 39 (Island Press, 2000), 18.

He also argued that landscape is much more likely to concern the man in the street or the woman in the field, than is biodiversity, and hence alluded to its democratic nature. As pointed out by Lowenthal, explicit or implicit in every people's favoured heritage are geographical traits felt integral to national identity. Countries commonly depict themselves in landscape terms. Landscapes have much in common, but each country values certain geographical features and elements of its own. Lowenthal notes that such criteria were once felt to be tainted by a geographical determinism that left inhabitants helpless to shape their own destinies. National patriotism traditionally reduced regional and local identities. Indeed, up until quite recently, it was widely felt that in Europe, landscape regulation and methodology were largely top-down, if not bureaucratic or mechanistic, and mainly concerned with scientific and expert views.[60]

Landscape also converges conceptually with the concept of 'commons'[61] which, conceived broadly, refers to shared natural and cultural resources which everyone has equal access to, but which no one can privately own. While Garrett Hardin predicted that the commons were doomed to failure in his famous essay 'The Tragedy of the Commons' in 1968,[62] Elinor Ostrom has shown that commons, if martialled successfully, can in fact lead to sustainable economic and social development.[63] The communitarian element to commons is aligned somewhat to the communitarian dimension of heritage (particularly since the concept of heritage has developed to reflect a more dynamic notion, one that incorporates intangible associations and emphasizes the interaction and relationships between people and place). Landscape and commons are aligned in the sense that they both represent an alternative relationship to land than one of private property (community forests are one such example). Heritage protection measures can help to protect commons, but they can also do the opposite when measures by the state to preserve a landscape interfere with commons based on collective use of lands. In 'Revisting the Commons', Ostrom et al. show how both privatization and

[60] Fairclough, 'Archaeologists and the European Landscape Convention', (n 57), 33.

[61] See, for example, Kenneth Olwig, 'Commons and Landscape', in Erling Berge and Lars Carlsson (eds), *Commons: Old and New: On Environmental Goods and Services in the Theory of Commons. Landscape, Law and Justice. Proceedings from a Workshop on Old and New Commons* (Centre for Advanced Study, Oslo, 2003), 15–22. Bas Pedroli, Saša Dobričič, and Amy Strecker, 'Common Goods from a Landscape Perspective', *I Quaderni di Careggi*, vol. 6:6 (2014), UNISCAPE.

[62] Garrett Hardin, 'The Tragedy of the Commons', *Science*, New Series, vol. 162, No. 3859 (1968), 1243–8.

[63] Elinor Ostrom, *Governing the Commons, The Evolution of Institutions for Collective Action* (Cambridge University Press, 1990).

government ownership can lead to more landscape degradation than community held common property regimes.[64]

The concept of 'common good' is another question, as it represents the common good as decided by the state. Yet deciding what constitutes 'common good' or public interest is an ideological question, which might be beneficial to one social group but detrimental to another.[65] This is particularly interesting when analysing the case law of human rights courts where the issue of landscape protection emerges as a legitimating factor impinging on other human rights general interest, yet this is an 'authorized' notion of common good, one that relates more to scene than to use or custom.[66]

2.5 The Culture–Nature Dichotomy

> When we say nature, do we mean to include ourselves?[67]
>
> Raymond Williams

Landscape had been the focus of ecology and other natural sciences since the beginning of the nineteenth century. It was the German geographer and biologist Alexander von Humboldt who first coined the scientific definition of landscape as a 'total character of a region of the earth'.[68] The term 'landscape ecology' was first employed in 1939 by Carl Troll, another German scholar.[69] Troll conceived a mosaic-like composition of the landscape and insisted on its anthropogenic components. Indeed, Troll's conception of landscape as anthropogenic was a precursor to the conception of landscape to occur much later in the social sciences. As Schama points out, 'even the landscapes that we supposed to be most free of our culture may turn out, on closer inspection, to be its product'.[70] The Dobris Assessment noted that this is particularly the case in Europe, where 'there are practically no areas that can be considered "natural" in the sense that there is no human influence whatsoever'.[71]

[64] Elinor Ostrom, et al. 'Revisiting the Commons: Local Lessons, Global Challenges', *Science*, 284 (1999), 278–82.

[65] Alan Hewitt, 'Privatizing the Public: Three Rhetorics of Art's Public Good in "Third Way" Cultural Policy', *Art & the Public Sphere*, (January 2011), 19–36.

[66] See the discussion on the case law of the European Court of Human Rights in Chapter 9.

[67] Raymond Williams, 'Ideas of Nature', *Problems in Materialism and Culture* (Verso Books, 1980), 67.

[68] See Wolfgang Haber, 'Concept, Origin and Meaning of "Landscape"', in Von Droste et al. *Cultural Landscapes of Universal Value* (n 1), 39.

[69] Ibid. [70] Schama, *Landscape and Memory* (n 52), 9.

[71] David Stanners and Philippe Bordeau, *Europe's Environment: The Dobris Assessment* (European Environment Agency, 1995), Chapter 8.

The term 'cultural landscape' was first employed by geographer Carl Sauer (1889–1975), who, in his much cited paper 'The Morphology of Landscape', stated that the 'cultural landscape is fashioned from a natural landscape by a culture group. Culture is the agent, the natural area the medium, the cultural landscape the result.'[72] Sauer and the Berkeley school were to influence other scholars such as John B. Jackson, whose conception of landscape was deeply humanistic. Jackson believed that landscapes should not just be viewed or preserved for purely aesthetic reasons, but in order to understand, experience, and appreciate landscapes in living terms.[73] Knut Faegri expanded on this viewpoint in the preface to an international symposium entitled 'The Cultural Landscape–Past, Present and Future', held in Norway in 1986.[74] In origin, the cultural landscape was the antithesis of unspoilt nature. However, modern attempts to protect untouched nature revealed that virgin landscapes were a fiction. The ensuing vegetation growth in protected areas showed that almost all landscapes are created or modified to varying degrees by humans.[75] As a physical category, cultural landscape is difficult to delimit, since all landscapes are bearers of culture.[76] Landscape is a complex phenomenon, understood differently by different disciplines.[77] In particular, the perception of the cultural landscape in the natural sciences diverges from that in the humanities.[78] For the former, the cultural landscape requires physical traces of human activity and the evolution of particular places in response to demographic and economic pressures. For the latter, people's mental perceptions of cultural landscapes are more significant. Tim Ingold disputes the notion of landscape as a datum of cultural and symbolic nature, separating the mental and material worlds.[79] He proposes instead a temporality of landscape that incorporates processes of social life as part of a dynamic process, of continuous exploitation. Ingold sees cultural landscape as stemming from what he terms 'taskscape'—a series of cyclical, interconnected processes, constituents of the landscape. 'Just as landscape is an array of related features,

[72] Carl Sauer as quoted by John Aitchison in B. Von Droste et al., *Cultural Landscapes of Universal Value* (n 1), 274.

[73] Ibid.

[74] Knut Fraegri. 'Preface', in Hilary H. Birks, H. J. B Birks, Peter Emil Kaland, and Dagfinn Moe (eds), *The Cultural Landscape–Past, Present and Future* (Cambridge University Press, 1988), 1.

[75] Ibid.

[76] See Michael Jones, 'The Elusive Reality of Landscape', in J. M. Fladmark, *Heritage: Conservation, Interpretation, Enterprise* (Donhead, 1993), 18.

[77] Ibid.

[78] Paul Claval, 'Changing Conceptions of Heritage and Landscape', in Whelan (ed.), *Heritage, Memory and the Politics of Identity* (n 22), 90.

[79] Tim Ingold, 'The Temporality of the Landscape', *World Archaeology*, 25 (2) (1993), 152–174.

so—by analogy—the taskscape is an array of related activities.'[80] His taskscape is typically analysed in five ways: mobility, habitat, economy, nature, and public space.

Alexandru Calcatinge points out that the terms 'cultural landscape' and 'landscape' have become almost synonymous, especially in academic literature, acknowledging that the whole landscape has cultural significance.[81] Jeffrey Blankenship argues that the cultural landscape idea emerged as a refuge for the diminished landscape idea (as theorized by Cosgrove).[82] As argued in the following pages, landscape has once again emerged as the preferred concept, with links to human rights, democracy, and public space. In subsequent chapters, when referring to landscape, it is understood to include cultural landscape, without explicitly making the distinction.

[80] Ibid.

[81] Alexandru Calcatinge, *The Need for a Cultural Landscape Theory: An Architect's Approach* (LIT Verlag, 2012), 73.

[82] Jeffrey D. Blankenship, *Reading 'Landscape': Mid-Century Modernism and the Landscape Idea* (UMass, 2011), 324.

3

Landscape and International Law

3.1 The Role of Law in Landscape Protection

National policies aimed directly at landscape protection tended to be overly conservationist before the mid-twentieth century, and since the 1990s have increasingly adopted a more pragmatic approach involving management, planning, and enhancement—in line with the principles of sustainable development. The antiquated approach often favoured the 'freezing' of landscape areas, which is understandable for places that are relatively untouched by human interference, such as Antarctica, but for most landscapes this is unrealistic, as landscapes themselves are the result of change. Graham Fairclough notes that while we may see the landscape as a construct of perception, intellectuality, and emotion, we know that the landscape has always changed, perhaps more than most perceptions admit, and we therefore accept that the landscape must continue to change.[1] However, we should work to influence and guide that change rather than merely standing by as mute witnesses to it.[2] While a conservationist approach can be indifferent or hostile to economic development, a sustainable development approach allows for a balance of interests. Therefore, any legitimate policy dealing with landscape must attempt to be democratic and take into consideration a number of interest levels (local, national, international) and dimensions (social, cultural, environmental), which is a very complex process. This is where law plays a vital role in landscape protection, and where consideration of other policies not directly aimed at landscape protection can affect a significant impact on the landscape. Salvatore Settis provides an example of just one such negative impact in the Italian context: the Trementi-bis law of 2001,[3] which introduced

[1] Graham Fairclough, 'Europe's Landscape: Archaeology, Sustainability and Agriculture', in Graham. Fairclough and Stephen Rippon (eds), *Europe's Cultural Landscape: Archaeologists and the Management of Change*. EAC Occasional Paper 2 (2003), 4.

[2] Ibid.

[3] Law 383 of 2001, Norme per incentivare l'emersione dell' economia sommersa', as cited in Salvatore Settis, *Paesaggio, Costituzione, Cemento* (Einaudi, 2010), 16–17.

tax reductions on commercial income for those who re-invested it in their business, particularly in the construction or expansion of property attached to their activities. The result was the construction of thousands of unused warehouses, particularly in the North-East of Italy, entailing not only in a waste of materials and resources, but also in an unsightly imprint on the landscape itself.[4] In his recent book *Paesaggio, Costituzione, Cemento* (Landscape, Constitution, Cement), Settis draws a parallel with the decline of civic sentiment and believes that the safeguarding of the landscape and the safeguarding of democracy are one and the same.[5] This sentiment is echoed by Carla Barbati.[6]

In Europe, national laws relating to landscape protection date back to the nineteenth century, the oldest being a Danish forestry law dating to 1805.[7] The first French law referring to landscape dates to 1906 and provides for by-laws to take landscape into consideration in the distribution of energy,[8] and in 1919 hydraulic companies were obliged to include measures for the protection of landscape in their specifications.[9] Likewise, a Swiss law of 1916 provides that power plants 'must not spoil the landscape'.[10] In Belgium, a specific law on the conservation of the beauty of landscapes dates as far back as 1911[11] and the first mention of landscape in Spanish law dates to 1916, in a law on national parks (which refers to 'remarkable natural landscapes').[12] While these early provisions emphasized an abstract notion of landscape beauty, they nevertheless illustrate a concern with damage to cultural or natural values of landscape. Four European countries directly refer to landscape in their constitutions. Article 9 of the 1947 Italian constitution refers to the 'safeguarding of landscape and the cultural and artistic heritage of the nation'. The German constitution of 1949 states that 'the federation is competent to legislate for the protection of nature and the management of landscape'.[13] The Swiss Constitution (1962) attributes the Cantons with the competence of nature and landscape protection, in particular with regard to maintaining the 'characteristic aspects' of the landscape.[14] The Portuguese Constitution of

[4] Ibid, 17. [5] Ibid, 282–3.

[6] Carla Barbati, 'Il Paesaggio como Realta Ético-Culturale', *Aedon Revista di Arte e Diritto* 2 (2007), 1127–1345.

[7] The Forest Reserve Act 1805. Lines of demarcation were drawn up and fixed, and the forests have since been a permanent feature of the cultural landscape. They were to be used for the production of timber and fuel, and were no longer to be utilized for grazing.

[8] Art. 19 loi du 15 juin 1906 sur la distribution de l'énergie.

[9] Art. 10.2 loi du 16 octobre 1919 relative à l'utilisation de l'énergie hydraulique.

[10] Art. 22 al. 2 of loi sur l'utilisation des forces hydrauliques du 22 décembre 1916 states usines 'ne doivent pas déparer ou doivent déparer le moins possible le paysage'.

[11] Loi du 12 aout 1911 sur La conservation de la beauté des paysages.

[12] Ley de Parques Nacionales 1916. [13] Art. 75. [14] Art. 24.

1976 obliges the state to take biologically sustainable landscapes into account in its territorial planning, as well as to guarantee the conservation of natural and cultural values.[15] A number of other European constitutions do not expressly mention 'landscape' but do refer to environment and culture.[16] Throughout the twentieth century landscape protection was attached to the national laws of European states in three ways: the first linked landscape to nature protection in the form of national parks or reserves; the second to the protection of historic monuments emphasizing the aesthetics or beauty of landscape;[17] and the third linked landscape to land-use planning in both rural and urban contexts. Today, almost all European states have laws relating to the protection of landscape and policies often combine the three approaches.[18]

International law began specifically to address the question of landscape protection in the 1960s and has seen a substantial amount of progress since the 1990s. The first and perhaps most visible role of international law in landscape protection is protected area designation. The concept of 'protected areas' derives from the nineteenth-century concern over loss of 'wilderness' and rapid changes in the lands of former European colonies. Initial attempts at conservation were based on the false premise that these lands had been untouched or pristine, when in fact they were the result of gradual human interaction with the environment over millennia. The national parks movement ensued with an emphasis on preserving impressive landscapes such as Yellowstone National Park or the Grand Canyon in the US, and increasingly the movement began to focus on the disappearance of species and ecosystems. Over time, the thinking on protected areas has come to the realization that humans are an integral part of the management of many 'natural' landscapes and that communities must be considered as important stakeholders in their protection and management. Protected areas are now recognized as being essential for the protection of the world's biological and cultural diversity.[19] The most successful internationally protected area regimes to date include the World Heritage Convention,[20] the Convention on

[15] Art. 66.

[16] Greece (Art. 24); Spain (Art. 45); Turkey (Art. 56); Netherlands (Art. 21); Slovakia (Arts 44 and 45); and Belgium (Art. 24).

[17] See Thomas F. King, 'Cultural Heritage Preservation and the Legal System with Specific Reference to Landscapes', in Ludomir R. Lozny (ed.), *Landscapes under Pressure. Theory and Practice of Cultural Heritage Research and Preservation* (Springer-Verlag, 2006), 243–54.

[18] Michel Prieur, 'Le Paysage en Droit Compare et en Droit International', *Environmental Policy and Law*, 27 (4)(1997), 355. Lionella Scazzosi, *Reading the Landscape. International Comparison/ Leggere il paesaggio. Confronti internazionale* (Gangemi, 2002).

[19] See Alexander Gillespie, *Protected Areas in International Law* (M. Nijhoff, 2007).

[20] Convention concerning the Protection of the World Cultural and Natural Heritage (opened for signature 16 November 1972, entered into force 17 December 1975), 1037 UNTS 151 (hereafter World Heritage Convention).

Biological Diversity,[21] the Ramsar Convention on Wetlands,[22] the Convention on Migratory Species,[23] and the United Nations Educational, Scientific and Cultural Organization (UNESCO) Man and Biosphere Programme. In addition, the International Union for the Conservation of Nature (IUCN), which is composed of both civil society organizations and governmental bodies and is one of the advisory bodies to UNESCO, has a number of categories of protected areas including the category of 'protected landscape'. Interestingly, this category is defined as a 'protected area where the interaction of people and nature over time has produced an area of distinct character with significant ecological, biological, cultural, and scenic value: and where safeguarding the integrity of this interaction is vital to protecting and sustaining the area and its associated nature conservation and other values.'[24] The world's protected areas contain specific plans and guidelines for the use and management of the landscape, and their classification places certain obligations on the states in whose territory the protected areas are situated.[25] The World Heritage Convention is the most relevant international treaty for the protection of cultural landscapes, particularly since the introduction of the specific category of 'cultural landscapes' within the scope of the Convention in 1992, further examined in Chapter 5.

The second area of international law of relevance to landscape protection is sustainable development, the principle that ties together the concern for natural systems with social and economic challenges facing humanity. While sustainable development is more of a guiding principle than a binding rule, a visible legal tool of sustainable development in practice is environmental impact assessment. Indeed, a number of important cases decided by the International Court of Justice have dealt with the issue.[26] Environmental impact assessment is the assessment of the possible positive or negative impacts that a proposed project may have on the environment, together consisting of natural, social, economic, and cultural aspects. The purpose of the assessment

[21] Convention on Biological Diversity (opened for signature 5 June 1992, entered into force 29 December 1993), 1760 UNTS 79.

[22] Ramsar Convention on Wetlands of International Importance Especially as Waterfowl Habitat (opened for signature 2 February 1971, entered into force 21 December 1975), 996 UNTS 245.

[23] Convention on the Conservation of Migratory Species of Wild Animals (opened for signature 23 June 1979, entered into force 1 November 1983), 1651 UNTS 333.

[24] More information concerning protected areas is available at <https://www.iucn.org/theme/protected-areas/about/protected-area-categories/category-v-protected-landscapeseascape> accessed 8 May 2018.

[25] See Gillespie, *Protected Areas in International Law* (n 19).

[26] See, for example, the Case concerning the Pulp Mills on the River Uruguay (*Argentina v Uruguay*), 20 April 2010, and the Case concerning the Gabcikovo-Nagymaros Project (*Hungary v Slovakia*), 25 September 1997.

is to ensure that decision-makers consider the ensuing environmental impacts when deciding whether to proceed with a project. While many international treaties provide for the carrying out of impact assessments,[27] in Europe it is EU legislation that is most rigorous in this regard,[28] although environmental impact assessment is becoming an increasingly accepted norm internationally.

The third area of international law implicated in landscape protection is that of human rights, substantive rights relating to culture, health, and property, and procedural rights such as the right to access information, to participate in decision-making processes, and to access justice. Participation of the public is central to good governance and the idea behind participation is that not only is it an equitable way of pursuing policy, but that it also avoids disputes at a later stage in the planning process. Human rights also play a role in landscape protection with regard to the rights of minorities and indigenous peoples, whose distinctive relationship with the landscape is often based on a use and dependency value, coupled with intangible values tied to cultural traditions and beliefs.

The fourth and most directly relevant area of international law is a branch containing a small number of soft law instruments and encapsulated in the European Landscape Convention that deals specifically with landscape protection. Neither a human rights treaty nor a 'protected areas' instrument, the European Landscape Convention (ELC) combines various aspects of previously mentioned instruments and its broad definition and conception of landscape encapsulates both cultural and natural values, while also combining it with a spatial justice dimension. For this reason, it has been stated that the European Landscape Convention 'democratizes' landscape.[29] The ELC is important because it recognizes the 'right' of people to enjoy quality landscapes and essentially promotes a notion of landscape as public space (which also connotes a 'polity' or 'community' of place). In this way, the ELC attempts conceptually to make up for the deficit left by the elevation of private property to the detriment of its social function. Many other areas of international law exist that impact upon the landscape, such as those regulating climate change, plant genetic resources, and water courses, just to mention a few, but these lie beyond the scope of this analysis.

[27] Convention on Environmental Impact in a Transboundary Context (opened for signature 25 February 1991, entered into force 10 September 1997) 1989 UNTS 310.

[28] Council Directive 2001/42/EC of 27 June 2001 on the assessment of the effects of certain plans and programmes on the environment, Art. 3.

[29] Riccardo Priore, 'La Convention Européenne du Paysage', *Revue européenne de droit de l'environnement*, No. 3 (2000), 285.

3.2 Rationale for the International Protection of Landscape

According to some legal scholars, landscapes cannot be considered as 'shared resources' when they are within the territory and under the sovereignty of a single state.[30] This view rests on the premise that, traditionally, the principle subjects of international law are states, that territory is subject to the sovereign authority of the state, and that there is a complete nexus between territory and sovereignty.[31] As will be illustrated further on, international law is relevant to the protection of landscape for a number of reasons. First, important elements of the cultural and natural heritage are considered not as mere private or public property, but as 'common heritage' of humankind. Certain landscapes form part of the cultural and natural heritage of humanity and as such place restrictions on the state. Second, the new global vision of landscape, as encapsulated in the ELC (discussed in Chapter 6), links the concept with human rights, democracy, and environmental justice. The concept of democracy and democratic institutions has been developed in recent years through the work of the Commission on Human Rights[32] and the Office of the UN High Commissioner for Human Rights, which gradually built a normative understanding of participation, democracy, the rule of law, and good governance in human rights terms.[33] Third, landscapes do not respect borders, as many landscapes straddle political boundaries (this in turn necessitates transfrontier co-operation and agreement). Furthermore, the rise of international environmental law has had an impact on landscape protection in so far as the general obligation to prevent environmental degradation entails a further limit on territorial sovereignty. For example, designation by UNESCO enabled the Australian government to rescue the southwestern Tasmanian temperate rainforest, along with its archaeological traces, from destructive development.[34] Fourth, the concept of intergenerational equity applies to landscapes because they not only contain the footprints of past civilizations,

[30] See, for example, Alexander Kiss and Dinah Shelton, *International Environmental Law* (M. Nijhoff, 2007), 147.

[31] Antonio Cassese, *International Law* (Oxford University Press, 2005), 56.

[32] The Commission has since become the Human Rights Council.

[33] See UN Commission on Human Rights, *Human Rights Resolution 2005/29: Strengthening of Popular Participation, Equity, Social Justice and Non-discrimination as Essential Foundations of Democracy*, 19 April 2005, E/CN.4/RES/2005/29; and UN Commission on Human Rights, *Human Rights Resolution 2005/32: Democracy and the Rule of Law*, 19 April 2005, E/CN.4/RES/2005/32, Part I.

[34] In this case, although it was held that the recommendations of the WHC Committee are not binding on sovereign government, the broad commitments undertaken by the government when signing the Convention could not be lightly dismissed. Accordingly, plans to build a hydroelectric

but they are also the living space of present generations and represent the condition of the earth that will be passed on to future generations.[35] Landscape also concerns the rights of life other than humankind, as some landscapes are home to ecosystems, habitats, and a diversity of wildlife. Unlike reserves or wilderness areas, however, the very notion of landscape implies a human presence. Lastly, landscape is the result not only of local custom but also of central and supra-national legislation. Part of the degradation of the European landscape has, for example, come from EU agricultural reforms, so it is logical that at supra-national level there is some common policy to tackle this.[36]

According to Antônio Augusto Cançado Trindade, 'traditional international law as purely inter-state has led to abuse of power by those who held it. Although states continue to play a predominant role at the international level, contemporary international law has been enriched with the overcoming of the old interstate dimension and the contributions of other subjects such as international organizations, individuals, and humankind.'[37] The late Antonio Cassese considered international law as being based on a universalist or cosmopolitan outlook, 'which sees at work in international politics a potential community of mankind'.[38] This reverses the rationale of Hobbes' Leviathan and the Westphalian tradition of international politics. States not only have responsibility towards other states—as in the classical intergovernmental tradition—but they also have obligations towards the international community as a whole, towards individuals and communities, and towards future generations.[39] Marco Gestri draws an interesting parallel between internal and external sovereignty; that is, in the same way that states are bound to uphold the public good in domestic law—which involves restrictions on certain rights and freedoms, such as the right to property—so must sovereignty be

dam, despite being supported by the government, were rejected as it was within a World Heritage site, to which international obligations applied. See *Commonwealth v Tasmania* [1983] 158 CLR. 1.

[35] Intergenerational equity is one of the founding principles of sustainable development. See Edith Brown Weiss, *In Fairness to Future Generations: International Law, Common Patrimony and Intergenerational Equity* (UN University, 1989). Edith Brown Weiss, 'Our Rights and Obligations to Future Generations for the Environment', *AJIL*, 84 (1990),198. Lothar Gundling, 'Our Responsibility to Future Generations', *AJIL*, 84 (1990), 207. Gary Supanich, 'The Legal Basis of Intergenerational Responsibility: An Alternative View—The Sense of Intergenerational Identity', *Yearbook of International Environmental Law*, 3 (1992), 94. Emmanuel Agius and Salvino Busuttil, *Future Generations and International Law* (Earthscan, 1998).

[36] Agricultural and other policies, however, will not be dealt with in detail. Exploring the complex matrix of policies affecting the overall landscape lies beyond the scope of this book.

[37] Antonio A. Cançado Trindade, *International Law for Humankind: Towards a New Jus Gentium* (M. Nijhoff, 2010), 177.

[38] Cassese, *International Law* (n 31), 3.

[39] See, for example, Karen Wellens, 'Revisiting Solidarity as (Re) Emerging Constitutional Principle', in Rudiger Wolfrum, *Solidarity: A Structural Principle of International Law* (Springer, 2010).

exercised in a way that promotes the general interest (of humankind) in the protection of common goods, i.e. landscape.[40] This line of reasoning forms one of the basic tenets of this analysis. Landscape, embodying both cultural and natural heritage and living space for communities, is at the very core of concepts that transcend the constraints of traditional inter-state law. These concepts will be scrutinized below as they underwrite much of the institutional framework for landscape protection. Developments made in cultural heritage law, environmental law, and evolving principles such as sustainable development, provide the contextual basis for the normative milieu without which landscape protection at the international level could not be envisaged.

> Two world views collide: the traditional view of the world consisting of sharply distinguished compartments (the national states) and a view of an interdependent world society with common values and with problems that can only be solved through common efforts and with respect for universal, hence supra-national, legal rules.[41]

Traditionally, international law focused on the sovereignty of states and the relations between them. The ultimate aim of this law was (and still is to a large extent) to preserve the self-interest of the state by ensuring peaceful co-operation and co-existence. International rules intend to strike a balance between rights and obligations of states and have a reciprocal state interest as their rationale, so that rules binding on the community as a whole were not originally created to protect general interests (beyond individual parties), but only the interests of each party, or of all the parties combined.[42] States only voluntarily limited the exercise of their external autonomy by accepting rules of treaty or customary international law. Contrary to national law, in international law states were—for the most part—the primary subjects, with individuals playing a limited role. In contrast to national law, the relations between states remained largely horizontal, lacking any central authority, with power being fragmented and dispersed.

Cassese pointed out that the traditional international order is unsatisfactory today as 'most components of national structures and of the international community (individuals, groups, associations, state-like entities, multinational corporations, transnational organisations) are so closely intertwined

[40] Marco Gestri, 'I Concetti di Patrimonio Comune dell'Umanità e di Risorse d'interesse Generale nel Diritto Internazionale', in G. Colombini (ed.), *I benei pubblici tra regole di mercato e interessi generali. Profili di diritto interno e internazionale* (Jovene, 2009).

[41] P. H. Kooijmans, Internationaal Publiekrecht in Vogelvlucht (2000), translation from Dutch by Marcel Brus in 'Bridging the Gap between state Sovereignty and International Governance: The Authority of Law', Gerard Kreijen (ed.), *State, Sovereignty and International Governance* (Oxford University Press, 2002), 359.

[42] Cassese, *International Law* (n 31), 12.

across national borders that they make up the phenomenon usually called "globalisation"'.[43] In this regard, international law is increasingly being viewed as a normative framework for 'international governance' or 'global governance', defined by the OECD as 'the process by which we collectively manage and govern resources, issues, conflicts and values in a world that is increasingly a "global neighbourhood"'.[44] Global governance has also been described as 'the complex of formal and informal institutions, mechanisms, relationships, and processes between and among states, markets, citizens and organizations, both inter - and non-governmental, through which collective interests on the global plane are articulated, rights and obligations are established, and differences are mediated'.[45] Marcel Brus notes that 'international governance' seems to constitute a fundamentally different basis for regulating international issues from the sovereignty of states.[46] He believes, nevertheless, that states are still the most important actors on the playing field, but that they have to adapt to the changing circumstances in present international society. State sovereignty, according to Robert Jennings, and the views about its nature and purpose, have necessarily varied from time to time because changing times require different approaches.[47] Jennings reminds us of the 1930s when, during the League of Nations period, the idea of sovereignty was considered as an obstacle to the development of international law and that what was needed was a so-called 'surrender of state sovereignty'.[48] This was the inter-war period when lawyers were faced with a system of international law which still recognized the sovereign legal right of a state to declare war on another in order to gain its political ends. The late Philip Jessup described this absolute sovereign state as 'the quicksand on which the foundations of traditional international law are built'.[49] The sovereign right to war was consequently abolished in the 1945 Charter of the United Nations. What Jennings points to, however, is that the 1930s' negative attitude towards sovereignty was suited to what was thought to be a principle need of those times. He also shows how this need changed after the Second World War, and during the period of de-colonization, when the attitude to sovereignty almost went

[43] Ibid.

[44] OECD, *Globalization: What Challenges and Opportunities for Governments?* OECD/GD (1996) 64.

[45] Thomas G. Weiss and Ramesh Thakur, *The UN and Global Governance: An Idea and its Prospects* (Indiana University Press, 2010).

[46] Marcel Brus, 'Bridging the Gap between State Sovereignty and International Governance: The Authority of Law', in Gerard Kreijen (ed.), *State, Sovereignty and International Governance* (n 41), 5.

[47] Robert Jennings, 'Sovereignty and International Law', in Kreijen (ed.), *State, Sovereignty and International Governance* (n 41), 27.

[48] Ibid. [49] Ibid, 29.

into reverse: it became again a respectable aim and represented the reasonable ambition of formerly colonized peoples. From this came the reinvention of Woodrow Wilson's political ideal of self-determination into the 'right of self-determination'.

In the post-decolonization and post-Cold War context of today, the classical concept of state sovereignty as exclusive and undivided has again become subject to criticism, but for different reasons than in the past—most of which have to do with the view that state sovereignty is less relevant to the needs of the global international community. Alfred Van Staden and Hans Vollaard note three main factors contributing to the demise of the Westphalian system: economic globalization, pushing us towards a borderless world; the awareness of our ecological interdependence, necessary for common survival; and the global cyberspace where chrono-politics takes over the role of geopolitics.[50] For these reasons, the view prevails that it is outdated to analyse contemporary politics in terms of actions and interactions of territorial units called states, which are supposed to exert supreme authority within their borders. The borders of nearly all modern societies have become so permeable and open to external influences that the traditional dividing line between domestic and foreign politics is becoming increasingly blurred.[51]

3.3 Common Heritage, Common Concern, Common Goods

> International law is not only rules. It is a normative system harnessed to the achievement of common values.[52]
>
> Rosalyn Higgins, 1994

The early notion of sovereignty and its correlation to *dominium* meant that any spaces not subject to the sovereignty of a state were classified in the Roman tradition as *res nullius*—no man's land—which could be occupied and appropriated, or *res communis*—those spaces which could not be appropriated, such as the oceans or high seas. Of course, *res communis* also

[50] Alfred Van Staden and Hans Vollaard, 'The Erosion of State Sovereignty: Towards a Post-territorial World?', in Gerard Kreijen (ed.), *Sovereignty and International Governance* (n 41), 165. See also Tuomas Forsberg, 'Beyond Sovereignty, Within Territory. Mapping the Space of Late-Modern (Geo)Politics', *Cooperation and Conflict* 31 (4), 355–86.

[51] Van Staden and Vollaard, 'The Erosion of State Sovereignty: Towards a Post-territorial World? (n 50), 169.

[52] Cited in Laura Westra, *Environmental Justice and the Rights of Indigenous Peoples* (Earthscan, 2012), 5.

implied freedom of use of the high seas, so that while no one sovereign could appropriate any part of this common space, each could dispose of its resources without limit.[53] This paradox led to the so-called tragedy of the commons,[54] the title of Garrett Hardin's 1968 article, whereby in the case of the high seas, the freedom to dispose of its resources by each and all has led to overfishing and depleted resources. The concept of the 'common heritage of mankind' emerged as a response to this. First coined in 1967 by Arvid Pardo, the Maltese representative at the United Nations, when referring to mineral resources recently discovered on the ocean bed, the term made its way into General Assembly Resolution 2749 of 15 December 1970 (XXV) according to which 'the seabed and the ocean floor, and the subsoil thereof, beyond the limits of national jurisdiction (the Area), as well as its resources "are the common heritage of mankind". No state can claim or exercise sovereignty or sovereign rights thereupon, and their use shall be for peaceful purposes only.' This was further elaborated in the United Nations Convention on the Law of the Sea (UNCLOS), adopted on 10 December 1982 at Montego Bay.[55] The common heritage of mankind as a concept was also asserted with regard to the International Law of Outer Space, in the 1979 Agreement Governing the activities of States on the Moon and Other Celestial Bodies.[56] The Moon Treaty proclaims the moon and its resources as the common heritage of mankind, and echoes an earlier agreement which determined the whole of outer space as being the 'province of all mankind', 'not subject to national expropriation by claim of sovereignty'.[57] The Antarctic Treaty of 1959, while it came before the above treaties and thus does not expressly mention the term 'common heritage', states in its preamble that its primary purpose is to ensure 'in the interest of all mankind that Antarctica shall continue forever to be used exclusively for peaceful purposes and shall not become scene or object of international discord'. This was further elaborated in the 1991 Madrid

[53] Hugo Grotius provided this distinction in his *Mare Liberum* 1609. *The Freedom of the Seas or the Right which Belongs to the Dutch to Take Part in the East Indian Trade, A Dissertation By Hugo Grotius, translated with a revision of the Latin Text of 1633 by Ralph Van Dem An Magoffin, Edited with an introductory note by James Brown Scott* (New York, 1916), 29.

[54] *The Tragedy of the Commons*, written by ecologist Garrett Hardin and first published in 1968, describes the dilemma in which multiple individuals acting independently and in their own self-interest, will ultimately deplete a shared limited resource, even when it is clear that it is in nobody's long-term interests for this to happen. *Science*, New Series, vol. 162, No. 3859 (Dec. 13, 1968), 1243–8.

[55] United Nations Convention on the Law of the Sea (opened for signature 10 December 1982, entered into force 16 November 1994), 1833 UNTS 396.

[56] Art. 11(1).

[57] Treaty on Principles Governing the Activities of States in the Exploration and use of Outer Space, Including the Moon and Other Celestial Bodies (opened for signature 19 December 1966, entered into force 10 October 1967), 610 UNTS 205, Art. 1(1) and 2.

Protocol to the Antarctic Treaty, which designates Antarctica as a 'natural reserve, devoted to peace and science'.[58] It has been argued that Antarctica is perhaps the only existing example of the implementation of the common heritage principle,[59] although Kemal Baslar sees this more of an implementation of the 'world park' idea, since he views common heritage as essentially an anthropocentric concept.[60]

Due to problems in the interpretation of 'common heritage'—which led to exploitation—a derivative concept, the 'common concern of mankind', emerged. The emphasis on 'concern' falls upon action and equitable sharing of burdens rather than the pursuance of benefits from exploitation of natural resources.[61] According to Horn, it is a 'global ethical concept which can focus on areas of concern for all humankind' and arguably, notes Shelton, 'could develop into an international norm which would prioritize 'environmental protection as a fundamental value of international society'.[62] The first explicit reference to 'common concern' was contained in UN General Assembly Resolution 43/53 on the protection of global climate for present and future generations of mankind, which recognized that 'climate change is a common concern of mankind, since climate is an essential condition which sustains life on earth'.[63] The fundamentals of the concept can be traced to various declarations and recommendations of the UN General Assembly, such as the 1972 Stockholm Declaration on the Human Environment, which referred to the 'common good of mankind'.[64] According to former Executive Director of United Nations Environment Programme (UNEP), the concept of common concern entails both spatial and temporal facets: spatial in so far as the concept implies the co-operation of states on matters of similar importance to all states and the international community as a

[58] Art. 2, Protocol on Environmental Protection to the Antarctic Treaty, 30 ILM 1455 (1991).

[59] Francesco Francioni, 'Legal Aspects of Mineral Exploitation in Antarctica', *Cornell Int'L.J*, 19 (1986), 163. For a more updated position after the Convention on the Regulation of Antarctic Mineral Resource Activities was adopted in 1988, see Francioni, 'Resource Sharing in Antarctica: for Whose Benefit?' *EUR J. Int'L*, 1 (1990), 258 and after the Madrid Protocol, Francioni, 'The Madrid Protocol on the Protection of the Antarctic Environment', *Tex. Int. Law Journal*, 28 (1993), 47–72.

[60] Kemal Baslar, *The Concept of the Common Heritage of Mankind in International Law* (M. Nijhoff, 1998), 261.

[61] UNEP, The Meeting of the Group of Experts to Examine the Concept of the Common Concern of Mankind in Relation to Global Environmental Issues (ed. D. J. Attard, Malta, 13–15 December 1990), Nairobi, Kenya (UNEP 1991), 19–47.

[62] Dinah Shelton, 'The Impact of Economic Globalization on Compliance', in Alexander Kiss and Dinah Shelton et al. (eds), *Economic Globalization and Compliance with International Environmental Agreements* (Kluwer 2003), 41.

[63] Resolution 43/53 on the protection of global climate for present and future generations of mankind, 70th plenary meeting, 6 December 1988, Operative para. 1.

[64] Para. 18.

whole.[65] The temporal aspect relates to the long-term effects of environmental issues affecting the rights and obligations of present and future generations.[66]

Given the existence of spaces that are neither fully public, nor entirely private, such as shared resources and common goods, property alone is no longer relevant for many governance strategies. Of course, ownership and control of resources may come in various shades and degrees, and while a piece of land might be privately owned in title, in practice its landscape is often the subject of collective use and management. Landscape is central to this notion, that is, it increasingly reflects a social order of land not governed solely by economic and property considerations, but also one which includes the 'common' shared aspects of the Earth's resources from ethical and social perspectives. Part of this emergence of common goods discourse can be demonstrated in the shift away from the nomenclature of cultural 'property' towards the idea of cultural 'heritage'.[67]

3.4 The Cultural Heritage of Humankind: From 'Property' to 'Heritage'

Throughout history, evidence can be found for the desire to protect places and objects held sacred to society, those things that identified a people or culture and bound them to a particular location or way of life. As far back as the second century AD, Greek historian Polybius stated that 'nobody can deny that the wanton destruction of temples, statues and other sacred things is pure folly'.[68] In Europe, up until the Renaissance, the Church was the main defender of sacred buildings and objects.[69] After the Peace of Westphalia in 1648, treaties began regularly to include clauses stipulating the restitution to their place of origin of archives and works of art seized in warfare.[70] One of

[65] Mostafa K. Tolba, *The Implications of the Common Concern of Mankind Concept on Global Environmental Issues,* Note of the Executive Director of UNEP to the Group of Legal Experts meeting, Malta, 13–15 December, 1990.

[66] Ibid, 3.

[67] See, for example, Federico Lenzerini and Ana Vrdoljak (eds), *International Law for Common Goods, Normative Perspectives on Human Rights, Culture and Nature* (Hart, 2014), especially Part II: 'Cultural Heritage', 139–249.

[68] Polybius as quoted in David J. Bederman, *International Law in Antiquity* (Cambridge University Press 2009), 262.

[69] Sue Williams, 'The Desire to Protect and Preserve', UNESCO *Sources* No. 80/ June 1996, 8.

[70] For example, the Treaties of Osnabrück and Munster (1648) ended the Thirty Years War in the Holy Roman Empire and the Eighty Years' War between Spain and the Republic of the Seven United Netherlands, to be followed by the Treaty of Oliva between Sweden and Poland (1662) and the Treaty of Whitehall between England and the Netherlands (1662). For more detail on the

the earliest governmental heritage programmes created in France in the wake of the Revolution determined which buildings from the nation's royalist past were worthy of being preserved, as opposed to being destroyed as reminders of the hated aristocracy. In 1794 the revolutionary government asked one of its members, the Abbé Grégoire, to write a response to a proposal to destroy all Latin inscriptions on monuments as they were seen as 'unrevolutionary'.[71] Grégoire produced three reports to the National Convention, each of which was intended to be an account of the losses sustained to the nation. Grégoire, however, decided to reflect on a question that had never before been the subject of legislative attention: why should caring for material culture and sites be the concern of the nation? Grégoire was the first to propose a rationale for preservation as a public duty based on the Revolution's self-proclaimed political values.[72] Grégoire reportedly stated that 'the productions of genius and the means of instruction are "common property"' and that 'national objects which, belonging to no one, are the property of all'.[73] He frequently used terms like 'common property' and 'common heritage' in his discourses. As pointed out by Joseph Sax, Grégoire's reports stand as the first expression of what was to become modern public policy on cultural property, and while his ideas were discarded at the time, his way of conceiving of cultural property set the terms of reference until this very day: preservation as a state responsibility, cultural property as belonging to the people of the nation even with no formal claim to ownership, and creative achievement as an asset of the state.[74] At the time, the Abbé Grégoire's ideals of preservation were not fulfilled. Cultural heritage became an instrument used to boost nation state ideology and imperialist power, and the Napoleonic Wars saw the pillaging of cultural goods on an unprecedented scale. When a state programme for the protection of historic monuments was finally established in 1830, it was under the restored monarchy of Louis-Philippe. Rather than adopt Grégoire's republican ideology, instead ancient castles, romantic ruins, mysterious abbeys, and an interest in a remote and heroic national past became the norm.[75] National pride revealed itself in a preference for ancestral glories, and even today preservation is often viewed as mere backward sentimentality. It appears from Sax's account that the Abbé Grégoire report never formally addressed the criteria on which to base a choice for preservation, but he vehemently opposed the politicization of art and the destruction of heritage, which he termed

subject see Stanislaw E. Nahlik, 'La protection internationale des biens culturels en cas de conflit armé', *Recueil des Cours* (1967) vol. I, 77 ff.

[71] Joseph Sax, 'Heritage Preservation as Public Duty: The Abbé Grégoire and the Origins of an Idea', *Michigan Law Review*, 88 (1989), 1142–69.

[72] Ibid. [73] Ibid. [74] Ibid. [75] Ibid.

'vandalism'.[76] He was thus highly progressive in his day because he linked tolerance for difference with respect for cultural heritage. In this sense, therefore, it could be said that Grégoire foresaw the rationale underpinning the international concern for the protection of cultural heritage, regardless of state politics, religion or ideology.

By the end of the nineteenth century most of Europe's built heritage was protected by national legislation and a concerted effort was being made to establish an agreement between European states to protect cultural heritage in times of war. The early Hague Conventions included various clauses prohibiting, as far as possible, the destruction of historical monuments and works of art and science during armed conflict.[77] The language did not change much from one instrument to the next and the structure remained the same; cultural property was to be protected unless in the case of military necessity and individuals responsible for offences to the cultural property were to be tried by the authorities in their own state. However, the Second World War saw cultural destruction on an unparalleled scale, with the loss of many hundreds of thousands of historic buildings, millions of cultural items, and whole historic zones, leaving desecrated landscapes in its wake. Three significant events then occurred: the founding of the United Nations in 1945, the Nuremberg Trials (1945–49),[78] and the adoption in 1954 of the Hague Convention for the Protection of Cultural Property in the Event of Armed Conflict.[79]

Established as an agency of the UN in 1945, UNESCO took over the work of the League of Nations in the field of intellectual co-operation and cultural heritage.[80] In the aftermath of the Second World War, and given the inadequacy of the earlier international treaties, the priority of the organization lay in the protection of cultural heritage during armed conflict: this resulted

[76] Ibid.

[77] See the Regulations annexed to the 1899 *Hague Convention Concerning the Law and Customs of War on Land (II),* as well as the 1907 Conventions (IV and IX). The protection is not absolute, as it is limited by a reservation concerning military necessity.

[78] For an account of the Nuremburg Trials and crimes committed against cultural property, see Jacqueline Nowlan, 'Cultural Property and the Nuremberg War Crimes Trial', *Humanitaeres Voelkerrecht,* 4 (1993), 221–3.

[79] Hague Convention for the Protection of Cultural Property in the Event of Armed Conflict (opened for signature 14 May 1954, entered into force 7 August 1956), 249 UNTS 240. It is worth noting that between the early Hague Conventions and 1954, a significant step was taken at the regional level in the form of the Treaty on the Protection of Artistic and Scientific Institutions and Historic Monuments (the Roerich Pact), which was signed in Washington in 1935 by twenty-one American states and to which the Hague Convention makes specific reference it its preamble.

[80] The United Nations Educational, Scientific and Cultural Organization was founded on 16 November 1945 by the representatives of 37 states which signed its founding treaty (in force 4 November 1946).

in the adoption of the 1954 Hague Convention. Not only was the Hague Convention the first instrument dealing with the protection of cultural property at the global level, but it was also the first time the encompassing notion of 'cultural property' was coined in an international legal instrument. It provides for both the safeguarding of cultural property against the possible effects of armed conflict through preparatory measures to be adopted in times of peace, and for the respect of such property in times of war and military occupation. The first articulation of the notion of the 'cultural heritage of mankind' was included in the preamble:

> [...] damage to cultural property belonging to any people whatsoever means damage to the cultural heritage of all mankind, since each people makes its contribution to the culture of the world.

The interpretation of the scope of the Convention regarding the extent of property to which it applies varies somewhat, mainly due to the elusive reference to cultural property in Article 1.[81] For Roger O'Keefe, the Convention's scope applies to the full complement of each contracting state's national cultural heritage, as defined by the state.[82] This is supported by the nature of the above cited preambular reference to the 'cultural heritage of mankind', to the fact that this be read in the wider sense,[83] and to the nature of following UNESCO instruments.[84] For John Henry Merryman, the language of the preamble is a 'charter for internationalism'.[85] However, while the attitude to cultural property in the Convention would appear independent of national jurisdiction and property rights,[86] and while the preamble is careful not to mention 'state', choosing instead the terms 'each people' and 'every people'; it still relies on the action of the state in the process of safeguarding and

[81] Cultural property is defined as being 'movable or immovable property of great importance to the cultural heritage of every people' and goes on to define such property.

[82] Roger O'Keefe, 'The Meaning of Cultural Property under the 1954 Hague Convention', *Netherlands International Law Review*, 46 (1), 26–56. O'Keefe deals with only cultural property qualifying for general protection, 30.

[83] O'Keefe quotes a former Judge of the International Court of Justice, Nagendra Singh, when he stated that 'the cultural objects and properties which make up [one state's] national heritage [are], consequently, the world's heritage', ibid.

[84] The author does not cite these instruments but he is most likely referring to the corpus of recommendations, declarations, and treaties that cite the importance of the cultural heritage for humankind.

[85] John H. Merryman, 'Two Ways of Thinking about Cultural Property', *American Journal of International Law*, 80 (4) (1986), 831–53, at 837.

[86] Art. 1 states that for the purposes of the Convention, 'the term "cultural property" shall cover, irrespective of origin or ownership:' and is therefore independent of property rights. This is in contrast to Art. 56 of the prior instruments that treated cultural property as private property.

protecting, not to mention the much-debated military necessity clause, which has been described as its 'one significant concession to nationalism'.[87]

In the following years, UNESCO began to focus on the protection of cultural heritage also in peacetime, and a number of declarations and recommendations were adopted to this end.[88] The 1966 Declaration on Principles of International Cultural Cooperation proclaims that 'all cultures form part of the common heritage of mankind' (Article 1(3)). However, while these developments added momentum to the idea of protection, cultural property remained essentially an affair of the state. This was reinforced by the UNESCO 1970 Convention on the Means of Prohibiting and Preventing the Illicit Import, Export or Transfer of Cultural Property, which, according to Francesco Francioni 'postulated a national idea of cultural heritage based on sovereignty and property rights'.[89] Nevertheless, the concept of cultural 'property', as it was still being termed, was beginning to change: the language appearing in the various international texts alluded to a value that went beyond that of the private interest of the individual holder or owner of a cultural object, to other values such as the national interest of the country of origin and the public interest of the international community in preventing the loss and dispersion of such objects.

A major turning point then came in 1972 with United Nations Conference on the Human Environment in Stockholm. For the first time, debates on preservation began to include the environment. Later that year, UNESCO's General Conference adopted the Convention Concerning the Protection of the World Cultural and Natural Heritage (hereafter World Heritage Convention).[90] For the first time the term 'world heritage' was used instead of 'cultural property' in the title of an instrument, marking the beginning of a conceptual shift which implied a radical change in perspective: the emphasis no longer being on the national interest of the state to which the property belongs, but on the general interest of humanity in preserving the cultural or natural site because of its universal importance, and as such deserving to be placed on a list of special international protection: the World Heritage List.

[87] Merryman, 'Two Ways of Thinking about Cultural Property' (n 86), 837. Merryman sees this as being in keeping with earlier Hague Conventions.

[88] See, for example, the Recommendation on International Principles Applicable to Archaeological Excavations (1956), the Recommendation concerning the Safeguarding of the Beauty and Character of Landscapes and Sites (1962) and the Recommendation concerning the Preservation of Cultural Property Endangered by Public or Private Works (1968), discussed in Chapter 4.

[89] Francesco Francioni, 'Introduction', in Francesco Francioni and Federico Lenzerini (eds), *The 1972 World Heritage Convention: A Commentary* (Oxford University Press, 2008).

[90] Convention concerning the Protection of the World Cultural and Natural Heritage (opened for signature 16 November 1972, entered into force 17 December 1975), 1037 UNTS 151.

As stated in the Preamble, 'considering that parts of the cultural or natural heritage are of outstanding interest' they 'therefore need to be preserved as part of the world heritage of mankind as a whole'. The Convention was also innovative for acknowledging the close links between nature and culture and for setting up a common regime of protection for both man-made and natural sites. The rationale for the World Heritage Convention owed itself in a great deal to two major events that occurred in the 1960s: one was the construction plan for the Aswan Dam which led to the flooding of the Upper Nile Valley, thus threatening the ancient Nubian monuments with submersion. UNESCO co-ordinated an international campaign which led to the relocation of the monuments to more elevated grounds, where they can still be seen today. What was striking about the campaign was that of the eighty million dollars it cost in total, over half of the sum was financed by some fifty countries. This showed the solidarity and sense of common responsibility for these cultural sites. The other event was the extensive flooding that occurred in Florence and Venice in November of 1966. The floods destroyed and damaged a significant amount of cultural property, including Renaissance paintings, sculptures, frescoes, and books. Given the great importance of the sites and objects affected, there was widespread international concern and a prompt and generous response by the international community to recover and restore what could be salvaged. However, this event, alongside that of the Nubian valley, illustrated that there was a gap in the peacetime protection of cultural heritage, which was still the domain of national law.[91]

'Heritage' would come to replace the use of property in later UNESCO instruments, reflecting the evolving concept of cultural and natural heritage, which could no longer be categorized by a term so laden with economic connotations. Furthermore, the term 'property' was becoming increasingly problematic in relation to natural heritage, as well as intangible cultural heritage and the heritage of indigenous peoples. Property does not invoke a duty to preserve or protect, whereas 'heritage' connotes a public and collective value. The inclusion of the category of cultural landscapes within the scope of the World Heritage Convention was emblematic of the evolving shift in the concept of heritage towards a more holistic notion encompassing beliefs and traditions, that is, intangibles, as well as the fact that often a site or property cannot be detached contextually from its surroundings. As will be illustrated, landscape is at the centre of this conceptual shift from property to heritage: although still a physical element of the cultural heritage, cultural landscapes bring us closer to the ethnographic information about

[91] Francesco Francioni, 'Thirty Years On: Is the World Heritage Convention Ready for the 21st Century?', *Italian Yearbook of International Law*, 12 (2002), 13–38.

the way of life of people as well as the close links existing between topographical and landscape features and cultural identity. This is somewhat paralleled in sacred cultural and natural spaces and places of memory inscribed on the Representative List for the Safeguarding of the Intangible Cultural Heritage.[92] In 2009, the sacred forests of Mijikenda Kaya were inscribed on the List of Intangible Heritage in Urgent Need of Safeguarding, one year after their inscription on the World Heritage List.[93] Apart from representing 75% of Kenya's biodiversity, the Kaya forests are culturally significant as they contain the traces of historic settlements of the Mijikenda ancestors, which serve as a focus of cultural and ritual activities continuing on the sites today.[94]

The universal common concern with the protection of cultural heritage became manifest in March 2001 with the destruction of the Buddhas of Bamiyan by the Taliban regime.[95] Prior to this act of destruction, the UN General Assembly adopted a resolution on 'the need to respect the common heritage of humankind'.[96] The UN stated it was 'deeply concerned and appalled by the Taliban edict ordering the destruction of all statues and non-Islamic shrines of Afghanistan, a destruction which would be 'an irreparable loss for humanity as a whole'.[97] The destruction of the Buddhas and the universal dismay in its wake led to the adoption by UNESCO, in 2003, of the Declaration concerning the Intentional Destruction of Cultural Heritage, which characterized 'intentional destruction' as:

> a violation of international law or an unjustifiable offense to the principles of humanity and dictates of public conscience, in the latter case so far as such acts are not already governed by fundamental principles of international law.[98]

[92] Article 2 defines the 'intangible cultural heritage' as the 'practices, representations, expressions, knowledge, skills—as well as the instruments, objects, artefacts and *cultural spaces* associated therewith—that communities, groups and, in some cases, individuals recognize as part of their cultural heritage' (emphasis added). Article 14(c) refers to the promotion of 'education for the protection of natural spaces and places of memory whose existence is necessary for expressing the intangible cultural heritage'.

[93] Decision of the Inter-governmental Committee: 4. COM 14.06.

[94] The nomination file refers to how the collective attitudes and beliefs of a rural society have shaped the landscape over time in response to prevailing needs. In particular, it states that 'the forests contain the traces of historic fortified settlements of the Mijikenda ancestors which serve as a focus of cultural and ritual activities continuing on the sites today. In a unique way, the intangible aspects of Mijikenda heritage are supported by physical cultural features of the kayas including paths, gate sites, burial grounds, settlement sites, ritual grounds etc. representing the material embodiment of their worldview and traditional belief systems. Nomination file 1231rev, available at <http://whc.unesco.org/en/list/1231/documents/> accessed 8 May 2018.

[95] Francesco Francioni and Federico Lenzerini, 'The Destruction of the Buddhas of Bamiyan and International Law', *European Journal of International Law*, 14 (2003), 619–51.

[96] UN General Assembly Resolution 55/243, of 9 March 2001.

[97] Ibid, paras 4 and 6.

[98] Operative part, section II, para. 2.

This Declaration is notable because it declares the destruction of cultural heritage in peacetime as a violation of international law. Significantly, the landscape of Bamiyan was inscribed as a Cultural Landscape on the World Heritage List, even in the absence of the Buddha statues, as a symbolic reminder of the appalling acts committed by the Taliban.[99] The symbolic power of landscape and its role as a *lieu de memoire* was thus affirmed by the World Heritage Committee (WHC). An attack on cultural heritage can symbolize an attack on the group as such, and indicates intolerance and hostility. This has become all the more evident in the recent conflicts in Mali, Iraq, and Syria, and is reminiscent of the deliberate destruction of cultural landscapes perpetrated during the War in the Former Yugoslavia.

3.5 Environmental Protection and Sustainable Development

The Stockholm conference adopted the 1972 United Nations Declaration on the Human Environment, a landmark instrument articulating twenty-six fundamental principles to guide the consolidation and evolution of international environmental law.[100] The Declaration dealt with a number of issues, such as the responsibility of states for transboundary environmental harm,[101] but it also went further by stressing the need for states to protect the environment for its own sake and for the benefit of future generations,[102] and by encouraging states to adopt an integrated and coordinated approach to environmental management.[103] It was an important catalyst for further efforts to expand environmental law, which led to a host of conventions,[104] soft law instruments,[105] and the World Commission on Environment and Development.[106] However, global environmental challenges such as climate

[99] Decision 27COM 8C.43. 'Cultural Landscape and Archaeological Remains of the Bamiyan Valley.'

[100] Louis B. Sohn, 'The Stockholm Declaration on the Human Environment', *Harvard International Law Journal*, 14 (1973).

[101] Principle 21. [102] Principles 2 and 4. [103] Principles 24 and 25.

[104] For example, the 1973 Convention on International Trade in Endangered Species of Wild Fauna and Flora (CITES) (opened for signature 3 March 1973, entered into force 7 January 1975), 993 UNTS 243; and the 1979 Convention on the Conservation of Migratory Species of Wild Animals (n 139).

[105] See especially the United Nations Principles of Conduct in the Field of the Environment for the guidance of states in the Conservation and Harmonious Utilization of Natural Resources Shared by Two or more States (1978); World Charter for Nature, GA Res. 37/7, UN Doc. a/37/51 (1982); and Hague Declaration on the Environment (1989) 28 ILM 1308.

[106] United Nations World Commission on Environment and Development, *Our Common Future—Brundtland Report* (Oxford University Press, 1987).

change and massive loss of biodiversity were not addressed until 1992 with the United Nations Conference on Environment and Development (UNCED), which adopted the Rio Declaration and keystone conventions on biological diversity and climate change.[107] The conference also endorsed Agenda 21, which set out a programme of action to address global environmental challenges in the 1990s and into the twenty-first century.[108] While former environmental conservation initiatives appeared hostile or indifferent to economic development, at times ignoring human rights considerations such as the needs of local communities dependent on natural resources, the approach adopted in the latter instruments is one of sustainable development, a concept first elucidated in the seminal Brundtland Report[109] and reiterated in almost all binding and non-binding international texts for the protection of the environment and natural and cultural heritage, (and even sometimes the economy) since then.[110] The Brundtland Commission describes it as development which meets the needs of the present without compromising the ability of future generations to meet their own needs, and as such represents a delicate balancing of competing interests—social, economic and environmental (the three pillars).[111] Christopher Weeramantry argues that a short-sighted bias is deeply entrenched in modern law, as most current legal systems concentrate on the rights of those who are living here and now.[112]

There is a belief on the part of many that sustainable development is simply soft law, and some even view the concept as purely 'aspirational'.[113] While the exact legal character of sustainable development remains unclear, Marie-Claire Cordonier Segger deems the concept to be a kind of 'interstitial' norm, where it is increasingly being used by international tribunals as a way of reconciling the right to economic development and the obligation to protect the environment.[114] In the case of *Gabčíkovo-Nagymaros*, for example, the

[107] 1992 Convention on Biological Diversity (n 137) and the 1992 United Nations Framework Convention on Climate Change: resolution adopted by the General Assembly, 20 January 1994, A/RES/48/189.

[108] UN Doc. A/CONF.151/26/Rev.1 (1992).

[109] *Our Common Future* (n 107).

[110] The World Trade Organization cites sustainable development among the aims of the institution.

[111] Indigenous people have argued through various international fora such as the United Nations Permanent Forum on Indigenous Issues and the Convention on Biological Diversity, that there are four pillars, the fourth being cultural.

[112] Christopher G. Weeramantry, Foreword, Mare-Claire Cordonnier Segger and A. Khalfan, *Sustainable Development Law, Principles, Practices and Prospects* (Oxford University Press, 2004).

[113] For example A. V. Lowe, *International Law* (Clarendon, 2007), and Lowe, 'Sustainable Development and Unsustainable Arguments', in Boyle and Freestone (eds), *International Law and Sustainable Development* (Oxford University Press, 1999), 19.

[114] Marie-Claire Cordonnier Segger and M. W. Gehring, *Sustainable Development in World Trade Law* (Kluwer, 2011), 135.

concept of sustainable development was deployed by the International Court of Justice as a meaningful way of reconciling these two conflicting norms of international law.[115] The case concerned a joint project between Slovakia and Hungary to construct an extensive dam and other works on a stretch of the Danube and treated the question of transboundary damage. Several arguments were made by Hungary regarding the potential impact of the project upon the down-stream environment and on supplies of drinking water in Hungary. As the court ultimately concluded that all the environmental matters could be addressed by ongoing co-operation between parties within the terms of a bilateral agreement, it did not offer any views as to any breach by Slovakia of an obligation to prevent transboundary harm. However, the ICJ repeated its statement in the *Nuclear Weapons* advisory opinion that 'the existence of the general obligation of states to ensure that activities within their jurisdiction and control respect the environment of other states or areas beyond national control is now part of the corpus of international law relating to the environment.'[116] Notably, the Court supported the importance of sustainable development and emphasized the procedural aspects of the concept, making explicit reference to the obligation of the parties to value, rethink, and monitor their projects in the light of environmental standards and sustainable development.[117]

Throughout the ages, mankind has, for economic and other reasons, constantly interfered with nature. In the past, this was often done without consideration of the effects upon the environment. Owing to new scientific insights and to a growing awareness of the risks for mankind—for present and future generations of pursuit of such interventions at an unconsidered and unabated pace new norms and standards have been developed, set forth in a great number of instruments during the last two decades. Such new norms have to be taken into consideration, and such new standards given proper weight, not only when states contemplate new activities but also when continuing with activities begun in the past. This need to reconcile economic development with the protection of the environment is aptly expressed in the concept of sustainable development.[118]

[115] *Gabcikovo-Nagymaros Project* case [1997] ICJ Rep 7, [53]. For further discussion see Duncan French, *International Law and Policy on Sustainable Development* (Manchester University Press, 2005) pp. 47–51; Philippe Sands, 'International Courts and the Applications of the Concept of Sustainable Development', *MaxPlanckYBUNL*, 3 (1993), 404; Alan E. Boyle, 'The Gabčíkovo-Nagymaros Case: New Law in Old Bottles', *YIEL*, 8 (1997), at 20.

[116] Gabcikovo-Nagymaros Project case [1997] ICJ Rep 7, [53].

[117] Patricia W. Bernie and Alan E. Boyle, *International Law and the Environment* (Oxford University Press, 2002), 96.

[118] Gabcikovo-Nagymaros Project case (*Hungary v Slovakia*) [1997] ICJ Rep 7, [37] ILM 162 (1998).

This reasoning was furthered more recently by the Permanent Court of Arbitration in the Iron Rhine case, which concerned the re-opening of an existing rail link between the Netherlands and Belgium.[119] In this case, the Netherlands had created nature reserves along the historic Iron Rhine railway line and sought to prevent its reactivation. Belgium argued that the upgrading of the line was part of a shift from road to rail transportation, assisting in the reduction of greenhouse gases in order to contribute to sustainable development. The Tribunal found that the application of environmental measures by the Netherlands could not amount to a denial of Belgium's transit right, nor could these measures render the exercise of such a right unreasonably difficult. While the Tribunal did not define or clarify the legal character of sustainable development, it nevertheless approached environment and development as mutually enforcing, integrated concepts—not as alternatives—and stated that development cannot be unlimited but is restricted by the significant harm it may cause to the environment.[120] Furthermore, the Tribunal held that the duty to prevent or mitigate such harm has now become a principle of international law.[121] In the 2006 Order on the Request for the Indications of Provisional Measures in the case Concerning Pulp Mills on the River Uruguay, the Court highlighted the importance of the need to ensure environmental protection of shared natural resources while allowing for sustainable economic development, in particular bearing in mind the reliance of the parties on the quality of the water of the River Uruguay for their livelihood and economic development.[122]

Sustainable development is also an agreed objective of many international trade treaties, including the WTO Institutional Agreement.[123] The concept has thus been referred to in a number of international trade disputes, among them the Shrimp–Turtle case before the WTO Appellate Body.[124] The dispute arose when the US imposed a restriction on the importation of shrimps from Asia due to the accidental destruction of sea turtles in the carrying out

[119] Permanent Court of Arbitration in the Arbitration Regarding the Iron Rhine ('Ijzeren Rijn') *Railway* (*Belgium v The Netherlands*) 2005 at 59, 114.

[120] Malgosia Fitzmaurice, *Contemporary Issues in Environmental Law* (Elgar, 2009), 85.

[121] (n 119).

[122] Case Concerning Pulp Mills on the River Uruguay (*Argentina v Uruguay*), request for Indication of Provisional Measures, Order of 13 July 2006 [2006] ICJ Rep. 19, at para. 80.

[123] For a further discussion on this aspect see Markus Gehring, 'Sustainable International Trade, Investment and Competition Law', in Marie-Claire Cordonnier Segger and Ashfaq Khalfan, *Sustainable Development Law: Principles, Practices and Prospects* (Oxford University Press, 2004), 281–94. See also, Duncan French, *International Law and Policy of Sustainable Development* (Manchester University Press, 2005), 168–211.

[124] WTO Doc.WTO/D558/AB/R, 12 October 1998.

of fishing activities. In 1997, India, Pakistan, and Thailand brought a joint complaint before the WTO Appellate Body. The WTO specifically mentioned the concept of sustainable development—recognized in the preamble of the WTO Agreement—to establish whether the measures taken to derogate from free trade were in the sense of article XX para. g of the General Agreement on Tariff and Trade (GATT). The Appellate Body made it clear that under WTO rules, countries have the right to take trade action to protect the environment and endangered species and that the WTO does not have to 'allow' them this right. It stated that the measures to protect sea turtles would be legitimate under GATT Article XX, which provides for the safeguarding of the environment as an exception to trade rules.[125] The concept of sustainable development has come a long way since it was first discussed in the 1980s, and it is now a significant concept in international discourse. However, the ambiguous formulation of the principle can give rise to divergent interpretations: one according supremacy to environmental protection and the other according supremacy to development. This remains a challenge to the concept of sustainable development, and it remains a constant tension in landscape disputes.

A principle shared by international law in the fields of cultural heritage, environment, and sustainable development is that of intergenerational equity. The idea that members of the present generation hold the earth in trust for future generations is now new. It was first relied upon as early as 1893 by the US in the Pacific Fur Seals arbitration and is referred to directly or indirectly in a number of early environmental treaties, such as the 1946 International Whaling Convention,[126] the 1968 African Conservation Convention,[127] and the 1972 World Heritage Convention.[128] The Rio Declaration states that 'the right to development must be fulfilled so as to equitably meet developmental and environmental needs of present and future generations'.[129] Responsibility

[125] The US lost the case, not because it sought to protect the environment but because it discriminated between WTO members. It provided countries in the western hemisphere technical and financial assistance and longer transition periods for their fishermen to start using turtle excluder devises.

[126] International Convention for the Regulation of Whaling (opened for signature 2 December 1946, entered into force 10 November 1948), 161 UNTS 72. The Preamble recognizes the 'interest of the nations of the world in safeguarding for future generations the great nature resources represented by the whale stock'.

[127] African Convention on the Conservation of Nature and Natural Resources, (opened for signature 15 September 1968, entered into force 16 June 1969), 1001 UNTS 3. The Preamble states that natural resources should be conserved, utilized, and developed 'by establishing and maintaining their rational utilisation for the present and future generations'.

[128] Art. 4: 'Parties agree to protect, conserve, present and transmit cultural and natural heritage to future generations'.

[129] Principle 3, Declaration on Environment and Development, Rio de Janeiro, June 1992, A/CONF.151/26 (Vol. I).

towards future generations is also mentioned in treaties dealing with flora and fauna,[130] the marine environment,[131] biological diversity,[132] and water and natural resources.[133] The UNESCO Declaration on the responsibilities of the present generations towards future generations expresses responsibility as both a precondition and an objective in its preamble.[134] Resources should not be exploited in a process of unjust enrichment, and there is a special obligation to maintain the planet's integrity because it has intrinsic worth and is essential to human survival.[135] The ability to pursue a rights-based approach has been extended to future generations in at least one case in which the Supreme Court of the Philippines granted standing to sue in obiter dictum, to present children on behalf of future generations.[136]

Brown Weiss' legal construct of trust is that 'each generation is a beneficiary of past generations and a trustee towards the future'.[137] In terms of natural resource terms, this imposes an obligation of stewardship, so that present enjoyment does not endanger future access and beneficial use. In legal philosophy, many scholars view intergenerational equity as both a moral principle—that current generations do not take priority over those to follow—and as a legal standard of equality among generations.[138] No generation has a superior claim to the earth's resources because humans did not create them. Human life emerged from and depends on the earth's natural resources, and is therefore inseparable from the environment. It is the separation of man from the earth, in the elevation of the concept of property to

[130] Preamble, Convention on International Trade in Endangered Species of Wild Fauna and Flora (CITES) (opened for signature 3 March 1973, entered into force 1 July 1975), 993 UNTS 243.

[131] Regional Convention for Cooperation on the Protection of the Marine Environment from Pollution (opened for signature 23 April 1978, entered into force 1 July 1979), 1140 UNTS 133 (Preamble). 1983 Cartagena de Indias Protocol, Preamble. 1982 Jeddah Convention, Art. 1(1).

[132] Convention on Biological Diversity (opened for signature 5 June 1992, entered into force 29 December 1993), 1670 UNTS 79 (Preamble).

[133] Convention on the Protection and Use of Transboundary Water Courses and International Lakes (opened for signature 17 March 1992, entered into force 4 August 2005), Art. 2(5)(c). 1985 ASEAN Convention, Preamble.

[134] Adopted at the 29th session of the General Conference of the United Nations Educational, Scientific and Cultural Organization meeting in Paris, 21 October to 12 November 1997.

[135] Dinah Shelton, 'Environmental Rights', in Philip Alston, *Peoples' Rights* (Oxford University Press, 2001), 182.

[136] Oposa v Factoran, 224 SCRA 792 (1993), in ILM 33 (1994), 173. See also, 'The Illusion of Intergenerational Equity: Oposa v Factoran as Pyrrhic Vistory', *Geo Int'L Env Law Review*, 15 (2003), 457.

[137] Edith Brown Weiss, *In Fairness to Future Generations: International Law, Common Patrimony, and Intergenerational Equity* (UN University, 1989).

[138] John Rawls, *A Theory of Justice* (Harvard University Press, 1970), 118; Dinah Shelton, 'Intergenerational Equity', *Solidarity: A Structural Principle of International Law* (Springer, 2009), 125.

the detriment of its social functions, which led to the current environmental problems we now face.[139]

With regard to cultural resources, we face the past generations in the spatial organizations and architectural details of our daily spheres of living, and this heritage is contested every time we make decisions concerning development. Memories are central to our identity constructions, and one cannot ignore physical milieus as central containers of these memories. When redeveloping historical places, we redevelop ourselves. It can be questioned as to whether sustainability is at all meaningful without appreciating the rights of past and future generations.[140]

3.6 Reconceptualizing Sovereignty and Dominion

After analysing the contemporary international context relevant for landscape protection, it can be deduced that the international legal order as traditionally conceived has undergone substantial changes in recent years. These changes alter the traditional notion of sovereignty, since states now have an obligation to safeguard the environment and elements of the cultural heritage for the benefit of humankind, including future generations. Here, I return to the discussion on the etymology of 'property' in Chapter 1, and the preliminary words on sovereignty at the start of this chapter, in order to shed light on the nature of these changes as they relate to landscape protection in international law. William Blackstone wrote in 1765 that the benefit of private property was the 'free use, enjoyment, and disposal of all his acquisitions, without any control or diminution'.[141] The right to private property in this view was the right to deprive others of a place and its resources. The similarity between the individual of liberalism and the sovereign was that they both claimed dominium:

> The dominium of Roman Law comprised both the legal title and the right of actual beneficial enjoyment. In other words, dominium treated as conceptually inseparable the owner's right to use, dispose of, and exclude others, from his property.[142]

[139] Landscape, as we have seen in preceding chapters, emerged as a symptom of this loss and an aesthetic value replaced a use and dependency value. Landscape itself can thus be read as a symptom of the demise of private property in terms of its social function.

[140] Ari Aukusti Lehtinen, 'Tracing Environmental Justice—On the Associations of Folk, Justice and the Environment', in Tina Peil and Michael Jones (eds), *Landscape, Law and Justice, Proceedings of a Conference* (Novus Forlag, 2003), 81–94 at 87.

[141] William Blackstone, *The Commentaries on the Laws of England*. Books 1 and 2 (Oxford University Press, 1966), 134.

[142] Kevin Gray, *Elements of Land Law* (Oxford University Press, 1993), 34.

The idea of dominium of private property meant that the private individual was as significant, if not more significant than, the public. 'So great moreover is the regard of the law for private property, that it will not authorise the least violation of it, not even for the general good of the whole community.'[143] The exclusion of others was the purpose of private property as it was of imperial and national sovereignty. Yet the fallacy of this notion of property is demonstrated by the social functions placed upon its use and enjoyment in practice (not to mention diverging considerably from its original etymological meaning—as discussed in Chapter 2). If we recall the restrictions that national laws place on private property, such as planning restrictions, it is clear that there no longer exists, if ever there did, a notion of property based on an exclusive right of 'dominium'. Therefore in the same way that dominion no longer characterizes property, nor does it exclusively characterize national sovereignty. In the same way as social obligations are placed on the possessor of property within the domestic sphere, so now (in theory) are duties placed on states within the international sphere. This correlation had already been raised by Marco Gestri in relation to the concepts of common heritage, common concern, and the cultural heritage of humankind.[144] Whether this is the case in practice is still to be seen, but any consideration of landscape protection in international law must necessarily consider this paradigm shift.

[143] Blackstone, *The Commentaries on the Laws of England* (n 141), 135.

[144] Marco Gestri, 'I concetti di patrimonio comune dell'Umanità e di risorse d'interesse generale nel diritto internazionale', in G. Colombini (ed.), *I benei pubblici tra regole di mercato e interessi generali. Profili di diritto interno e internazionale* (Jovene, 2009).

4

Institutional Framework for Landscape Protection

4.1 Early Initiatives and Soft Law

This part of the book analyses the institutional measures dealing with landscape protection at the international level, which can be roughly divided into three phases. The first, outlined in Chapter 4, is characterized predominantly by soft law instruments adopted under the auspices of UNESCO and the Council of Europe, and a strong conceptual dependency upon aesthetics and nature. This began to change in the early 1990s due to the influence of the cultural landscapes concept (explored in Chapter 5), and a number of normative developments in other regimes began to reflect this. The second phase, analysed in Chapter 5, is encapsulated in the UNESCO World Heritage Convention, particularly since 1992, with the introduction of the category of 'cultural landscapes' within the Convention's scope. Chapter 6 then deals with the third phase, beginning with the adoption of the European Landscape Convention in 2000, which has in turn influenced other normative developments in the field of international law governing the natural and cultural environment.

4.2 UNESCO Recommendations

In the early international soft law instruments concerned with landscape protection, the cultural and natural dimensions to landscape were largely dealt with separately.[1] The UNESCO Recommendation concerning the Safeguarding of the Beauty and Character of Landscapes and Sites of 1962,[2]

[1] Soft law generally refers to legal instruments such as declarations, recommendations, and other policy guidelines that may carry political weight but are not legally binding *senso strictu*.

[2] UNESCO *Recommendation concerning the Safeguarding of the Beauty and Character of Landscapes and Sites*, adopted 11 December 1962.

for example, focused on the aesthetic value and beauty of landscapes to be safeguarded and protected. Emphasis of the Recommendation was on 'preservation and restoration' of landscapes and sites. Terms such as 'virgin land' and 'dangers which threaten' are emblematic of the concern within the Recommendation of the acceleration of modern society and the effects of industrial and commercial development, but also of the misconception that landscape is predominantly a 'natural' construct, somehow external to human interaction.

A further UNESCO initiative followed in 1968 with the adoption of the Recommendation concerning the Preservation of Cultural Property Endangered by Public or Private Works,[3] which refers to immovables such as archaeological and historic or scientific sites, as well as their 'setting'. The Recommendation sets down general principles for the preventive and corrective measures aimed at protecting cultural property from public or private works likely to damage or destroy it, including, inter alia, the 'construction and alteration of highways which are a particular danger to sites or to historically important structures or groups of structures',[4] the 'construction of dams for irrigation',[5] pipelines,[6] farming operations, and afforestation.[7] An innovative feature of the Recommendation was the provision to carry out surveys—essentially impact assessments—in advance of any public or private works that might endanger cultural property, to determine measures to be taken to preserve and the amount of salvage operations to be carried out.[8] In particular, the Recommendation places emphasis on the preservation *in situ* of cultural property endangered by public or private works 'in order to preserve historical association and continuity'.[9]

The Recommendation concerning the Safeguarding and Contemporary Role of Historic Areas of 1976[10] does not mention the word landscape itself, although it indirectly relates to landscape protection by referring to a variety of historic areas and open spaces.[11] The preamble notes the 'human dimension' to landscapes by emphasizing the importance of historic areas for the 'daily environment of human beings everywhere' which 'represent the living presence of the past which formed them, [...] provide the variety in

[3] UNESCO *Recommendation concerning the Preservation of Cultural Property Endangered by Public or Private Works*, adopted 19 November 1968.

[4] Art. 8(d). [5] Art. 8(e). [6] Art. 8(f). [7] Art. 8(h). [8] Art. 22.

[9] Art. 9. [10] Adopted on 26 November 1976.

[11] Article 1(a) states that 'Historic [...] areas shall be taken to mean any groups of buildings, structures and open spaces including archaeological and paleontological sites, constituting human settlements in an urban or rural environment, the cohesion and value of which, from the archaeological, architectural, prehistoric, historic, aesthetic or socio-cultural point of view are recognized. [...]'

life's *background* needed to match the diversity of society, and that by doing so they gain in value and acquire an *additional* human dimension' (emphasis added).[12] It can be observed that the 'human dimension' referred to is seen as an appendage to the site in question, rather than intrinsically part of it, and that historic areas are part of life's *background*, rather than foreground. Accordingly, in the early instruments, the measures to be adopted by the state relate mostly to preservation, conservation, and restoration. The Recommendation concerning the Safeguarding of the Beauty and Character of Landscapes and Sites, for example, extends the scope of its measures to the whole territory,[13] its measures being solely of a protective and preservation nature: yet it is inconceivable that the whole territory might be preserved. However, the Recommendation concerning the Safeguarding and Contemporary Role of Historic Areas of 1976 did have some innovative features for its time: it noted the role of local, regional, and national planning, as well as the responsibilities of citizens, and notably, Article 13 established the obligation to provide 'machinery for appeal against arbitrary or unjust decisions.'

The Recommendation concerning the Protection, at National level, of the Cultural and Natural Heritage (1972) adopted by UNESCO at its seventeenth session to complement the World Heritage Convention recognized that 'cultural and natural heritage should be considered in its entirety as a homogenous whole, comprising not only works of great intrinsic value, but also more modest items'.[14] The duty to preserve—and *a fortiori* not to destroy—cultural and natural heritage was recognized because 'every country in whose territory there are components of the cultural and natural heritage has an obligation to safeguard this part of mankind's heritage and to ensure that it is handed down to future generations'.[15] A notable feature of the Recommendation is its inclusion of provisions on land-use and its mention of the productive use of the land,[16] something that was not referred to in the text of the World Heritage Convention (was it deemed to be of national relevance?). The scope of the Recommendation was understandably wider, given that it applies to all cultural and natural heritage—even the more 'modest items'. However, the mention of land use and production in such an early instrument was to foresee some of the developments being made later at UNESCO, when discussion on agricultural landscapes began. Interesting to note, however, is that one of the provisions relating to land use in the Recommendation refers only to natural, not cultural, heritage: 'member states should develop short and long-range plans, based on inventories of

[12] Preamble. [13] Art. 3. [14] Art. 5. [15] Preamble.
[16] Arts 37 and 38.

their *natural* heritage, to achieve a system of conservation to meet the needs of their countries'.[17] The following provision provides for an 'advisory service to guide non-governmental organisations and owners of land on national conservation policies consistent with the productive use of land', which inherently recognized the role of famers and associations. Yet the omission of 'culture' from the article on planning failed to consider the range of cultural heritage present in a rural context.

4.3 Council of Europe Instruments

Landscape is implicated in a number of treaties adopted under the auspices of the Council of Europe, namely, the Berne Convention on the Conservation of European Wildlife and Natural Habitats (1979),[18] the European Convention on the Protection of the Architectural Heritage (Granada, 3 October 1985),[19] and the European Convention on the Protection of the Archaeological Heritage, also known as the Valletta Convention (Valletta, 16 January 1992).[20] In addition, a number of Council of Europe recommendations deal directly (and indirectly) with the issue of landscape protection: Recommendation R(95)9 of 11 September 1995 of the Committee of Ministers on the integrated conservation of cultural landscape areas as part of landscape policies; Recommendation 79(9) of the Committee of Ministers concerning the identification and evaluation for the protection of natural landscapes; Recommendation R(89)6 of the Committee of Ministers of 13 April 1989 relating to the protection and enhancement of rural architectural heritage; and Recommendation R(80)16 on the specialized training of architects, town planners, civil engineers, and landscape designers.

The Berne Convention on the Conservation of European Wildlife and Natural Habitats was adopted with the aim of conserving wild flora and fauna and their habitats, as well as the monitoring and control of endangered and vulnerable species. Its preamble states that wild flora and fauna represent a natural heritage of aesthetic, scientific, cultural, recreational, and economic value, which must be preserved and transmitted to future generations, and

[17] Art. 37.

[18] Council of Europe, Convention on the Conservation of the European Wildlife and Habitats (opened for signature 19/9/1979, entered into force 1/6/1982), ETS No. 104.

[19] Council of Europe, Convention on the Protection of the European Architectural Heritage (opened for signature 3/10/1985, entered into force 1/12/1987) ETS No. 121.

[20] Council of Europe, European Convention on the Protection of the Archaeological Heritage (opened for signature 16/1/1992, entered into force 25/5/1995), ETS No. 143.

the measures needed to protect them necessarily include landscape.[21] The Convention led to the creation in 1998 of the Emerald Network of Areas of Special Conservation Interest, an ecological network covering large tracts of the territory of the states parties—almost all Council of Europe member states. It operates alongside the EU's Natura 2000 Network, which is based on the Habitats and Birds Directives, and although not dealing directly with landscape protection per se, its impact on the landscape is substantial given that large areas of European territory fall within its lines of demarcation.[22]

Landscape is implicated as cultural heritage in both the European Convention on the Protection of the Architectural Heritage and the European Convention on the Protection of the Archaeological Heritage. In relation to the former, landscape is connected to the setting of architectural sights and thus the aesthetic experience of the site in its context. The definition of the architectural heritage in the Convention includes 'sites: the combined works of man and nature, being areas which are partially built upon and sufficiently distinctive and homogeneous to be topographically definable and are of conspicuous historical, archaeological, artistic, scientific, social or technical interest'.[23] Article 7 provides that: 'in the surroundings of monuments, within groups of buildings and within sites, each Party undertakes to promote measures for the general enhancement of the environment'. Both articles obviously imply landscape considerations and the approach adopted by the Convention is a conservationist one, concerned with the increased homogeneity of building materials and the loss of vernacular character.[24] Recommendation R(89)6 of the Committee of Ministers of 13 April 1989 relating to the protection and presentation of rural architectural heritage is based on the fact that the evolution of agricultural production and social changes that result threaten the traditional rural architecture and, as a result, the landscape.

The European Convention on the Protection of the Archaeological Heritage (Valletta Convention) of 1992 replaced the earlier London Convention (1969)[25] and introduced a number of changes: when comparing the old and the revised texts, the main difference is to be found in the change

[21] This was confirmed in Recommendation 25 of 6 December 1991 of the Standing Committee for the Convention, which contained several references to the landscape outside the designated protected areas, made on the basis of a report by Cyrille de Klemn, *La conservation des milieux en dehors des aires protégées* (Council of Europe 1992).

[22] For information on the extent of the Natura 2000 Network, <http://ec.europa.eu/environment/nature/natura2000> accessed 30 January 2018.

[23] Art. 1(3).

[24] See Arts 10–13.

[25] Council of Europe, European Convention on the Protection of the Archaeological Heritage, ETS No. 66 (n 20).

of perspectives from excavations and finds to the archaeological heritage in a much wider sense, as part of the cultural landscape. No direct reference to landscape is made in the Convention, yet the obligations imposed on states parties regarding the identification and measures for protection involve landscape as an indirect concern. Article 2, for example, states that each party shall provide for 'the maintenance of an inventory of its archaeological heritage and the designation of protected monuments and *areas*' and to create '*archaeological reserves,* even where there are no visible remains on the ground or under water, for the preservation of material evidence to be studied by later generations'.[26] Article 4 requires States parties 'to implement measures for the physical protection of the archaeological heritage, making provision [...] for the acquisition or protection by other appropriate means by the authorities of areas intended to constitute archaeological reserves' and 'for the conservation and maintenance of the archaeological heritage, preferably in situ'.[27] Article 5 provides for the integration and consideration of the archaeological heritage in development plans. Another central idea is the 'participation of the public at large' and the 'promotion of access to archaeological sites'.[28] While the emphasis in the early London Convention rested heavily on archaeological excavation, illicit trade, and thus archaeology as property,[29] the Valletta Convention is more concerned with archaeology as a common resource, and thus its heritage value—note the change from the term 'civilizations' to 'mankind' in the preamble,[30] as well as the provision for the preservation of 'archaeological reserves' for 'later generations' in Article 2.

As Lyndel Prott and Patrick O'Keefe have pointed out, this concept of inheritance and handing on is central to the notion of 'heritage', whereas 'property' does not incorporate concepts of duty to protect and preserve.[31] The relevance of the Valletta Convention for landscapes relates to those of archaeological value and can be split into three levels of interest: scientific considerations (there has been a gradual shift away from the antiquarian focus on the alienated artefact towards a concern with the social and spatial context and a widening interest in the settings within which artefacts are found);

[26] Art. 2(i) and 2(ii). [27] Art. 4(i) and 4(ii). [28] Art. 9.

[29] The terms 'remains' and 'objects' are used to a greater extent than 'sites' throughout the Convention and the preoccupation is clearly on illicit excavation, which is mentioned in several articles: Art. 3(a), Art. 5(b), (c), (d), and Art. 6 para. 2.

[30] The 1969 Convention states in its preamble 'Affirming that the archaeological heritage is essential to a knowledge of the history of civilization' whereas in the preamble to 1992 Convention this has been changed to 'Recalling that the archaeological heritage is essential to a knowledge of the history of mankind'.

[31] Lyndel V. Prott and Patrick J. O'Keefe, 'Cultural "Heritage" or Cultural "Property"?', *International Journal of Cultural Property*, vol. 1, issue.1 (2002), 307.

contextual considerations; and symbolic value, which in the case of landscape is perhaps the most powerful of the three. Very often it is the associative dimension to a particular landscape (not only archaeological landscapes), which makes it so unique.

Perhaps the most elaborate initiative adopted under the auspices of the Council of Europe prior to the European Landscape Convention was Recommendation R(95)9 of 11 September 1995 on the integrated conservation of cultural landscape areas as part of landscape policies.[32] The Recommendation outlines a European strategy for action to conserve and manage cultural sites, delimited topographically, which attest to the presence of physical traces reflecting former uses of land and distinctive activities, skills, or traditions, or the artistic or literary representations inspired by them, or the significance of places for the historical events that took place there.[33] The concept of landscape is broadened substantially in this instrument and it can be seen as a precursor to the European Landscape Convention in its structure, scope, and aims.

The foregoing instruments, while they introduced some innovative features and acted as precursors for further developments by UNESCO and the Council of Europe in relation to landscape protection, did not at this stage form any kind of binding obligations in relation to landscape protection. The above recommendations relating to landscape provided policy guidelines and examples of best practice, yet these were largely aspirational and had little effect on state practice. The European Conventions on the Protection of Archaeological and Architectural Heritage did affect state policies towards both these dimensions to the heritage (architectural and archaeological), but this is merely one aspect of the cultural landscape. Likewise, the Berne Convention, while innovative and influential for its time, only applies to the natural landscape in the context of nature protection.

4.4 Other Initiatives: Towards a People-Centred Approach

The early conceptual dependency of landscape upon nature is also evident in some other regional international instruments. The Convention on the Protection of the Alps (1991), for example, makes clear that landscape is

[32] Adopted by the Committee of Ministers, 11 September 1995 at the 543rd meeting of the Ministers' Deputies.

[33] Art. 1.

never considered alone but always connected to nature,[34] and its Protocol Concerning Environmental Protection and Landscape Management also comes under the title of 'Nature and the Countryside'—implying that the terms 'landscape' and 'countryside' are synonymous.[35] At this stage, the protection of landscape was patchwork at best, and the protection of natural and cultural heritage remained separate.

Around the same time that the Alpine Convention was adopted, however, discussions were underway on the inclusion of mixed sites within the World Heritage Convention (discussed in Chapter 5). The involvement of the IUCN in this process (in addition to ICOMOS and the IFLA) is evident by the broadening concept of IUCN categories of protected areas. The work of the IUCN led to a shift in its focus from nature reserves and national parks to a full range of protected areas, including the category of 'protected landscapes'.[36] The definition of this kind of protected area was obviously influenced by the 'cultural landscapes' concept. It differs significantly from the definition of other protected areas in the sense that it is designed to foster a close relationship between nature and people, with the physical attributes of an area integrated with its associated social, cultural, and traditional values. This category defines the protected landscape as an 'area of land, with coast or seas as appropriate, where the interaction of people and nature over time has produced an area of distinct character with significant aesthetic, ecological and/or cultural value, and often with high biological diversity. Safeguarding the integrity of this traditional interaction is vital to the protection, maintenance and evolution of such as area.'[37] The other five IUCN categories of protected areas include 'strict nature reserve/wilderness area', 'national park', 'natural monument', 'habitat/species area', and 'managed resource area'. It is significant that the landscape category should specifically combine both nature *and* people, and in this way, the definition reflects the essence of

[34] Art. 2(2).

[35] An exception to the rule was the Benelux Convention on Nature Conservation and Landscape Protection (Brussels, 8 June 1982), which acknowledged the human dimension of landscape. Article 1 defines landscape as 'a tangible part of the earth defined by the relation and interaction of various factors: soil, relief, water, climate, flora, fauna and man. [...] The landscape may be considered as a reflection of the attitude of the community to its natural environment and the way in which it interacts with its environment'.

[36] See IUCN Management Guidelines for *Category V 'Protected Landscape/Seascape'* available at <https://www.iucn.org/theme/protected-areas/about/protected-areas-categories/category-v-protected-landscapeseascape> accessed 30 January 2018.

[37] The Management Guidelines also include the objective 'to support lifestyles and economic activities which are in harmony with nature and the preservation of social and cultural fabric of the communities concerned', 'to bring benefits to and contribute to the welfare of the local community'. IUCN, *Management Guidelines for IUCN Category V*, (2002), 23, 29.

landscape as a twofold relationship, an interface between nature *and* culture. Category V areas (protected landscapes) have been embraced by a number of other regimes such as the 2003 African Convention,[38] the Man and Biosphere Programme (MAB),[39] and the International Tropical Timber Organization Guidelines on the Conservation of Biological Diversity.[40] The twofold relationship between culture and nature was also enunciated in the Convention on Biological Diversity (CBD) (Rio, 1992), which mentions the role inhabitants can play in the protection of biological diversity in Article 8(j):

> States shall, subject to its national legislation, respect, preserve and maintain knowledge, innovations and practices of indigenous and local communities embodying traditional lifestyles relevant for the conservation and sustainable use of biological diversity and promote their wider application with the approval and involvement of the holders of such knowledge, innovations and practices and encourage the equitable sharing of the benefits arising from the utilization of such knowledge, innovations and practices.

In particular, the CBD has focused on the link between cultural diversity and biological diversity in the practices and traditions linked with land. A working group on article 8(j) was established in 1998 by the fourth meeting of the Conference of the Parties (COP) to the CBD. At its fifth meeting in 2000, the COP agreed to enhance the role and involvement of indigenous and local communities in the achievement of the objectives of the Convention. Of particular significance for landscape are the Akwé: Kon 'Guidelines for the conduct of cultural, environmental and social impact assessments regarding developments proposed to take place or which are likely to impact on sacred sites and on lands and waters traditionally occupied or used by indigenous and local communities'.[41] The guidelines are intended to provide a collaborative framework to ensure the involvement of indigenous and local communities in the assessment of cultural, environmental, and social concerns and interests of indigenous and local communities of proposed developments. The preamble to the Guidelines recognizes the negative impacts of many developments on sacred sites and traditionally occupied lands, and the loss of communities' traditional knowledge, innovations, and practices as a

[38] It places strong emphasis on 'sustainable development' and the mix of economic, social, cultural considerations. See Preamble and Art. V.

[39] The overarching objective of the biosphere reserve is 'sustainable development' and its essence is that people are not excluded from the protected area, and are an intricate part of the management and conservation of the area and its surroundings. The MAB is one of the few regimes that does not necessarily view concentrations of humans around a core zone of protection to be inimical to the goals of species and ecosystems protection.

[40] IUCN, *Management Guidelines for Category V* (2002), 30.

[41] COP 7 Decision VII/16.

result.[42] Accordingly, governments are encouraged to 'initiate a legal and institutional review of matters related to cultural, environmental, and social impact assessment, with a view to exploring options for incorporation of these guidelines into national legislation, policies, and procedures, bearing in mind that nothing in these guidelines should adversely affect biodiversity and the livelihoods of other communities, and that they should be implemented in a manner that is consistent with international law and with other international obligations.'[43]

The approach adopted of the CBD working groups, the IUCN, and other international organizations in the 1990s can be seen to have been influenced by the United Nations Conference on Environment and Development, or the Earth Summit, which took place in Rio de Janeiro in June 1992, and which propounded more social environmentalism through the idiom of sustainable development. The conceptual convergence between landscape (land + people) and sustainable development is clear.

[42] Ibid, at 57. [43] Ibid, at 58.

5

The 1972 UNESCO World Heritage Convention

5.1 Natural Landscapes and the First Twenty Years

The Convention on the Protection of the World Cultural and Natural Heritage (hereafter World Heritage Convention) was adopted by UNESCO at its seventeenth General Assembly in 1972.[1] Recognized as the flagship programme of UNESCO's activities in the field of culture, the original aim of the Convention was to ensure the identification, protection, conservation, presentation, and transmission to future generations of cultural and natural heritage of 'outstanding universal value'.[2] The rationale behind the Convention was that the 'deterioration or disappearance of any item of the cultural or natural heritage constitutes a harmful impoverishment of the heritage of all the nations of the world' (preamble). The World Heritage Convention now has 193 states parties,[3] which makes it the world's most universal legal instrument in the field of conservation.[4] To be nominated for inclusion in the World Heritage List, sites must be of 'outstanding universal value' and meet at least one out of ten selection criteria.[5] Outstanding universal value 'means cultural and/or natural significance which is exceptional enough to transcend

[1] Convention concerning the Protection of the World Cultural and Natural Heritage (opened for signature 16 November 1972, entered into force 17 December 1975), 1037 UNTS 151 (hereafter World Heritage Convention).

[2] Art. 4.

[3] Ratification status as of January 2018 <http://whc.unesco.org/en/statesparties> accessed 8 May 2018.

[4] For an overview of the Convention's inception and development, see Francesco Francioni, 'Thirty Years On': Is the World Heritage Convention Ready for the 21st Century?', *Italian Yearbook of International Law*, 12 (2002), and Francesco Francioni and Federico Lenzerini (eds), *The World Heritage Convention: A Commentary* (Oxford University Press, 2008).

[5] Outlined in para. 77 of the Operational Guidelines for the Implementation of the World Heritage Convention, WHC. 08/01, January 2008.

national boundaries and to be relevant and of importance to the global community now and in the future'.[6]

It is fair to say that the World Heritage Convention has received a disproportionate amount of attention—both scholarly and popular—compared to other UNESCO treaties. This is due to a number of reasons, including it being the earliest international treaty dealing with the peacetime protection of cultural heritage, its high visibility and widespread recognition, and for the way in which it has influenced heritage discourse and heritage standards globally. The Convention has been commented upon, and indeed critiqued, from various disciplinary standpoints.[7]

Although the World Heritage Convention was innovative for its time because it provided for the protection of *both* natural and cultural sites—a fact discernible from the use of the term 'heritage' instead of 'property' in its title[8]—selection criteria were nevertheless separated into natural and cultural sites at the time of drafting. Nature conservationists believed that the less human interference there had been in a given area, the 'better' or more authentic it was.[9] Thus cultural heritage was divided into monuments, groups of buildings, and sites.[10] Natural heritage was divided into natural features, geological, and physiographical formations and natural sites.[11] Cultural sites had

[6] Operational Guidelines, para. 49.

[7] The World Heritage Convention has been a topic of investigation in many disciplinary fields, including critical heritage studies, tourism studies, indigenous rights, landscape studies, cultural geography, archaeological heritage management, global governance, environmental studies, and urban planning.

[8] For a discussion on the transformation from cultural property to cultural heritage in international law, see Francesco Francioni, 'Des biens culturels au patrimoine culturel: l'évolution dynamique d'un concept et de son extension', in Abdulqawi. A. Yusuf (ed.), *Elaboration de règles internationales sur l'éducation, la science et la culture* (UNESCO 2007).

[9] Peter Fowler, *Landscapes for the World* (Windgather Press, 2004), 4 (hereafter Fowler, *Landscapes for the World*).

[10] Monuments include 'architectural works, works of monumental sculpture and painting, elements or structures of an archaeological nature, inscriptions, cave dwellings and combinations of features, which are of outstanding universal value from the point of view of history, art or science'. Groups of buildings include 'groups of separate or connected buildings which, because of their architecture, their homogeneity or their place in the landscape, are of outstanding universal value'. Sites include 'works of man or the combined works of nature and man, and areas including archaeological sites, which are of outstanding universal value from the historical, aesthetic, ethnological or anthropological point of view' (Art. 1).

[11] Natural features consist of 'physical and biological formations or groups of formations, which are of outstanding universal value from the aesthetic or scientific point of view; geological and physiographical formations and precisely delineated areas which constitute the habitat of threatened species of animals and plants of outstanding universal value from the point of view of science or conservation; natural sites or precisely delineated natural areas of outstanding universal value from the point of view of science or conservation; natural sites or precisely delineated natural areas of outstanding universal value from the point of view of science, conservation or natural beauty' (Art. 2).

to meet the criteria of authenticity and natural sites the criteria of integrity.[12] What constitutes either of these terms has been a contentious issue since the Convention's inception.

The first Operational Guidelines stated that authenticity involves 'matters of design, material, workmanship or setting'.[13] Both criteria have been expanded substantially by the World Heritage Committee (WHC) over the years, and the single paragraph defining authenticity in the first Operational Guidelines now incorporates some eight paragraphs in the most recent Guidelines (2017).[14] 'Properties nominated under criteria (i) and (iv) must now meet the conditions of authenticity, and the Nara Document on Authenticity is cited as a practical basis for measuring this.[15] All properties nominated for inscription must possess the conditions of integrity.[16] Integrity is described as 'a measure of the wholeness and intactness of the natural and/or cultural heritage and its attributes', and requires the assessment of a number of elements.[17] It is usually taken to mean physical and/or contextual and/or environmental integrity. Examples would include an archaeological or architectural complex which was more or less complete, or a ruin, which had not been subsequently developed upon. Development in or around a site which strips it of an essential integrity, for example, a road dividing an architectural work from its gardens, would cause the loss of integrity. On the other hand, continuous and harmonious development over time could maintain integrity and enhance a site.

Although no explicit mention was made of landscapes in the original text of the Convention, the Operational Guidelines referred to landscapes under the criteria for natural heritage, namely as examples of the 'interaction between man and his environment', with 'terraced agricultural landscapes' provided as an example.[18] Landscape was also referred to under cultural criteria but only in relation to 'garden and landscape design'. A new paragraph was

[12] Operational Guidelines for the Implementation of the World Heritage Convention (1), CC-77/CONF.001/8 Rev, para 11.

[13] Ibid, para. 9.

[14] Operational Guidelines for the Implementation of the World Heritage Convention. WHC. 17/01 12 July 2017. 41 COM 11.

[15] Operational Guidelines for the Implementation of the World Heritage Convention, WHC. 16/01, para 79. The Nara Document on Authenticity was adopted in Nara (Japan), 1–5 November 1994 and was conceived in the spirit of the Charter of Venice of 1964 and expands on it in response to the evolving scope of cultural heritage concerns.

[16] Decision 20 COM IX. 13.

[17] Operational Guidelines for the Implementation of the World Heritage Convention, WHC. 16/01, para 88.

[18] Operational Guidelines for the Implementation of the World Heritage Convention, CC-77/CONF.001/8 Rev, para. 10 ii(c).

introduced into the 1980 Operational Guidelines emphasizing the importance of 'mixed sites',[19] and the reference to 'terraced agricultural landscapes' was removed from the list of natural criteria. In 1984 it returned, however, when the issue of mixed natural/cultural sites and rural landscapes was raised by the Rapporteur—reference being made to 'exceptionally harmonious, beautiful, man-made landscapes as epitomised by the terraced rice-fields of South East Asia, the terraced fields of the Mediterranean Basin or by certain vineyard areas in Europe'. Despite this reference to mixed sites, in the following years most landscapes were inscribed on the World Heritage List under natural criteria only. The inscription of some landscapes under natural criteria excluded the recognition of people who for generations had lived there and who had managed the landscape (and for whom the landscape was sacred in some cases). Indeed, in the early years of the Convention's implementation, there was an assumption that natural heritage was pristine, without the influence of humanity.[20] Due to these problems, the WHC requested the IUCN, ICOMOS, and the International Federation of Landscape Architects to form a task force with the aim of developing guidelines for the identification and nomination of mixed natural and cultural sites.[21] A first meeting was held in 1985 and guidelines were drafted, although when the UK put forward the nomination of the Lake District National Park in 1987 as a potential mixed natural/cultural landscape, the Committee opted not to make a decision until specific criteria could be developed for cultural landscapes.

5.2 World Heritage 'Cultural Landscapes'

In 1992, the first expert meeting on World Heritage cultural landscapes was held in La Petite Pierre (France).[22] On the basis of the recommendations of

[19] As the combination of 'natural and cultural sites'. Operational Guidelines for the Implementation of the World Heritage Convention (1980) UNESCO Doc WHC/2 Rev, p. 4, para. 13.

[20] See, for example, UNESCO 1st Session of the World Heritage Committee: CC-77/CONF.001/9. 19 October 1977.

[21] Mechtild Rössler, 'UNESCO and Cultural Landscape Protection' in Bernd von Droste et al. (eds), *Cultural Landscapes of Universal Value* (Gustav Fisher Verlag with UNESCO 1995), 42–49. Peter Fowler, *World Heritage Papers 6. World Heritage Cultural Landscapes 1992–2002*, (UNESCO World Heritage Centre 2003).

[22] Report of the Expert Group on Cultural Landscapes (La Petite Pierre, France, 24–26 October 1992). WHC-92/CONF.202/10/Add. See also, on the genesis of the concept within the World Heritage Convention: Mechtild Rössler, 'Linking Nature and Culture: World Heritage Cultural Landscapes', *Cultural Landscapes: the Challenges of Conservation*, World Heritage 2002, Shared Legacy, Common Responsibility; Associated Workshops, 11–12 November 2002 (Ferrara), 10.

the meeting, the Operational Guidelines were subsequently revised to officially include 'cultural landscapes' within the scope of the Convention, and were adopted by the sixteenth session of the WHC.[23] Cultural landscapes were defined as 'cultural properties representing the combined works of nature and of man designated in Article 1 of the Convention. They are illustrative of the evolution of human society and settlement over time, under the influence of the physical constraints and/or opportunities presented by their natural environment and of successive social, economic, and cultural forces, both external and internal.'[24]

They should be selected on the basis both of their outstanding universal value and of their representativity in terms of a clearly defined geo-cultural region and also for their capacity to illustrate the essential and distinct cultural elements of such regions.[25] [...] The term embraces a diversity of manifestations of the interaction between humankind and its natural environment.[26]

The inclusion of the category of 'cultural landscapes' within the scope of the World Heritage Convention reflected the evolving concept of 'heritage' and recognized the fact that many sites cannot be separated into criteria of culture or nature. It also recognized the cultural and social importance attached to landscapes, which had, until then, been designated as 'natural' heritage.[27] Prior to this, the text of the Convention favoured a 'monumental' vision of heritage, corresponding to Western aesthetic canons. 'Out of step with over twenty years of progress made in the human sciences, it risked losing its credibility by privileging the monuments of a few cultural basins'.[28] From an analysis of those in attendance at the first expert meeting in La Petite Pierre, it appears that the Australian experience of managing indigenous landscapes had an influence on the conceptualization of cultural landscapes for

Peter Fowler, World Heritage Cultural Landscapes, 1992–2002: A Review and Prospect, ibid, 17. Mechtild Rössler, 'World Heritage Cultural landscapes: A UNESCO Flagship Programme 1992–2006', *Landscape Research*, *31* (4) 333–53. John Aitchison, 'Cultural Landscapes in Europe, a Geographical Perspective', in Bernd von Droste et al (eds), *Cultural Landscapes of Universal Value* (1995), 272. David Jacques, 'The Rise of Cultural Landscapes', *International Journal of Heritage Studies*, 1 (1995).

[23] Decision 16COM XIII. 1–3.

[24] Operational Guidelines for the Implementation of the World Heritage Convention, 1994, para 36, available at <http://whc.unesco.org/archive/opguide94.pdf> accessed 30 January 2018.

[25] Ibid, para. 36. [26] Ibid, para. 37.

[27] UNESCO 1st Session of the WHC. CC-77/CONF.001/9. 17 Oct. 1977, 3. UNESCO Expert Review on Evaluation of General Principles and criteria for Nominations of Natural World Heritage Sites. WHC-96/CONF.202/INF.9. 15 April 1996, 4.

[28] Sophie Boukhari, 'Beyond the Monuments: A Living Heritage', *UNESCO Sources*, No. 80 (June 1996), 7.

the purposes of redefining the Convention's criteria.[29] Three categories of cultural landscapes were incorporated into the revised Operational Guidelines:[30]

i. *clearly defined landscapes* designed and created intentionally by man. This embraces garden and parkland landscapes characteristically constructed for aesthetic, social, and recreational reasons which are often but not always associated with religious or other monumental buildings and ensembles;

ii. *organically evolved landscapes* resulting from an initial social, economic, administrative, and/or religious imperative and have developed their present form by association with and in response to the natural environment. Such landscapes reflect that process of evolution in their form and component features. They fall into two sub-categories:
   a) *relict (or fossil) landscapes* in which an evolutionary process came to an end at some time in the past, either abruptly or over a period. Their significant distinguishing features are, however, still visible in material form:
   b) *continuing landscapes* which retain an active social role in contemporary society closely associated with a traditional way of life. They are continuing to evolve while, at the same time, exhibit significant material evidence of their historic evolution;

iii. *associative cultural landscapes* with definable powerful, religious, artistic, or cultural associations with the natural element rather than material cultural evidence, which may be insignificant or even absent.

The criteria concerning continuing and associative landscapes were significant because they gave recognition to continuing tradition, customary practices, and the associative dimension to landscapes. As noted by Rössler, 'the primary difference was the acceptance of communities and their relationship with the environment'.[31] The inclusion of both continuing landscapes and associative landscapes were certainly influenced by arguments raised by Indigenous peoples in response to the 'natural' heritage nominations of well-known heritage sites in Australia and New Zealand, most notably Uluru and Tongariro National Park. Tongariro National Park had been inscribed under natural criteria from 1990 before it was known that the 'natural' environment was not only the homeland of a community but also that the natural features

[29] Report of the Expert Group on Cultural Landscapes, La Petite Pierre (France) 24–26 October 1992 (n 22).

[30] Defined in para. 39. Operational Guidelines 1994.

[31] Rössler, 'World Heritage Cultural Landscapes: A UNESCO Flagship Programme 1992–2006' (n 22).

were imbued with great importance for their culture. Moreover, it was the presence of this community and their care and maintenance of the natural environment that gave the site its characteristic qualities. Tongariro was re-inscribed as an associative landscape in 1993 to mark the fundamental role the landscape plays in the oral tradition and cultural identity of the Maori people. According to Chief of the Ngati Tuwharetoa: 'these sacred mountains are to be owned by no-one and yet are for everyone'.[32]

Likewise, Uluṟu and its surrounding landscape had initially been inscribed on the World Heritage List as a natural site in 1987, but was re-inscribed in 1994 as a cultural landscape in recognition of the close cultural associations between the Uluṟu landscape and the Aṉangu people. Uluṟu played an important role in shaping the definitions of cultural landscape in 1992 and thereafter. As stated by the Australian Government's renomination: 'The significance of the landscape is not measured only by individual locations . . . they are interconnected by the *iwara* (tracks) of the heroic beings active during the *Tjukurpa* (the Law).'[33] 'It is a complex concept because it relates not only to the era of the travels of the ancestral figures, but also to the Law as a force in the lives of the living. It does not reflect the Western concept of time.'[34] Many of the striking rock features of Uluṟu 'are the transformed bodies or implements of the creative heroes of the Aṉangu religion. The conservation and management of the Uluṟu Kata Tjuṯa National Park are guided by Aṉangu law and involves for example, the spacing of groups more evenly across the landscape ensuring that overexploitation of particular wild foods does not occur.'[35] For the Aṉangu and many other indigenous peoples, the landscape is not only a natural entity, but also a cultural one.

Aside from the recognition of intangible values and the spiritual relationship between local communities and nature, the cultural landscapes category acknowledged that sites are not isolated islands, but that they have to be seen in the ecological system and their cultural linkages in time and space beyond single monuments and strict nature reserves. Furthermore, cultural landscapes highlighted the importance of unique land-use systems, the continued work of people over centuries and sometimes millennia to adapt to the natural environment, also recognized as enhancing biological diversity.[36]

[32] Chief of the Ngati Tuwharetoa, as cited in Fowler, *Landscapes for the World* (n 9), 33.

[33] Renomination of Uluṟu-Kaṯa Tjuṯa National Park, reproduced in Fowler, *Landscapes for the World* (n 9), 34.

[34] Ibid.

[35] Sophie Boukhari, 'Beyond the Monuments: A Living Heritage', *UNESCO Sources* 80 (June 1996), 9.

[36] Mechtild Rössler, World Heritage—Linking Cultural and Biological Diversity, Paper for the Seventh US/ICOMOS Symposium: *Learning from World Heritage*, Natchitoches, Louisiana, 25–27 March 2004.

Key world crops developed in spectacular agricultural systems in the High Andes (e.g. potatoes, corn), terraced rice paddies in Asia (rice, fish, vegetables), and oasis systems in the Sahara (dates). The global importance of these systems and the genetic varieties in diverse cultural landscapes was acknowledged. In some cases they represent models for sustainable land use and community stewardship, including the marketing of specific agricultural products or traditional arts and crafts. The third cultural landscape to be inscribed on the World Heritage List represented one such example. The Rice Terraces of the Philippine Cordilleras were inscribed as a cultural landscape (organically evolved continuing) in 1995.[37] Described as the result of the interaction between the people their customary activities and traditional practices of rice production dating back centuries, the decision to inscribe the Cordilleras was based on their illustration of a 'remarkable degree of harmony between humankind and the natural environment', their 'great aesthetic appeal', as well as their demonstration of 'sustainable farming systems in mountainous terrain, based on careful use of natural resources.'[38] 'Owing to the difficult terrain, the Cordillera mountain tribes are among the few peoples of the Philippines who successfully resisted foreign domination and preserved their tribal culture'.[39] The steepness of the slopes means that all tilling and maintenance has been carried out manually for the last 2000 years. The complex system of dams, sluices, canals, and bamboo pipes transfer water from the highest terrace to the lowest, draining into a river or stream at the bottom of the valley. However, while the designation of an agricultural landscape such as the Cordilleras as World Heritage was based on humanizing principles, the effects of such designation are arguably contrary to such ends.

Maintaining the integrity of a cultural landscape implies an obligation on the people living there to maintain their customs and traditional farming practices, yet this can be difficult, if not burdensome, in the face of external market forces, poverty, and environmental problems. The Cordilleras were placed on the List of World Heritage in Danger in 2001 due to landscape management issues stemming from the abandonment of terraces, dispossession of property rights, and resource management conflict.[40] The underlying challenge for the landscape of the Cordilleras landscape was (and still is) socio-economic in nature.[41] After a number of fact-finding missions, benchmarks were set in 2006 by the World Heritage Centre and the advisory bodies ICOMOS and IUCN. These benchmarks returned to the core of the

[37] Decision 19COM VIII.C.1. [38] Ibid. [39] Ibid.

[40] Rachel Guimbatan, 'Managing our Changing World Heritage: The Philippines Rice Terraces Experience' IOP Conference Series: *Earth and Environmental Science*, vol. 6 (2009), session 57.

[41] Ibid.

landscape's problems and sought to consider local peoples' perceptions, local development aspirations of the communities, and functional governance mechanisms.[42] In order for the landscape of the Cordilleras to maintain its legitimacy, it must fulfil socio-economic benefits and provide a livelihood for the communities who live there. After efforts were made by the state party to remedy the situation, the Cordilleras were withdrawn from the List of World Heritage in Danger in 2012.[43] Yet the case represents one of the challenges in the designation of living landscapes deemed to be of outstanding universal value, where that value implies restrictions on the fundamental rights of its inhabitants—namely that of development and self-determination, to be discussed further later in the chapter.

5.3 Landscape Diversity and Representativeness of the List

The Operational Guidelines refer to the great variety of landscapes representative of the different regions of the world.[44] The problem of geographical cover and under-representation have marred the World Heritage Convention since its inception. There was, and still is, a preponderance of categories of cultural items that essentially pertain to European civilization, archaeological sites, historic sites, and Christian monuments, while vernacular heritage and cultural landscapes represented less than 10% of the whole List.[45] In addition, cultural sites have always massively outnumbered natural sites on the World Heritage List.[46] Thus, the listing system may appear rather ad hoc, driven by national interests. In an attempt to remedy this somewhat, in 1994 at its eighteenth session, the WHC adopted a Global Strategy for a more representative list.[47] The strategy aimed to encourage more under-represented countries to become states parties to the Convention

[42] Expert Meeting of the World Heritage Convention on Benchmarks and Chapter IV of the Operational Guidelines, Paris, 2–3 April 2007.

[43] Decision 33 COM 7A.24.

[44] Para. 47 and annex 3. Operational Guidelines for the Implementation of the World Heritage Convention, WHC. 16/01.

[45] H. Stovel, 'The Evaluation of Cultural Properties for the World Heritage List', *Nature and Resources*, 28 (3) (1992), 30; Henry Cleere, 'The Uneasy Bedfellows: Universality and Cultural Heritage', in Robert Layton, Julian Thomas, and Peter G. Stone (eds), *Destruction and Conservation of Cultural Property* (Routledge, 2001), 22, 26.

[46] This is still the case. As of January 2018, there are 832 cultural sites compared to 206 natural sites.

[47] Report of the Meeting on the Global strategy and Thematic Studies for a Representative World Heritage List (20–22 June 1994), UNESCO Doc. WHC-94/CONF.003/INF. 6.

and develop tentative lists. Since then World Heritage nominations are not considered unless previously inscribed on the Tentative List by a state party.[48] Later, it was decided to examine only two complete nominations per state party per year, provided that at least one of the nominations concerned a natural property, and the annual limit on the amount of nominations to be reviewed was set at forty-five.[49]

As previously stated, the World Heritage Convention focuses on cultural properties of 'outstanding universal value' and selection for nomination for inscription of a property on the World Heritage List must come from the states parties. This has caused some criticism of the Convention,[50] in that the listing of a few may signal to governments that they are at liberty to do as they wish with any site not on the List, and hence deemed to be of lesser historical, cultural, or social importance. Yet not all cultural properties or sites deemed to be important could feasibly be listed. 'Outstanding universal value' is a means of selection of a number of representative sites, which because of their exceptional quality are of more concern for the international community. Furthermore, the Convention's Article 12 provides that 'when a property belonging to the cultural heritage has not been included in the List, this shall in no way be construed to mean that it does not have an outstanding universal value for the purposes other than those resulting from inclusion'. Federico Lenzerini's analysis of Article 12 points out that a 'cultural property may be of outstanding universal value, being thus included within the scope of the Convention *ratione materiae*, even in the event that it is not inscribed on the World Heritage List'.[51] This is also emphasized by Guido Carducci, who argues that the Convention 'applies to heritage as defined by Articles 1 and 2 situated on the territory of states parties, whether or not this heritage is listed under Article 11'.[52] Arguably, states parties to the Convention are under the obligation to respect the provisions of the Convention also with regard to those cultural properties not included in any of the two lists established by Article 11, if they objectively satisfy the conditions and requirements for being

[48] Paras 62–63 Operational Guidelines for the Implementation of the World Heritage Convention, WHC.08/01, January 2008.

[49] This procedure takes place on an experimental basis of four years, leaving the state party the decision on the nature of the nomination, see para. 61(a) Operational Guidelines 2008.

[50] David Lowenthal, 'Cultural Landscapes', *The UNESCO Courier: A Window Open on the World*, 50 (9) (1997), 18–20.

[51] Federico Lenzerini, 'Article 12. Protection of Properties not Inscribed on the World Heritage List', in Francioni and Lenzerini (eds), *The 1972 World Heritage Convention. A Commentary* (Oxford University Press, 2018), 202.

[52] Guido Carducci, Articles 4–7, 'National and International Protection of the Cultural Heritage', in Francioni and Lenzerini (eds), *The 1972 World Heritage Convention. A Commentary* (n 51), 113.

considered of 'outstanding universal value'.[53] The Buddhas of Bamiyan, for example, were not inscribed on the List at the time of their wilful destruction by the Taliban, yet as pointed out by Pierre-Marie Dupuy, Afghanistan had ratified the Convention in 1979 and the importance of the Buddhas did not depend on their inscription on the List (and even if it did, it would unlikely have deterred the Taliban from destroying them).[54] Indeed, there are cultural landscapes in many regions of the world which are not of 'outstanding universal value' but which may be highly representative or important at national or international levels.[55] There are also many world heritage sites that are essentially cultural landscapes, although not inscribed as such. Archaeological landscapes such as Stonehenge and Avebury—as relict or fossil landscapes—or garden and park landscapes such as Versailles would be clear examples. Fowler notes that the cultural landscape concept is not the opposite of an area or structure which is thought to be of only local interest, as every landscape has its locally significant features and finds validity as a local place. The difference is that a potential World Heritage Site must satisfy the criterion of being 'outstanding' in so far as it must have a demonstrable quality over and above the merits of something of only local heritage interest.[56] The rationale behind the designation of cultural landscapes as a World Heritage category was a noble one, an attempt to make the List more credible, representative, and more relevant outside Europe. However, as the example of the Cordilleras shows, it is not without problems, since designating a living landscape as heritage can bring with it various socio-economic challenges for sustainability and spatial justice. What follows is an examination of the typology of cultural landscapes inscribed on the List.

5.4 A Typology of World Heritage Cultural Landscapes

While cultural landscapes are defined as the 'result of the combined work of nature and man', they are nevertheless categorized as cultural or mixed heritage. Since the inclusion of cultural landscapes within the scope of the WHC in 1992, a total of 102 such landscapes have been inscribed on the World Heritage List (one of which has been delisted). Many sites inscribed

[53] Ibid, 205.

[54] Pierre-Marie Dupuy, 'The Impact of Legal Instruments adopted by UNESCO on General International Law', in Abdulqawi A. Yusuf (ed.), *Standard-Setting in UNESCO, Vol. 1, Normative Action in Education, Science and Culture. Essays in Commemoration of the Sixtieth Anniversary of UNESCO* (UNESCO 2007), 351, 360.

[55] Although, other categories exist to this end, including IUCN Protected areas V for example.

[56] Fowler, *Landscapes for the World* (n 9), 1.

prior to 1992 would classify as cultural landscapes, as previously mentioned. Peter Fowler notes that prior to 2002, over 100 cultural landscapes had been inscribed on the List, yet only thirty of these were in the cultural landscapes category.[57] Another study carried out more recently in 2007 revealed that over 360 sites on the World Heritage List could be described as a landscape complex.[58] For the purposes of examining the typology, however, only those World Heritage sites defined as cultural landscapes within their site description will be addressed here. The first fact worth noting is that, of the 101 sites currently inscribed as cultural landscapes, ninety-one are classified as cultural heritage, and only twelve as mixed sites. Almost half of these cultural landscapes can be found in Europe and North America (fifty-four), followed by Asia and the Pacific (nineteen), Africa (twelve), Arab States (eight), and Latin America and the Caribbean (eight). A common thread of cultural landscapes is that most of them bear a toponym in their nomination title (valley, mountain, hill, archipelago, grove) or demarcated unit (region, park, settlement). However, cultural routes also feature, even though they do not represent a defined topographical area or spatial complex per se. It is difficult to separate cultural landscapes into the three categories originally conceived in the Operational Guidelines because many landscapes share multiple typologies, and the selection criteria for ascertaining the outstanding universal value of landscapes have since been incorporated into a set of ten criteria for all World Heritage nominations.[59] However, it can be observed that the most represented form of cultural landscapes on the List is the second category, that is, *organically evolved cultural landscapes*, which can be split into *relict (or fossil) landscapes* and *continuing landscapes*. The former refers to ancient cultural landscapes that emerged in the prehistoric or historic period but which were later abandoned by humans or which are no longer used for the original purpose. Their material evidence is represented in the archaeological remains or ruins in the landscape. The continuing landscape, however, continues to function and evolve over time. Broadly speaking, the category of organically evolved cultural landscapes includes agricultural landscapes, industrial landscapes, historical townscapes, historic memorial landscapes, and

[57] Peter Fowler, World Heritage Cultural Landscapes 1992–2002, *World Heritage Papers 6* (UNESCO World Heritage Centre, 2003), 140.

[58] Marina Kuleshova (Chief of the Cultural Landscapes Management Department, Heritage Institute, Moscow), Cultural Landscapes in the World Heritage List, paper presented at the Regional Seminar for CIS countries '*Safeguarding the World Heritage in the Context of New Global Challenges*', 1–3 March 2011, Moscow.

[59] Until the end of 2004, World Heritage sites were selected based on six cultural and four natural criteria. The Operational Guidelines were then revised to include only one set of ten criteria, available at <http://whc.unesco.org/en/criteria/> accessed 30 January 2018.

sacred landscapes. For the most part, particularly in the case of agricultural landscapes inscribed on the List, they are supposed to illustrate a harmonious interaction between humans and the environment over time, such as the Rice Terraces of the Philippine Cordilleras or the Cinque Terre. However, there are exceptions to this rule, for example, Las Medulas historic mining landscape in Spain.[60] Las Medulas is the result of Roman exploitation of gold deposits using a technique based on hydraulic power, which impacted heavily on the landscape, leaving sheer faces in the mountainsides and vast areas of tailings, which are now used for agriculture. There was substantial objection at the time of nomination from some delegations, who believed not only that Las Medulas did not correspond to the definitions of cultural heritage in Article 1 of the Convention, but that this landscape was the result of destructive human activities as well as 'harmful to the noble cause of environmental promotion and protection'.[61]

The next most represented category of cultural landscape on the List is the *associative cultural landscape*, now represented in criterion VI of the ten selection criteria, according to which a landscape must be 'directly or tangibly associated with events or living traditions, with ideas, or with beliefs, with artistic and literary works of outstanding universal significance'. It must be noted that this criterion is for the most part not considered in isolation but combined with other criteria in assessing the outstanding universal value of landscape for inscription. The first cultural landscapes formally inscribed on the List, Tongariro National Park in 1993 and Uluṟu Kaṯa Tjuṯa in 1994 (previously discussed) were both re-inscribed under this category in recognition of the close cultural associations between these landscapes and the indigenous people for whom they hold special value. Of the thirty-one landscapes inscribed under the 'associative' criterion, the majority (twenty-six) are located outside Europe—in Asia and the Pacific, Africa, and Central America. The majority of these represent sacred landscapes, for example, in the form of sacred mountains (China, Japan, Kyrgyzstan),[62] sacred hills (Madagascar, Zimbabwe),[63] and sacred forests (Kenya).[64] Other historic, literary, and artistic associations are represented in a small number of associative landscapes

60 Decision 21COM VIII.C.

61 This was the position of Thailand with agreement from Germany and Finland. Report of the 21st session of the Committee, WHC-97/CONF.208/17.

62 Mount Wutai Sacred Buddhist Mountain (China), Decision 33COM 8B.7; Sacred Sites of the Kii Mountain Range (Japan), Decision 28COM 14B.28 and the Salaimon-Too Sacred Mountain (Kyrgystan), Decision 33COM 8B.16.

63 Royal Hill of Ambohimanga (Madagascar), Decision 25COM XA; Matobo Hills (Zimbabwe), Decision 27COM 8C.38.

64 Sacred MijiKenda Kaya Forests (Kenya), Decision 32COM 8B.50.

in Europe, the Val d'Orcia being an example of a landscape with artistic and literary associations;[65] the Þingvelli National Park in Iceland as a landscape with historic and literary associations—it was the seat of Norse governance from 930 until the eighteenth century and is celebrated in medieval Icelandic sagas.[66] The remaining of the three categories of cultural landscapes, that is, *clearly defined landscapes* designed and intentionally created by man, is the least represented on the official list of cultural landscapes, all of which are located in Europe, as expected. This category covers garden and parkland landscapes, with a strong emphasis on aesthetics, often associated with building ensembles. Example of such a landscape includes Sintra in Portugal,[67] the Royal Botanic Gardens in the United Kingdom,[68] or the Garden Kingdom of Dessau-Worlitz in Germany.[69]

5.5 Institutional Framework and Implementation

The Operational Guidelines, although not mentioned in the Convention's text, play an essential role in the daily implementation of the Convention by the secretariat.[70] They set out the procedure for the inscription of sites and landscapes on the World Heritage List, include updated criteria for the protection and conservation of World Heritage sites, for the granting of international assistance through the World Heritage Fund, and for the mobilization of national and international support for the Convention, among other things. They are periodically revised to reflect the decisions of the WHC—the most recent Guidelines were adopted in 2017.[71] The Operational Guidelines are 'flexible working documents', a tool of UNESCO 'governance'[72] and, in so far as they foster a uniform administrative practice of the states parties, especially regarding nominations of

[65] Val d'Orcia (Italy); Decision 28 COM 14B.51.

[66] Þingvelli National Park (Iceland) Decision 28 COM 14B.41.

[67] Decision 19COM VIIIC.1.

[68] Decision 27COM 8C.32.

[69] Decision 24COMXC.1.

[70] Peter Strasser, 'Putting Reform into Action': Thirty Years of the World Heritage Convention: How to Reform a Convention without Changing its Regulations', *International Journal of Cultural Property*, 2 (2002), 246. Armin von Bogdandy and D. Zacharias, 'Zum Status der Weltkulurerbekonvention im deutschen Rechtsraum—ein Beitrag sum internationalen Verwaltungsrecht, Neue Zeitschrift fur Verwaltungsrecht', *NVwZ*, 26 (2007), 5, 527.

[71] WHC.17/01, Decision 41 COM 11.

[72] Sabine Von Schorlemer, 'Compliance with the World Heritage Convention: Reflections on the Elbe Valley and the Dresden Waldschlössen Bridge', *German Yearbook of International Law*, 51 (2008), 9.

properties for inscription, they have also been compared to an 'administrative act'.[73]

Under the terms of Section III, articles 8 through 14 of the World Heritage Convention, implementation and oversight of the Convention are entrusted to the WHC, which meets once a year and consists of twenty-one representatives from the states parties to the Convention. The Committee is supported by a secretariat at the World Heritage Centre, UNESCO headquarters in Paris, and by three advisory bodies: the International Council of Monuments and Sites (ICOMOS), the International Union for the Conservation of Nature (IUCN),[74] and the International Council for the Conservation and Restoration of Monuments (ICCROM). ICOMOS plays the largest role in the case of cultural landscapes and works closely with the IUCN. The main functions of the Committee are to examine the nominations put forward by states parties for inscription on the World Heritage List, to examine the state of conservation of the properties inscribed on the List through reactive monitoring, decide which properties should be inscribed on the World Heritage in Danger List, and decide whether a property should be deleted (which has only occurred twice, to be discussed later), to determine how resources are to be used and to review and report on the implementation of the Convention.[75] Views on the effectiveness of the WHC vary between scholars and along disciplinary lines. On the one hand, the Committee has been described as a 'guardian of the general interest'[76] and the Convention is generally perceived as having a strong system of 'international governance'.[77] On the other hand, however, the Committee has come under scrutiny for its increasing politicization, with voting based on geopolitical alliances rather than on safeguarding the general interest.[78] In addition, recommendations of the Advisory Bodies are increasingly

[73] Laurance Boisson de Chazour, 'Treaty Law-Making and Non-Treaty Law Making: The Evolution Structure of the International Legal Order', in Rudiger Wolfrum and Volker Roben (eds), *Development of International Law in Treaty Making* (Springer 2005), 463, 473.

[74] Full title: 'The International Union for the Conservation of Nature and Natural Resources'.

[75] Operational Guidelines for the Implementation of the World Heritage Convention, WHC. 08/01. Paras 6–7.

[76] Gionata Buzzini and Luigi Condorelli, 'Article 11, List of World Heritage in Danger and Deletion of a Property from the World Heritage List', in Francioni and Lenzerini (eds.), *The 1972 World Heritage Convention: A Commentary* (n 4), 187.

[77] Diana Zacharias, *The International Regime for the Protection of the World Cultural and Natural Heritage* (Shaker Verlag 2007), 32.

[78] See, for example, Lynn Meskell, 'UNESCO's World Heritage Convention at 40. Challenging the Economic and Political Order of International Conservation', *Current Anthropology*, 54 (4) (2013), and Lynn Meskell, 'The Rush to Inscribe: Reflections on the 35th Session of the World Heritage Committee, UNESCO Paris, 2011', *Journal of Field Archaeology*, 37 (2) (2012), 145–51.

overturned and publicly derided.[79] Lynn Meskell argues, for example, that sites are being transformed into transactional commodities with exchange values that transcend their cultural values.[80]

Periodic reporting consists in the reporting by states parties to the UNESCO General Conference (through the Committee) on the legislative and administrative provisions they have adopted for the application of the Convention, including the state of conservation of the World Heritage sites located on their territories. States parties can request expert advice from the advisory bodies and the secretariat. Periodic reporting is important for the long-term conservation of the properties as well as for ensuring the credibility of the implementation of the Convention. The procedure and format for such reporting is set out in detail in the Operational Guidelines.[81] Reactive monitoring consists in the reporting by the secretariat and the advisory bodies to the WHC on the state of conservation of sites inscribed on the List that may be under threat. A further layer of supervision in the form of 'reinforced monitoring' was established by the Committee in 2007.[82] States parties are invited to inform the Committee of their intention to undertake or authorize any major restoration or construction work that may affect the outstanding universal value of the property. The Committee may inscribe a property on the List of World Heritage in Danger if the site is threatened by serious and specific danger; if major operations are necessary for the conservation of the site and if assistance under the Convention has been requested for the site.[83] Although, in practice, the Committee has proceeded to enlist some properties on the World Heritage in Danger List also without state consent, for example, the City of Dubrovnik in 1991.[84] A number of criteria are set out in the Operational Guidelines to determine whether the site is deemed to be in danger. These include, inter alia, threatened effects of armed conflict, or effects of regional planning and town planning projects that seriously impair the authenticity or integrity of the

[79] Jukka Jokilehto, 'World Heritage. Observations on Decisions related to Cultural Heritage', *Journal of Cultural Heritage Management and Sustainable Development*, 1 (2011), 61–74.

[80] Meskell, 'UNESCO's World Heritage Convention at 40. Challenging the Economic and Political Order of International Conservation' (n 78) and Lynn Meskell, 'World Heritage and WikiLeaks: Territory, Trade, and Temples on the Thai-Cambodian Border', *Current Anthropology*, 57 (1) (2016), 72–95.

[81] Decision 22 COM VI.7, set out in Section V.B. *Operational Guidelines for the Implementation of the World Heritage Convention*, WHC. 11/01.

[82] Decision 31COM 5.2.

[83] *Operational Guidelines for the Implementation of the World Heritage Convention*, WHC. 16/01, para. 177

[84] Decision 15COM VII.

site.[85] In the past, the information provided by states parties, particularly looking at the requirements of the conservation reports by the secretariat and the advisory bodies, was often incomplete.[86] The frequency of the reporting was regarded as insufficient to monitor the implementation of decisions. Reinforced monitoring was adopted by the Committee to clarify the rules and responsibilities pertaining to World Heritage status and to improve compliance.[87] Reinforced monitoring may be activated when implementation requires more robust monitoring and reporting beyond the standard requirements; the main difference between reinforced and reactive monitoring being the frequency of the information gathering activities and in the detail of the reporting process. States parties have the 'responsibility' (stronger language) to provide all relevant information to the WHC on the implementation of its decisions and to co-operate in this regard.[88] In extreme circumstances, where the site has deteriorated to the extent that it has lost the characteristics which determined its inclusion in the World Heritage List, and where the corrective measures have not been taken by the state party, the Committee may propose the deletion of the site from the World Heritage List.[89] According to UNESCO's former Director General Matsuura, deletion is 'never a satisfactory solution as UNESCO's World Heritage Convention and World Heritage List have been created to ensure the preservation and enhancement of our shared heritage'.[90] Deletion has in fact only occurred twice in the Convention's history, to be discussed further below.

The approach by UNESCO in ensuring compliance of states parties with the Convention has generally been of 'low level' intensity, through persuasion or political pressure on governments, through placing a property on the List in Danger or through technical and financial assistance. This approach has been successful in many cases where the integrity of landscapes or sites has been seriously compromised by proposed development projects (see examples below). Although the Committee can issue formal expressions of concern to national governments and the international community, and may hold extraordinary sessions, it is 'powerless to intervene directly against the will of the

[85] *Operational Guidelines for the Implementation of the World Heritage Convention*, WHC. 16/01, para. 179(b).

[86] WHC-07/31.COM/5.2. Paris 15 June 2007 'Mechanism proposed by the Director-General to ensure proper implementation of the World Heritage Committee decisions', paras 1 and 3.

[87] Ibid. [88] Decision 31COM 5.2.

[89] *Operational Guidelines for the Implementation of the World Heritage Convention*, WHC. 16/01, paras 192–198.

[90] UNESCO Press Releases, 31 January 2008, available at www.whc.unesco.org/en/news/412 accessed 8 May 2018.

state party concerned in order to protect our universal heritage'.[91] The tension between state sovereignty on the one hand, and the international community interest on the other, has been a constant concern since the Convention's adoption.[92]

5.6 World Heritage and the Global Governance of Landscape

The World Heritage Convention, despite its shortcomings, has undoubtedly had an impact on the global governance of landscapes. First, World Heritage status appears to weigh on domestic practice in cases of landscapes under threat from destructive large-scale project development. Second, it has proved instrumental in international cases dealing with landscape degradation (particularly in cases of investor–state arbitration and international criminal law) and third, the concept of the 'cultural landscapes' category itself has influenced other normative developments in the fields of international environmental law and cultural heritage law.[93]

World Heritage status has been used in many cases attempting to protect landscapes from environmentally or culturally destructive projects. Non-European examples include the Tasmanian rain forests, the location of a state-backed hydro-electric dam in the 1980s, which would have seriously harmed the integrity of the landscape. The case eventually made its way to the Australian High Court, where a four to three majority ruled in favour of the federal government and compliance with the Convention's obligations.[94] More recently, in 2014, the Tasmanian forests became again the focus of a dispute over proposals for modifications to the boundaries of the Tasmanian Wilderness to accommodate logging activity, made by Australian government on foot of election promises. Ultimately, the influence of the WHC, backed by domestic scrutiny and popular support, led to the cancellation of the proposed changes and protection of the Tasmanian Wilderness.[95] In a similar case, a major copper mining operation was planned

[91] Christina Cameron, 'The Strengths and Weaknesses of the World Heritage Convention', *Nature and Resources*, 28 (3) 21.

[92] Art. 6 of the World Heritage Conventions reaffirms the sovereignty of states parties, as well as the property rights provided by national legislation. For a discussion on sovereignty and the World Heritage Convention see Francesco Francioni, 'World Cultural Heritage List and National Sovereignty', *Humanitäres Völkerrecht* (1993), 195.

[93] Discussed in Chapter 4 and Chapter 6.

[94] See *Commonwealth v Tasmania* [1983] 158 CLR. 1.

[95] BBC News, 'Australia Drops Tasmanian Wilderness Logging Campaign' <http://www.bbc.com/news/world-australia-35854980> accessed 30 January 2018.

for the Glacier Bay National Park, located at the junction of the Tatshenshini and Alesk rivers in British Columbia. The Tatshenshini-Alesk was part of an area including Canadian and US territory, inscribed on the World Heritage List in 1994 for its spectacular glacier and ice-field landscapes, as well as for the importance of grizzly bear, caribou, and Dall sheep habitat (under natural criteria VI through X). Because the mining (and consequent acid mine damage predicted by environmental impact assessment) would violate the World Heritage Convention, in addition to the Migratory Birds Convention, the Pacific Salmon Treaty, and the US–Canada Boundary Waters Treaty, a coalition of fifty conservation organizations urged British Colombia's provincial government to create the Tatshenshini-Alsek Provincial Wilderness Park to protect the region.[96]

The World Heritage Convention has also been cited in a number of international investment disputes to justify the breaking of bilateral investment treaties (BITs) in order to protect cultural landscapes from destructive development. A wide variety of activities carried out by a state may interfere with an investor's property rights and since investment agreements do not provide protective exemptions for environment or cultural heritage, regulatory measures aimed at protecting landscape may be considered as tantamount to expropriation, leading to a dispute. As illustrated by Valentina Vadi,[97] the public purpose of a given regulation has been subject to only a limited exploration by tribunals and is not per se a defence to a claim of expropriation. While historically the basic content of BITs has almost entirely focused on investment protection, in recent years public policy concerns have begun to be incorporated more frequently into BIT provisions, concerns such as health, safety, security, and environmental protection.[98] The protection of World Heritage landscapes has been the subject of two International Centre for the Settlement of Investment Disputes (ICSID) Tribunal cases in which the importance of international cultural heritage obligations was considered and in which inscription on the World Heritage List affected the outcome: *SPP v Egypt* and *Parkerings v Lithuania*.

[96] M. Chiglieri, 'How the Tatshenshini-Alsek Wilderness Avoided Mining Disaster,' <https://www.oars.com/blog/how-the-tatshenshini-alsek-wilderness-avoided-mining-disaster/> accessed 30 January 2018.

[97] Valentina Vadi, 'Cultural Heritage and Investment Law: A Stormy Relationship?', *International Journal of Cultural Property*, 15 (1)(2008), 1–24, 5. Vadi makes a case for the inclusion of cultural exceptions into IIAs.

[98] See Catherine A. Rogers and Roger P. Alford (eds), *The Future of Investment Arbitration* (Oxford University Press, 2009), and R. Dolzer and C. Schreuer (eds), *Principles of International Investment Law* (Oxford University Press, 2008).

SPP v Egypt and *Parkerings v Lithuania*

The case of *Southern Pacific Properties Limited v Arab Republic of Egypt*[99] involved the development of a tourist village at the pyramids of Giza by Southern Pacific Properties Limited. After the investment had been approved, Egypt applied for the area to be inscribed on the World Heritage List and cancelled the development project with a view to gaining World Heritage status, which was subsequently granted in 1979.[100] The ICSID recognized that the registration of these areas occurred belatedly in the context of the dispute, but that Egypt's acts, which were contemporaneous with the cancellation of the project, indicated the genuineness of its concerns for the heritage at the project site. One of these acts was Decree No. 90 of 1978 which declared landscape on the project site to be 'public property'.[101] The Tribunal sustained the claimants' argument that the public purpose of the expropriation could not alter the obligation to pay fair compensation. However, it also added that the claimants' activities on the Pyramids Plateau would have become internationally unlawful in 1979, but that it had significant consequences in other respects,[102] namely, following 1979 when the Pyramids Plateau was enlisted as World Heritage, 'sales in the areas registered with the World Heritage Committee under the UNESCO Convention would have been illegal under [...] international law', and that the allowance of *lucrum cessans* may only involve those profits which are legitimate.[103] Thus as a result of World Heritage status for the site, compensation could be radically affected.[104] The notion of World Heritage and its implications was further elaborated in the dissenting opinion of Judge Mohamed Amin El Mahdi, who opined that 'the uniqueness of the site on which the project was finally intended to be implemented, mandated to take into consideration this element of 'public international interest or need' as regards the issue of the dispute'.[105] In his opinion, the two Parties in the dispute did not underestimate the obligation to preserve any vestige of the Ancient Civilization on the Pyramids Plateau. By choosing the site of the project on the Plateau proper and in the vicinity of the monuments themselves, those who opted for that choice, instead of the site proposed by the Respondent, were necessarily aware of the high risks undertaken. 'It was in

[99] *Southern Pacific Properties (Middle East) Limited v Arab Republic of Egypt*, ICSID Case No. ARB/84/3, Award on the Merits, 20 May 1992, 8 ICSID Rev—FILJ (1993), at 328.

[100] Decision CONF 003 XII.46.

[101] *Southern Pacific Properties (Middle East) Limited v Arab Republic of Egypt*, ICSID Case No. ARB/84/3, Award on the Merits, 20 May 1992, 8 ICSID Rev—FILJ (1993) at 156.

[102] Ibid, at 157. [103] Ibid, at 190. [104] Ibid.

[105] Dissenting Opinion of Judge El Mahdi, at 2(c).

fact and in law a 'contrat à grand risque' he stated, with all the consequences that emanate from that *qualification juridique*'[106] and extended this further by implying there was a prior obligation regarding the preservation of cultural heritage in the interest of the international community and that this obligation constitutes an element of the international public order.[107] As pointed out by Riccardo Pavoni, the case was significant because the ICSID Tribunal unhesitatingly accepted the WHC as relevant applicable law. In addition, the Tribunal's terminology and overall structure of its reasoning imply that state measures adopted to safeguard heritage sites already registered on the World Heritage List would override investor protections and that investors should take notice of host states' WHC obligations and become aware of the possible cultural and natural sensitivity of areas where they implement their activities.[108]

In the case of *Parkerings v Lithuania*,[109] the ICSID Tribunal adopted a different approach and found that Lithuania's cancellation of a project justified different treatment on the grounds of cultural heritage. The case involved a Norwegian investor Parkerings, who had entered into a contract to build and maintain multi-story parking facilities in the historic old town of Vilnius. The dispute erupted when the contract was terminated by the municipality, following legislative changes that brought the agreement into conflict with Lithuanian law.[110] The claimant alleged that Lithuania had breached, among other things,[111] the most-favoured nation treatment provision of the BIT and drew a contrast between the treatment it received and the treatment enjoyed

[106] Ibid.

[107] 'In my opinion, I consider that the interest of the International Community as regards its Human Cultural Heritage implied a non-codified international obligation binding upon both the International Community and the States even before the entry into force of the UNESCO Convention. I may just refer here, in this context, to the fact that when Egypt, in the early sixties, had no alternative but to take the hard and painful decision to sacrifice certain monuments, *inter alia* the temple of Abu Simbel, as an inevitable consequence to the construction of the Aswan Dam, the international community saw to it, financially and technically, that these monuments be protected and preserved. This action, that dates thirty years ago, yet reveals *un Etat d'esprit* of the International Community behind its strive to preserve its own Cultural Heritage and for the least an international obligation in the making.' Ibid.

[108] Ricardo Pavoni, 'Environmental Rights, Sustainable Development, and Investor-State Case Law: A Critical Appraisal', Pierre-Marie Dupuy, Francesco Francioni and Ernst-Ulrich Petersmann (eds), *Human Rights in International Investment Law and Arbitration* (Oxford University Press 2009), 536. The *Santa Elena* award displayed a hostile approach to the WHC and other environmental obligations and was a major setback for international environmental law.

[109] ICSID Case No. ARB/05/8. Award of 11/09/2007.

[110] The changes involved the law on local fees and charges, the decree on clamping and the law on self-government, which were all amended in 2000. Ibid, at 327.

[111] Parkerings also alleged a violation of the duty of equitable and reasonable treatment, a violation of the obligation of protection and a violation of the prohibition of expropriation.

by a Dutch firm, Pinus Proprius.[112] However, counsel for Lithuania argued that the two projects differed in important respects: notably in the public opposition to the Parkerings project on archaeological and environmental grounds, and the fact that the project infringed deeper into the city's Old Town as defined by UNESCO, sparking concern from the State Monument Protection Commission over the impact on the city's cultural heritage.[113] The Tribunal ultimately ruled that Lithuania was not in breach of its obligations under the Norway–Lithuania BIT and held that the archaeological and environmental concerns attached to the Parkerings project justified different treatment. Notably the Tribunal found it 'decisive' that the Parkerings Project 'extended significantly more into the Old Town as defined by UNESCO'[114] and added:

> Indeed, the record shows that the opposition raised against the BP projected multistory car park were important and contributed to the Municipality decision to refuse such a controversial project. The historical and archaeological preservation and environmental protection could be and in this case were justification for the refusal of the project.[115]

Thus, the ICSID Tribunal held that characteristics such as different historical, archaeological, and environmental impacts of two foreign investment projects may contribute to a finding that two projects do not share like circumstances for comparison purposes. In this respect the Tribunal was praised by the Centre for International Environmental Law for giving 'proper weight to environmental factors', one observer adding that tribunals have differed in their approaches to interpretation of like circumstances, some treating them as mere exceptions while others in this case, as proper justifications.[116] The fundamental difference between the case of *SPP v Arab Republic of Egypt*

[112] At a superficial level, the two projects were comparable: Pinus Proprius, a competing foreign firm, also had an agreement to build a parking complex in Vilnius under a similar joint-activity agreement with the city.

[113] Ibid, at 385. On 20 October 2000, the State Monument Commission of Lithuania objected to the parking plan for a number of reasons, stating, inter alia that 'the planned garages would change the character of the Old Town of Global value; destroy large areas of unexplored cultural layer. Also, the intensity of traffic and air pollution in the Old Town is likely to increase. The Old Town might become less attractive in terms of tourism and to the residents and visitor, and this would be a great loss.' Likewise, the Urban Development Department of the Vilnius Municipality also objected to the project stating that 'the city's humanitarian community would psychologically not accept this proposal. [...] In terms of the townscape, the site of the square is very important in the formation of the area of Cathedral Square.' Ibid, at 386.

[114] Ibid, at 392. [115] Ibid.

[116] See remarks by Marcos Orellana, Attorney with the Centre for International Environmental Law, which has often intervened as an amicus curiae in such cases to raise public concerns. *Investment Treaty News*, 28 September 2007, <http://www.iisd.org/pdf/2007/itn_sep28_2007.pdf> accessed 30 January 2018.

and that of *Parkerings v Lithuania* is that while in former, the site had not yet been inscribed in the World Heritage List at the time the parties entered into the investment agreement, in the latter, the Old Town of Vilnius already had World Heritage status, which lent more weight to the overall argumentation of the respondent state, ultimately leading to a different outcome in the award. While the two cases indirectly dealt with the question of cultural landscape, that is, the pyramids, and surrounding area in the former, and the townscape of Vilnius in the latter, they both concerned the international 'public interest' in their preservation, the community interest in their protection, not as property of the state but as legacy of humankind, thereby illustrating the positive influence of World Heritage status.

Prosecutor v Strugar (ICTY), Prosecutor v Al Mahdi (ICC)

In addition to investor–state arbitration, the influence of the World Heritage Convention can also be seen in the jurisprudence of international criminal law. Two cases stand out in this regard: the first dates from the war in the Former Yugoslavia and concerns the deliberate shelling of the Old Town of Dubrovnik by the Yugoslav Peoples' Army in 1991. The Trial Chamber of the International Criminal Tribunal for the Former Yugoslavia (ICTY) recognized the attacks as independent counts of criminal liability under the laws and customs of war. Specifically, the Trial Chamber observed that 'the Old Town of Dubrovnik in its entirety was entered onto the World Heritage List in 1979 upon the nomination of the SFRY. The properties inscribed on the World Heritage List include those, which because of their architecture, their homogeneity or place in the landscape, are of outstanding universal value from the point of view of history, art or science. [...] The Chamber therefore concludes that the attack launched by the JNA forces against the Old Town on 6 December 1991 was an attack directed against cultural property within the meaning of Article 3(d) of the Statute.'[117] Thus, the World Heritage status of Dubrovnik proved instrumental in the ICTY judges' construing the site as cultural property for the purposes of interpreting the court's statute.

The significance of World Heritage status was emphasized to a much greater extent in a more recent case involving an attack on a World Heritage site (arguably a cultural landscape, although not inscribed on the List as such). On 27 September 2016, the International Criminal Court (ICC) convicted Ahmad Al Faqi Al Mahdi for the deliberate targeting and attack of historic and religious monuments during the occupation of Timbuktu (Mali)

[117] *Prosecutor v Pavle Strugar* (Trial Judgment), IT-01-42-T, International Criminal Tribunal for the Former Yugoslavia (ICTY), 31 January 2005, para 327.

in 2012, when armed groups took control of the city and forcibly imposed Sharia Law on the population. Mr Al Mahdi was a member of Ansar Dine and head of the 'hisbah'—the morality brigade—under the occupation of Timbuktu by AQMI (Al Qaeda Organization in the Islamic Maghreb) and Ansar Dine. Central to the prosecution's argument was that the destruction of important cultural heritage sites not only affected the local inhabitants, but was also an affront to the values of humanity as a whole. The Prosecutor noted that 'humanity's collective conscience was shocked by this senseless destruction of its common heritage.[118]

The fact that all but one were UNESCO World Heritage sites proved an aggravating factor in the case against Al Mahdi. As noted by the Court, 'all sites but one were UNESCO World Heritage sites, and, as such their attack appears to be of particular gravity as their destruction does not only affect the direct victims of the crimes, namely the faithful inhabitants of Timbuktu, but also people throughout Mali and the international community.'[119] This fact was clear with the reaction to many similar acts of destruction, for example, during the war in the former Yugoslavia at the shelling of Dubrovnik and Mostar, at the deliberate destruction of the Buddhas of Bamiyan by the Taliban in 2001, and more recently at the attack on Palmyra and other heritage sites in Syria, Iraq, and beyond. However, humanity as a whole is a somewhat ephemeral victim in this instance, the real victims being the local inhabitants of Timbuktu whose cultural heritage and cultural rights were being targeted. While Al Mahdi was aware of the World Heritage status of the shrines in question,[120] it is not clear whether World Heritage status served as a reason for their targeting. In essence, what was targeted was the sacred, associative landscape of the people of Timbuktu, even if what gained attention was the World Heritage status of those sites. Thus, the rationale of the Court in emphasizing universal values over the more relativist ones is not entirely logical in this case.[121]

What the foregoing cases illustrate is that World Heritage status can and does play a role in decisions involving landscape protection at the international level, whether through diplomatic channels and their influence on domestic

[118] Office of the Prosecutor (OTP), Statement of the Prosecutor of the International Criminal Court, Fatou Bensouda, at the opening of the confirmation of charges hearing in the case against Mr Ahmad Al-Faqi Al Mahdi, 1 March 2016, available at <https://www.icc-cpi.int/Pages/item.aspx?name=otp-stat-01-03-16> accessed 8 May 2018.

[119] *Prosecutor v Ahmad Al Faqi Al Mahdi*, ICC-01/12-01/15, para. 39.

[120] *Prosecutor v Ahmad Al Faqi Al Mahdi*, ICC-01/12-01/15-171, Judgment of 27 September 2016, Trial Chamber VIII, para. 46.

[121] Paige Casaly, '*Al Mahdi* before the ICC: Cultural Property and World Heritage in International Criminal Law', *International Criminal Justice*, 14 (5)(2016), 1199-1220.

decisions, as in the case of Tasmanian Wilderness and the Glacier National Park, or through its use by states as a legitimate aim to rescind on trade agreements, or more recently as an aggravating factor in international criminal cases concerning the intentional destruction of cultural landscapes. These examples contribute to a general *opinio juris* on the binding character of the principles prohibiting the deliberate destruction of landscapes of significant importance for humanity. Francesco Francioni and Federico Lenzerini cite the almost universal ratification of the World Heritage Convention, as well as the authoritarian character of UNESCO recommendations—representing the near totality of states that participate in the General Conference—as corroborating factors for this *opinio juris*.[122] Roger O'Keefe recalls the obligation to protect in Article 4 as an obligation owed to 'all states parties to the Convention, and "established for the protection of a collective interest of the group" as laid down in Article 48(1)(a) of the International Law Commission's Articles on the Responsibility of States for Internationally Wrongful Acts'.[123] It is, in O'Keefe's view, an obligation *erga omnes*. Furthermore, the nature of the 'protection of cultural heritage as a matter of public interest, and not only as part of private property rights, is recognized in most of the mature domestic legal systems of the world'.[124] This represents some of the positive influence of the World Heritage Convention on global landscape governance. The impact of World Heritage status on local landscapes is significantly more complex.

5.7 The World Heritage Convention and Local Landscape Governance

According to Mechtild Rössler, the opening of the World Heritage List to cultural landscapes related to a shift towards 'people and communities'.[125] Yet what this means in practice is not clear sixteen years after the introduction of the cultural landscapes category. The shift to people and communities does not avoid the fact that landscapes are inherently contested, perhaps even

[122] See, for a further discussion on this point: Francesco Francioni and Federico Lenzerini, 'The Destruction of the Buddhas of Bamiyan and International Law', *European Journal of International Law*, 14 (4)(2003), 635.

[123] See also, Roger O'Keefe, 'World Cultural Heritage: Obligations to the International Community as a Whole?' *International and Comparative Law Quarterly*, 53 (1) (2004), 190.

[124] Francioni and Lenzerini, (n 122).

[125] Rössler, 'World Heritage Cultural Landscapes: A UNESCO Flagship Programme 1992–2006' (n 22), 333–53.

more so than other forms of heritage sites or monuments, due to the fact that many cultural landscapes are lived-in places. Cultural geographers use the term 'contested landscape' to suggest that no one looks at the landscape completely objectively, without preconceptions and biases.[126] Contested landscapes are essentially about the unequal distribution of power, in which the views of some groups are deemed acceptable, while others are marginalized and ignored. Two European cases illustrate such tensions with cultural landscape inscription. The first is the cultural landscape of the Dresden Elbe Valley, one of only two sites to have been deleted from the World Heritage List, after the local authorities of Dresden decided to proceed with the construction of a controversial bridge across the valley.[127] The second is the cultural landscape of the Val d'Orcia, which concerned the construction of a tourist development in the town of Monticchiello.

Dresden Elbe Valley

The Dresden Elbe valley was inscribed on the World Heritage List as an outstanding cultural landscape in 2004, for the way in which it integrated 'the celebrated Baroque setting and suburban garden city into an artistic whole within the river valley', as well as being 'an example of land use, representing an exceptional development of a major Central European city'.[128] The cultural landscape comprises both the urban centre of Dresden, as well as the valley stretching eighteen kilometres along the Elbe river from Ubigau Palace and Ostragehege fields in the north west, to Pillnitz Palace and the Elbe River Island in the south east. In 2005, it was revealed that documents supplied to support nomination of the site did not contain all the correct information regarding the location and dimensions of the Waldschlössen bridge, one of a number of bridges planned for the valley contained within the nomination dossier. After additional information had been supplied by the Mayor and the local administration, UNESCO stated that 'this valley crossing is no longer an urban bridge, but instead an important road connection resembling a motorway which would result in tearing apart the affected areas of the city and mostly the valley area of the river Elbe'.[129] A meeting was held in January

[126] Barbara Bender, 'Stonehenge—Contested Landscapes', in B. Bender (ed.), *Landscape Politics and Perspectives* (Berg, 1993), 245–80.

[127] The first site which was the subject of delisting was the Arabian Oryx sanctuary in Oman. The government encroached upon 90% of the reserve, and despite reservations and warnings, it was delisted in 2007. Decision 31COM 7B.11.

[128] Description available at <http://whc.unesco.org/en/list/1156> accessed 30 January 2018.

[129] ICOMOS World Report 2006/2007 on Monuments and Sites in Danger, Heritage at Risk (2008), 64.

2006 at UNESCO's headquarters, with a variety of stakeholders, including the mayor of Dresden, where he agreed to commission a visual impact study. This was followed by a second meeting during which the mayor decided to suspend works until the outcome of the next session of the WHC. In the meantime, however, the Regional Government—the Land of Saxony—intervened and ordered construction of the bridge to proceed.[130]

At its thirtieth session in 2006, the WHC expressed great concerns over the bridge project and the results of the visual impact study. The study showed that the construction of the project would have a major visual impact on the core area of the cultural landscape.[131] The Committee then decided to place Dresden on the World Heritage in Danger List, with the intention of deletion should the authorities decide to proceed. Germany was requested to review the project(s) in the core zone and to provide an updated report to UNESCO by 2007. In a reinforced monitoring mission to the Dresden Elbe Valley in 2008, the importance of sensitive development was stressed by UNESCO: 'In terms of authenticity and integrity, it is important to recognize that the cultural landscape of the Dresden Elbe Valley developed over centuries of gradual accumulation and is therefore a living, evolving urban site where a certain degree of change is acceptable by definition.'[132] It was also emphasized that over the centuries there was constant and conscious preservation of special panoramic views through careful planning of developments, i.e. certain fundamental features of the landscape 'appear to have been intentionally retained and even enhanced over time because they were seen as constituting the essence of the place'.[133] At its thirty-first session, the Committee decided to delete Dresden from the List, but gave Germany a further four months to find an acceptable solution. The solution offered by the authorities entailed slight modifications to the original design, which were not deemed to be enough by UNESCO to mitigate the impact of the bridge on the landscape. Eventually, after another year of attempted dialogue, the Dresden Elbe Valley was delisted.[134]

At the root of the dispute was the fact that the original planning decision of the Land of Saxony for the bridge had been approved before UNESCO had agreed to inscribe the Dresden Elbe Valley as a World Heritage site.

[130] See paras 113–115 and 116 ('Ersatzvornahme', execution by substitution) of the Gemeindeordnung für den Freistaat Sachsen (SächsGemO), 18 March 2003 (SächsGVBl., 55).

[131] State of Conservation (Dresden Elbe Valley) Decision 30 COM 7B.77.

[132] Giovani Boccardi (World Heritage Centre) and Jaroslav Killian (ICOMOS), Reinforced Monitoring Mission to the Dresden Elbe Valley World Heritage Property Germany, 4–5 February 2008, Mission Report, available at <http://archiv.welterbe-erhalten.de/pdf/080310_UNESCO_Report.pdf> accessed 30 January 2018.

[133] Ibid. [134] Decision 33 COM 7A.26 Dresden Elbe Valley (Germany) (C 1156).

Yet the information provided by the nomination file was incomplete and did not provide full information regarding the bridge's dimensions and location. According to Rössler, there were 'misunderstandings' and 'misinformation'.[135] The original application dossier supplied to the World Heritage Centre contained no precise proposal, only a map with various bridge models. Apparently there was another, internal document in German, which was not official, since all official documents have to be written in one of the working languages—English or French. 'When a major construction project is pending, this project has to be presented to UNESCO for review, including the blueprints. This did not happen, and we only learned about this specific bridge belatedly'.[136] It was described as an urban bridge, when it resembled a four-lane motorway. Furthermore, there was an assumption on the part of the authorities that because Dresden was not listed at the time, they were at liberty to pursue their own planning projects irrespective of potential breaches of the Convention and the international responsibility ensuing. The regional authorities relied on the fact that there had been a citizen's referendum in 2005, which asked whether or not the citizens of Dresden were in favour of the bridge proposal. The outcome of the referendum was a majority in favour of the bridge.

When mediation failed, a number of cases were brought before local and regional administrative and constitutional courts.[137] These culminated in Dresden City Council bringing a constitutional challenge and urgent motion to the Supreme Constitutional Court of Germany.[138] The court upheld the referendum and the decision of the Saxon Higher Administrative Court, which ordered construction of the bridge to commence immediately. Sabine Von Schorlemer views the actions of the German state as puzzling.[139]

[135] Interview with Mechtild Rössler, 'Dresden-UNESCO Dispute. There were Misunderstandings'. *Spiegel*, 7 February 2007.

[136] Ibid.

[137] Administrative Court Dresden, Decision of 30 August 2006, 12 K 1768/06, decision on provisional measures in favour of the City Council who suspended the construction of the bridge. This was overturned by the Higher Administrative court of Bautzen. Administrative Court Dresden, Decision of 19 June 2007, 12 K 1139/07 (rejection of the petition by the mayor of Dresden Lutz Vogel to prevent the continuation of construction work to increase the chances for compromise with UNESCO). See also, Higher Administrate Court Bautzen Decision of 9 March 2007, 4 BS 216/06 (repeal of permission to suspend the construction of the bridge), and Higher Administrative Court Bautzen, Decision of 16 July 2007, 4 BS 243/07 (confirming the refection of the petition of the Mayor of Dresden).

[138] BVerfG, Decision of 29 May 2007, 2 BvR 695/07.

[139] Sabine Von Schorlemer, 'Compliance with the World Heritage Convention: Reflections on the Elbe Valley and the Dresden Waldschlössen Bridge', *German Yearbook of International Law*, 51 (2008), 3.

She cites the fact that Germany applied to have the valley inscribed on the List only a number of years previously, yet did not intervene with the Land of Saxony to try to halt the project.[140] In addition, she argues that Germany had been party to the World Heritage Convention since 1976, is one of the world's most developed countries which supports other less-developed nations in the field of cultural co-operation, and in the past has modified plans for development projects on other World Heritage sites due to concerns voiced over integrity.[141] Likewise, the Foreign Federal Ministry warned that the loss of World Heritage Status would constitute 'a serious loss of credibility for Germany in the field of international co-operation'.[142] Von Schorlemer also points to an alternative to the bridge that existed in the form of a tunnel, which was supported by the WHC.[143] Yet what is missing in her analysis is that it is precisely Germany's so-called puzzling actions that lead us to critically examine the delisting of Dresden, in particular, the implications of cultural landscape designation as weighed against the needs and desires of local populations. It could be argued that the decision to delist the cultural landscape only aggravated the situation and led to a loss of credibility, not for Germany as a state party, but rather of the World Heritage regime and its perceived unrealistic expectations. This was not a case of intentional heritage destruction, but one where initial misunderstandings, lack of proper oversight, and failed compromise led to a drastic decision, the effect of which had no influence on the original design of the bridge. The case raises the issue as to whether urban areas such as Dresden are suitable for cultural landscape designation. Dresden differs substantially from the case of the only other World Heritage site to have been delisted: the Oryx sanctuary in Oman, whereby the state approved operations on 90% of the reserve, threatening the Oryx species and their natural habitat. This was a fully informed decision on the part of Oman to encroach on the sanctuary in question, thereby rendering its continued viability as a habitat untenable.

[140] On the contrary, the Constitutional Court upheld the Land of Saxony's motion to proceed with construction.

[141] For example, the plans to construct a car park in the old city of Mamburg (ICOMOS, World Heritage at Risk, 2004/2005, 78), or the plans to destroy the old town of Quedlinberg.

[142] Marja Einig-Heidenhof, Head of Cultural and Educational Division at the Federal Ministry of Foreign Affairs, quoted in the Report of the Foreign Ministry to the 67th General Assembly of the German Commission for UNESCO (Dessau 27–28 June 2007).

[143] Although, admittedly, a tunnel would have considerable costs because of the funds already spent on the bridge project.

Monticchiello and the Val d'Orcia

The Val d'Orcia was also designated a World Heritage cultural landscape in 2004. Inscribed under criteria (iv) and (vi), its site description notes that the Val d'Orcia is 'part of the agricultural hinterland of Siena, re-drawn and developed when it was integrated in the territory of the city-state in the fourteenth and fifteenth centuries to reflect an idealized model of good governance and to create an aesthetically pleasing picture. The landscape's distinctive aesthetics, flat chalk plains out of which rise almost conical hills with fortified settlements on top, inspired many artists. Their images have come to exemplify the beauty of well-managed Renaissance agricultural landscapes.'[144] In 2006, a town located in the heart of the Val d'Orcia, Monticchiello, became the centre of controversy over a 20,000 square metre development of ninety-five individual housing units in what was termed a 'lotizzazione contestata' (contested housing development).[145] Aside from the inappropriate location of the houses—a brand new land sub-division located just under the castle and the historic village, with implications for access to water and sustainability—the development was originally intended to provide social housing for local couples who could no longer afford to live within the city walls. It was thus envisaged as an initiative to halt the population decline of the village. However, once the project received planning permission, the social aim of the project was subverted within a number of years to become an exclusive tourist development of semi-detached houses and villas well beyond the affordability of the locals. In the meantime, the Val D'Orcia was designated a protected area in 1999 and inscribed on the World Heritage List as a cultural landscape in 2004, presumably with the details of the development contained in the supporting documentation (in its original intended state as social housing units).[146] The development began to receive increased criticism on foot of an opinion piece produced in *La Repubblica* by intellectual and Monticchiello resident Asor Rosa in 2006,[147] which coincided with the initial construction phase of the project. Widespread debate ensued, with emphasis placed on the fact Monticchiello was a UNESCO World Heritage site and as such belonged to 'the cultural heritage of humanity'.[148] As a result, the Ministro dei Beni

[144] Decision 28 COM 14B.51. Site description available at <http://whc.unesco.org/en/list/1026> accessed 30 January 2018.

[145] Stefano Chiarini, 'Una lottizzazzione contestata in un paese patrimonio UNESCO', *Il Manifesto*, 5 January 2007.

[146] Decision 28 COM 14B.51.

[147] Alberto Asor Rosa, 'Il cemento assale la Val d'Orcia', *La Repubblica*, 24 August 2006.

[148] Although, somewhat incongruously, the advertising for the 'exclusive residence' used this to promote the marketing of the site.

Culturali initiated talks with the responsible local authority—the Commune of Pienza—in order to mitigate the development and propose a solution to the problem. A high-level meeting was tabled between the Ministry, the Regione Toscana, and the Director of the World Heritage Centre Francesco Bandarin, and a national conference was held in the Val d'Orcia in 2006.[149] This led to the eventual injunction of the last phase of construction by Minister Francesco Rutelli.[150] The action was welcomed by UNESCO representatives.[151] Since then, recent changes in the national Landscape Code have introduced a number of measures affecting the protection and management of the landscapes, with the aim of preventing another case like Monticchiello.[152]

Yet, as often happens in a landscape dispute, the community at the centre became divided over the issue. In Monticchiello, the housing development became the subject of an annual play by the Teatro Povero—a theatre composed of the inhabitants themselves—in 2007; the programme for 'A(h)ia!' reads:

> in the houses, a focus of scandal and division within the community, the hopes and fears of the villagers suddenly found a concrete form: on the one hand there was the hope of a future which would be more prosperous, vital and concrete, divorced from aesthetic preoccupations which seemed to belong to a museum or a tombstone; on the other hand, there was the massive intrusive impact of the buildings themselves, in a setting which is sensitive to say the least.[153]

The concerns of the inhabitants not wanting to live in a 'museum' are wholly legitimate, yet at the same time, it is questionable as to whether this particular development would have been of real benefit to the local community in the long term. Aside from the dimensions of the development (which is not a massive intrusion in the landscape but is out of proportion with the castle and its town), its 'exclusive' nature made it likely that most of the units would be occupied by seasonal visitors, ironically looking for an 'authentic' Tuscan experience in a World Heritage site. It did not offer any solutions to the declining population of the town itself, nor provide a sustainable means

[149] Convegno Nazionale: 'Monticchiello, Toscana: Il Paesaggio Italiano', 28 October 2006.

[150] Rutelli's measure was seen as the most viable solution. Salvatore Settis had called for the local authorities to place a compulsory purchase order on the already-built houses and then demolish them.

[151] See 'Monticchiello, stop alle construzioni. Rutelli firma il vincolo paesaggistico', Cronaca, *La Repubblica*, 23 January 2007.

[152] Decreto legislativo 24 marzo 2006 n. 157 alters Part III (dealing with landscape) of the Codice dei Beni Culturali e del Paesaggio; and reduces the identification process (Art. 138), lends more weight to organs of the State in protection and management (Art. 146); and rationalizes the system of sanctions (Art. 167).

[153] Teatro Povero programme of 2007, author's copy.

of income. Monticchiello is one of a number of land-use planning disputes to have taken place in Tuscany in recent years, which have been used as an example in one research project to illustrate how the land-use planning system has changed from being based on solidarity to being interest-based, the result of poor governance on the part of elected officials who equate business interests with the public interest.[154]

The cases of Monticchiello and Dresden can be contrasted for the way in which the situation was dealt with by the respective authorities. In the latter, the local and regional authorities made no attempt at a real compromise, and World Heritage status did not appear to weigh sufficiently upon them in order to do so; on the contrary, the regional authorities of Saxony attempted to turn the dispute into one of local democracy versus 'foreign domination', with the Mayor of Saxony even stating that UNESCO World heritage status 'punishes' the citizens of Dresden.[155] Nor did the German state intervene in this regard, and perhaps rightly so. One author argues that the main problem is scarce knowledge—particularly on the local and regional level—of the implementation and compliance tools existing for the World Heritage Convention.[156] She cites the frequent misinterpretations of the Convention as being related to the question of who is in the position to nominate a site and the legal consequences of such inscription. Indeed, in an interview with Der Spiegel, Mechtild Rössler pointed to the 'misunderstandings' and 'misinformation' as contributing factors to the dispute, which highlights the need for greater communication with authorities and stakeholders regarding the Convention's obligations. There is no provision in the Convention for dispute settlement.

However, there is also a popular perception that the World Heritage Convention can be a tool to 'defend' a site, but as the case of Dresden shows, this is only possible with the political will of the state party. Regarding the Convention's obligations, there are various interpretations among stakeholders as regards compliance with the obligations of inscription on the World Heritage List. Edith Brown Weiss rightly points out that 'highly educated' and mobile transnational elites may feel comfortable with decision-making

[154] Anna Marson, Land-use planning 'scandals' in Tuscany: mismanagement or underestimation of general public interests, *Politische Italien Forschung Occasional Papers*, No. 09/2010.

[155] Press Release Staatskanzlei (State Chancellery), 25 June 2007: 'kommt Erpressung nahe', see also member of the German Parliament (CDU) *Arnold Vaatz*, Interview of 4 July 2008 'Erpressungspotential' <http://www.dradio.de/dlf/sendungen/interview_dlf/811475> accessed 30 January 2018.

[156] Sabine Von Schorlemer, 'Compliance with the World Heritage Convention: Reflections on the Elbe Valley and the Dresden Waldschlössen Bridge', *German Yearbook of International Law*, 51 (2008), 3.

at the international level, but this may evoke a visceral reaction from local communities who may be hostile to international institutions.[157] If local residents are excluded from the decision-making process and dictated to rather than listened to, suspicion and hostility inevitably arise from certain obligations pertaining to inscription and site management. This is why communication and participatory mechanisms are important from the onset. Indeed, in assessing ten years of cultural landscape protection, it was recommended by experts that increased co-operation be established with local and regional bodies and that there be greater communication with people.[158] As stated by a well-known cultural landscapes expert, 'one of the main lessons learnt from cultural landscapes is that the best way in most cases to secure the future of that which we wish to maintain is to involve the residents'.[159] It is of no surprise that the most successfully managed World Heritage Sites are those in which the inhabitants have an active role in the management (for example, Cinque Terre or Wachau[160]), for they alone can sustain the living landscape. The notion that people are central to any landscape policy is perhaps the principle tenet of the European Landscape Convention, the focus of the next chapter.

In 2011, UNESCO adopted a Recommendation on the Historic Urban Landscape,[161] which explicitly mentions 'using participatory planning and stakeholder consultations', the establishment of appropriate partnerships, and local management frameworks for conservation and development projects, as well as the 'coordination of public and private actors' in its text. Its stated purpose is to act as an additional tool to integrate policies and practices of conservation of the built environment into the wider goals of urban development and represents a much more dynamic instrument than some of the previous UNESCO soft law instruments on landscape adopted thirty years ago.

[157] Edith Brown Weiss, 'The Rise or Fall of International Law?', *Fordham Law Review*, 69 (2000), 345, 360.

[158] World Heritage Centre, *Cultural Landscapes: The Challenges of Conservation*, World Heritage Papers 7.

[159] Fowler, *Landscapes for the World* (n 9), 31.

[160] The Wachau is a stretch of the Danube Valley between Melk and Krems, 'is an outstanding example of a riverine landscape bordered by mountains in which material evidence of its long historical evolution has survived to a remarkable degree.' It was inscribed under criterion (ii) and (iv) in 2000. CONF 204 X.C.1

[161] UNESCO Recommendation on the Historic Urban Landscape, 10 November 2011.

6

The European Landscape Convention

6.1 Origins of the ELC

The European Landscape Convention (ELC) was adopted on 20 October 2000 in Florence.[1] Largely the initiative of the Council of Europe's Congress of Local and Regional Authorities (CLREA), it was borne out of a concern over the increasing degradation and fragmentation of Europe's rural landscapes. The roots of the Convention can be traced to a number of occurrences in the early 1990s: the first was the Mediterranean Landscape Charter (also known as the Seville Charter), adopted by the regions of Andalusia (Spain), Languedoc-Roussillon (France), and Tuscany (Italy) in 1993.[2] The second was a detailed report published by the European Union's Environment Agency entitled 'Europe's Environment: the Dobris Assessment', a document on the state of the environment in greater Europe and its prospects for the future.[3] The text devotes an entire chapter to landscapes and contains a proposal for drafting an international convention on rural landscapes under the auspices of the Council of Europe. In 1994, the IUCN published 'Parks for Life: Actions for Protected Areas in Europe', similarly advocating an international convention on rural landscape protection in Europe.[4] A central idea behind these documents was that distant policies (in particular, EU agricultural directives) negatively affect local landscapes, yet local people have little input into the decision-making process.[5]

[1] Council of Europe, European Landscape Convention (opened for signature 20/10/2000, entered into force 1/3/2004), ETS No. 176.

[2] Resolution 256 (1994) of the Standing Conference of Local and Regional Authorities of Europe.

[3] David Stanners and Philippe Bourdeau, *Europe's Environment: The Dobris Assessment* (European Environmental Agency, 1995).

[4] IUCN Commission on National Parks and Protected Areas (CNPPA), *Parks for Life, Action for Protected Areas in Europe* (IUCN, 1994), full text available at <https://portals.iucn.org/library/sites/library/files/documents/1994-023.pdf> accessed 30 January 2018.

[5] Report on the Preliminary Draft European Landscape Convention. Strasbourg, 5 May 1997, CG (4) 6 Part II.

On foot of these recommendations, the Congress of Local and Regional Authorities of the Council of Europe initiated the drafting process for a European Convention on Landscape and an ad hoc drafting group was established.[6] The drafting group included, inter alia, Council of Europe committees on cultural heritage and biodiversity, the UNESCO World Heritage Committee (WHC), the IUCN, the Committee of Regions of the European Commission, and the three regional authorities that had signed the Mediterranean Landscape Charter. After several meetings and draft texts spanning a number of years, a final version of the ELC was approved and opened for signature in Florence in 2000. As stated in Recommendation 40 on the draft ELC of 1998, the demand for such a convention derived from the 'importance that Europe's citizens attach to their environment [...], the fact that citizens have come to realise that the quality and diversity of many landscapes are declining [...] and that this is having an adverse effect on their everyday lives.'[7] Furthermore, it was felt that 'landscape should become a mainstream political project, since it plays an important role in the well-being of Europe's citizens, for whom it is no longer acceptable that their surroundings are transformed by technical and economic changes on which they have no say'.[8]

6.2 Paradigm Shift: Landscape as Public Space

The ELC is the first international treaty solely dealing with the protection and enhancement of landscape and is innovative for a number of reasons, not least because of the definition of landscape provided in Article 1(a) of the Convention:

> Landscape means an area, as perceived by people, whose character is the result of the action and interaction of natural and/or human factors.

This definition recognizes the duality of landscape: both the physical tangible area of land and its added layer of associations as perceived by people. It mentions both natural and human factors. In a notable departure from the approach of the World Heritage Convention, no categories or criteria are provided. Instead, the Convention applies to all landscapes—hence the use of the term 'landscape' in the singular. The ELC focuses not only on outstanding

[6] Ibid.

[7] Report on the Preliminary Draft European Landscape Convention. Strasbourg, 5 May 1997, CG (4) 6 Part II.

[8] Ibid.

landscapes but also on 'every day or degraded landscapes'[9]—the places where most people live and work. Accordingly, it applies to the entire territory [...] and covers natural, rural, urban, and peri-urban areas. It includes land, inland water and marine areas.[10] It follows that the measures foreseen by the ELC include not only protection, but also the management and planning of landscapes.[11] Furthermore, the public are encouraged to participate in the formulation of landscape plans and policies.[12] For these reasons, it has been said that the ELC 'democratizes' landscape.[13] The underlying rationale of the ELC is that a purely conservationist approach helps deflect attention from the forces leading to change elsewhere, and thus neglects those areas not afforded protection.

By stating that the landscape is a basic component of the European natural *and* cultural heritage, the ELC departs from the apparent culture/nature dichotomy present in most international legal instruments. As the explanatory report points out, the ELC 'is not confined to either the cultural, man-made or natural components of the landscape'.[14] Notably, it makes explicit reference to a number of instruments in its preamble, including the Berne Convention on the Conservation of European Wildlife and Natural Habitats, the European Convention for the Protection of the Architectural Heritage, the European Convention on the Protection of the Archaeological Heritage, the Convention on Biological Diversity, and the World Heritage Convention. The preamble also notes the various fields of public interest in the landscape as being the 'cultural, ecological, environmental and social'. The Convention obliges each State party: 'to recognise landscapes in law as an essential component of peoples' surroundings, as an expression of the diversity of their shared cultural and natural heritage, and as a foundation of their identity;[15] and to establish and

[9] Article 2 states 'this Convention applies to the entire territory of the Parties and covers natural, rural, urban and peri-urban areas. It includes land, inland water and marine areas. It concerns landscapes that might be considered outstanding as well as every day or degraded landscapes'.

[10] Ibid.

[11] Ibid, at Art. 3. Interestingly, a list was included in the Draft ELC yet this was omitted in the final text.

[12] Ibid, at Art. 5(c). This involves interest groups at the national and community level, as well as local and regional authorities.

[13] Riccardo Priore, 'La Convention européenne du Paysage', *Revue européenne de droit de l'environnement*, 3 (2000), 285. See also, Graham Fairclough, 'New Heritage Frontiers', in *Launching Colloquy of Heritage and Beyond: A Publication on the Contribution of the Council of Europe Framework Convention on the Value of Cultural Heritage for Society*, Lisbon, 20 November 2009, 31, available at <http://www.coe.int/t/dg4/culutreheritage/heritage/identities/SpeechesLisbon/> accessed 30 January 2018.

[14] Council of Europe 'European Landscape Convention: Explanatory Report', available at <http://conventions.coe.int/Treaty/EN/Reports?Html/176.htm> accessed 30 January 2018.

[15] Art. 5(a).

implement landscape policies aimed at landscape protection, management, and planning through the adoption of the specific measures.[16] These measures include training and education, awareness raising, identification and assessment, establishing landscape quality objectives,[17]establishing procedures for the participation of the public,[18] and the integration of landscape in town and regional policies.[19]

The Preamble to the ELC acknowledges that landscape contributes to 'human well-being' and that it is 'a key element of individual and social well-being'.[20] The fact that the preamble links 'well-being' to landscape is significant. Well-being is, as Yves Luginbühl puts it, 'being well disposed in mind and body'.[21] The concept of well-being reflects the concept of health as defined by the World Health Organization (WHO): 'Health is a dynamic state of complete physical, mental, spiritual, and social well-being and not merely the absence of disease or infirmity'.[22] The Convention's linkage of landscape with well-being also acknowledges the theoretical underpinnings of much of the literature emanating from the humanities and environmental psychology since the 1980s: landscape is more than a naturally produced canvas to be primed over. It is deeply imbedded in the consciousness with strong emotive and associative elements. For this reason, if we recall the words of Adrian Philips, 'landscape is much more likely to concern the man in the street or the woman in the field, than is biodiversity'.[23] Geographer Elisée Reclus commented in the nineteenth century that 'individuals seek their reflection in the landscape of the place where they live'.[24] This acknowledgement of links between landscape and a person's attachment to place where he/she lives is nevertheless more difficult to deal with, because it brings into play factors which make public intervention difficult.[25] However, individual and social well-being are inextricably linked and social well-being is perhaps more attainable if landscape is the result or expression of the efforts of the authorities

[16] Art. 5(b). [17] Art. 6. [18] Art. 5(c). [19] Art. 5(d).

[20] Preamble, European Landscape Convention and its explanatory report in English.

[21] Council of Europe, *Landscape and Sustainable Development: Challenges of the European Landscape Convention* (Council of Europe Publishing, 2006), 32.

[22] Report of the Executive Board of the World Health Organization, 1998. See Maguelonne Dejeant-Pons and Marc Pallemearts, *Human Rights and the Environment* (Council of Europe, 2002), 271.

[23] Adrian Philips, IUCN, 'Landscape Conservation Law. Present Trends and Perspectives in International and Comparative Law', *Environmental Policy and Law*, Paper No. 39, (IUCN, 2000), 58.

[24] Elisée Reclus, Du sentiment de la nature dans les sociétés modernes, *Revue des deux Mondes*, Paris, 1866.

[25] Not every individual can be taken into consideration of course, and there is the obstacle of NIMBYism (not in my back yard) to contend with.

to ensure that inhabitants have an input into decisions affecting them, which brings us to one of the principle aims of the Convention.

The ELC requires its states parties to define a genuine landscape policy in partnership with the public.[26] In particular, Article 5(c) of the Convention provides that 'each party undertakes to establish procedures for the participation of the general public, local and regional authorities, and other parties with an interest in the definition and implementation of landscape policies'. Article 6(d) further adds that 'Each party undertakes to define landscape-quality objectives for the landscapes identified and assessed after public consultation in accordance with Article 5(c).'[27] The Convention specifically refers to the Aarhus Convention on Access to Information, Public Participation in Decision-Making and Access to Justice on Environmental Matters (25 June 1988)[28] in its preamble. As Michel Prieur points out:

> The reason for the European Landscape Convention's insistence on the participative approach is a desire not so much to fall in with prevailing fashion as to give legal recognition to the special features of landscape [. . .] Democratisation of the landscape is not just a question of the new scope which the Landscape Convention introduces; it is also reflected in this collective and individual appropriation of all landscapes, through the requirement that there be direct participation for all in the phases of decision-making regarding landscape alteration, supervision of landscape evolution and prevention of reckless destruction.[29]

While other texts also highlight the importance of public participation in the definition and implementation of landscape policies,[30] the ELC explicitly

[26] The 'public' is taken to mean civil society in a broad sense.

[27] In the context of heritage, Ruth Gavison lists the dimensions of 'publicness' as: accessibility, ownership, control, accountability, effect and intimacy, while Benn and Gaus reduce these to three: access, agency and interest. See John Carman, *Against Cultural Property, Archaeology, Heritage and Ownership* (Bloomsbury, 2005), 49.

[28] Convention on Access to Information, Public Participation and Access to Justice in Environmental Matters, Aarhus, 25 June 1998. 2161 UNTS 447. Entry into force 30 October 2001. Text available at <http://www.unece.org/env/pp/treatytext.htm/> accessed 30 January 2018.

[29] Michel Prieur, 'Landscape Policies: Contribution to the Well-Being of European Citizens and to Sustainable Development—Social, Economic and Ecological Aspects', *Second Conference of the Contracting and Signatory States to the European Landscape Convention, Strasbourg*, 10 October 2002, T-FLOR 2 (2002), 20.

[30] IUCN Management guidelines for IUCN category V Protected Areas—Protected Landscapes / Seascapes, September 2002; Committee of Ministers Recommendation No. R (95) 9 of 11 September 1995 on the integrated conservation of cultural landscape areas as part of landscape policies; Committee of Ministers Recommendation (2002)1 of 30 January to Member States on the guiding principles for sustainable development of the European Continent, The Convention on the Protection of the Alps, 7 November 1991, in the Chambéry Protocol of Application of 20 December 1994 and the Aarhus Convention as seen above.

lays out the specific measures to be taken.[31] The ELC diverges from previous environmental approaches to landscape, which often neglected the social dimension to the landscape by excluding inhabitants from living or conducting activities in certain areas. The history of the idea of nature demonstrates how the white middle class demarcated nature as aesthetic landscape to be viewed from a distance. Landscapes thus represented the areas of power where indigenous inhabitants were often forced to leave their homelands in accordance with the designation of national parks.[32] This was the case, for example, with the designation of the Yellow Stone and Yosemite National Parks in the US. While acknowledging the landscape as both natural *and* cultural heritage, and while referring to environmental treaties in its preamble, the Convention places people at the centre of landscape and can thus be seen for the most part as an anthropocentric treaty. However, it refrains from using the term 'cultural landscape', as the European landscape is by definition cultural.

6.3 Subsidiarity and Local Landscape Governance

The ELC makes an explicit reference to the principle of subsidiarity and to the European Charter of Local Self Government in its text.[33] Article 4 states that 'Each Party shall implement this Convention, in particular Articles 5 and 6, according to its own division of powers, in conformity with its constitutional principles and administrative arrangements, and respecting the principle of subsidiarity, taking into account the European Charter of Local Self-government'. The principle of subsidiarity establishes that governmental activities must be carried out by the public authorities nearest to citizens and that they be delegated to higher governmental levels (regions, states) only if they can provide a better or more suitable service. Subsidiarity was first established as a key element of the European Charter of Local Self Government, adopted under the auspices of the Council of Europe in 1985: 'Public responsibilities shall generally be exercised, in preference, by those authorities which are closes to the citizen. Allocations of responsibility to another authority should weigh up the extent and nature of the task

[31] Such as landscape character assessment, a new form of surveying and assessing landscape features using Geophysical Information Systems technology combined with public perception surveys.

[32] Ari Aukusti Lehtinen, 'Tracing environmental Justice—On the Associations of Folk, Justice and the Environment', in T. Peil and M. Jones (eds), *Landscape, Law and Justice, Proceedings of a Conference* (Novus Forlag, 2003), 81–5.

[33] Council of Europe, European Charter of Local Self-Government of 15 October 1985, European Treaty Series No 122, available at <http://conventions.coe.int/> accessed 8 May 2018.

and requirements of efficiency and economy'.[34] Since being enshrined in the Treaty of Maastricht in 1992, it has also become a fundamental principle of the European Union.

Subsidiarity is increasingly seen as a 'structural tool to mediate the polarity of pluralism and the common good' and as 'a conceptual alternative to the idea of state sovereignty'.[35] Indeed, one of the paradoxes of an increasingly fragmented and globalized social order is the return to regionalism.[36] In light of the approach adopted by the ELC, that is, its focus not only on the protection of special landscapes, but also on the improvement of everyday and degraded landscapes,[37] the involvement of local/regional authorities is not only desirable but necessary from a practical perspective. Accordingly, the ELC commits contracting parties to establish procedures for local and regional authority participation in defining and implementing landscape policies,[38] and requires local authority involvement in identifying and assessing landscapes.[39] Therefore, the states parties that have signed up to the Convention must undertake to involve local and regional authorities in the establishment and implementation of landscape policies, landscape identification/assessment, as well as the definition of quality objectives. The importance of this aspect of the ELC was highlighted by Keith Withmore, Chair of the Sustainable Development Committee of the Council of Europe Congress of Local and Regional Authorities:

> This is a political project which is undoubtedly ambitious, given that what is sought is a major shift in the relationship between citizens or the public and their local areas. For the project to succeed, the authorities must ensure that, like a liquid flowing through a complex structure, the Convention's principles penetrate the inner workings of society. Without co-operation of national, regional and local authorities, the liquid in question will remain in its exalted European container, where it will be put on display by a small number of particularly inspired or zealous politicians and officials.[40]

While the roots of the ELC are largely to be found in the commitment to landscape protection on the part of Europe's local and regional authorities, and while subsidiarity is certainly a favourable form of governance in many instances, it must be noted that local and regional authorities are often viewed

[34] Art. 4, para. 3.

[35] Paolo G. Carozza, 'Subsidiarity as a Structural Principle of International Human Rights Law', *American Journal of International Law*, 97 (2003), 38.

[36] Fred Powell, *Think Globally, Act Locally: Sustainable Communities, Modernity and Development*, paper presented to the Irish Social Science Platform Summer School, Sligo, 23–25 June 2008.

[37] Art. 2. [38] Art. 5. [39] Art. 6.

[40] Keith Withmore, Draft Speech at the Conference on the occasion of the entry into force of the European Landscape Convention, Strasbourg, 17 June 2004.

in a negative manner where planning and the protection of the landscape are concerned. In this respect, the implementation of the ELC is a highly ambitious political project. It is important to distinguish between local democracy on the one hand and the complete delegation of powers to local administration on the other. Indeed subsidiarity means that activities should be carried out nearest to the citizens and that they be delegated to higher levels of government only if they can provide a better service. A better service includes being better equipped to make sensitive planning decisions, and in cases of major interventions in the landscape, this would imply several levels of government involvement.

6.4 Landscape Beyond Borders

One of the reasons international law is relevant for landscape protection is due to the fact that landscapes transcend property divisions and straddle political borders. The ELC acknowledges this: Article 9 provides that Parties 'shall encourage transfrontier co-operation on local and regional levels and, wherever necessary, prepare and implement joint landscape programmes'. A number of previous treaties already indirectly apply here: the European Convention on Transfrontier Co-operation between Territorial Communities or Authorities (Madrid, 21 May 1980),[41] the Benelux Convention on Nature Conservation and Landscape Protection,[42] the Alpine Convention and its Protocol Concerning Environmental Protection and Landscape Management,[43] and the Framework Convention on the Protection and Sustainable Development of the Carpathians (22 May 2003),[44] all of which involve the harmonization of local and regional policies in the interests of protection and management of the environment and implicitly, landscapes. Indeed, the preamble to the ELC makes explicit reference to the European Convention on Transfrontier Co-operation between Territorial Communities or Authorities and its additional protocols.[45]

[41] Model Agreement on the Creation and Management of Transfrontier Parks (see para. 1.9) Model Agreement on the Creation and Management of Transfrontier Rural Parks (see para. 1.10).

[42] Benelux Convention on Nature Conservation and Landscape Protection, Brussels, 8 June 1982.

[43] The Alpine Convention was signed on 7 November 1991 in Salzburg by Austria, France, Italy, Germany, Switzerland, Lichtenstein, and the EU. Slovenia and Monaco signed later.

[44] Framework Convention on the Protection and Sustainable Development of the Carpathians, Kiev, 22 May 2003.

[45] Council of Europe, European Treaty Series No. 106.

However, as noted by Michel Prieur, despite the considerable progress facilitating transfrontier co-operation, landscape problems rarely constitute the subject of such co-operation.[46] The ELC could provide an opportunity to give new impetus to transfrontier co-operation by encouraging states and local authorities to share experiences and enter into new agreements devoted exclusively to common landscape programmes, in line with Article 9.[47] A further aspect attributed to the transcendental character of landscape is the fact that many landscapes, particularly those with discernible pre-historic values, are the remaining vestiges of a past that existed long before the existence of the nation state and convey symbols about regions and different political, social, and cultural constellations not confined within the borders of modern states.

Since its adoption in the year 2000, the ELC has received significant attention outside Europe, particularly from Southern Mediterranean countries, Australia, and Latin America.[48] This has led to the adoption, in 2016, of a protocol amending the ELC.[49] Article 1 of the Protocol amends the title of the Convention to 'Council of Europe Landscape Convention'. Article 2 of the Protocol adds a new paragraph to the text of the ELC expanding its geographical scope to non-members of the Council of Europe:

> wishing to enable the application of the values and principles formulated in the Convention to non-European States who so desire.[50]

As stated by the Committee on Social Affairs, Health and Sustainable Development, examples of successful transfrontier co-operation in the framework of the ELC abound across Europe. They mainly concern joint projects for ecotourism, landscape conservation, restoration, and development through protected areas or parks, protection against floods, sustainable forest and land management, and tackling the cross-border impact of pollution, as

[46] Michel Prieur, 'Landscape and Policies, International Programmes and Transfrontier Landscapes', in Council of Europe, *Landscape and Sustainable Development: Challenges of the European Landscape Convention* (2006), 121–53, at 144.

[47] In the same spirit, UNESCO, in the context of the 'Cultural Landscapes' workshop for the 30th Anniversary of the World Heritage Convention, extended an invitation to 'establish a solid legal framework for transfrontier initiatives and co-operation between local authorities', World Heritage Report, Paris 2003.

[48] Doc. 13916, Reference 4167 of 27 November 2015. 2016—March Standing Committee.

[49] Council of Europe, Protocol Amending the European Landscape Convention (opened for signature 1 August 2016), European Treaty Series No. 219.

[50] New para. 13.

well as pilot activities for improving the integrity of transboundary watersheds and ecosystems.[51]

A further positive aspect of the ELC is the clause contained in Article 12, which recognizes the supremacy of other existing or future international conventions, provided that such conventions enshrine stricter provisions concerning landscape protection, management, or planning.[52] In other words, it affirms the primacy of any treaty that is more demanding or more favourable than the ELC where landscape matters are concerned. It follows that states parties affirm the pre-eminence of the ELC over any other instrument that contains provisions which are less demanding—although in practice this is unlikely as the measures foreseen by the ELC are not overly rigorous. The originality of Article 12 is that it affirms superiority of any rule that is more favourable to landscape, whether that rule be in other conventions or in domestic law.

6.5 Institutional Framework and Implementation

The ELC entered into force on 1 March 2004, after it received the required ten ratifications. As of January 2018, thirty-nine states parties have ratified the ELC and two have signed the treaty.[53] Article 10 of the ELC provides that existing competent Committees of Experts shall be responsible for monitoring the Convention's implementation and that these committees shall propose the criteria for conferring and the rules governing the landscape award of the Council of Europe, as well as propose amendments to the Convention.[54] The committee of experts charged with monitoring the implementation of the Convention was finally established in 2008 with the creation of the Steering Committee on Cultural Heritage and Landscape

[51] Committee on Social Affairs, Health and sustainable Development, *Draft Protocol Amending the European Landscape Convention*, B. Explanatory memorandum by Mr Schennach, Rapporteur, Report, Doc. 13989, 18 February 2016, para. 6.

[52] Art. 12 states: 'The provisions of this Convention shall not prejudice stricter provisions concerning landscape protection, management and planning contained in other existing or future binding national or international instruments.'

[53] Andorra, Armenia, Azerbaijan, Belgium, Bosnia and Herzegovina, Bulgaria, Croatia, Cyprus, Czech Republic, Denmark, Estonia, Finland, France, Georgia, Greece, Hungary, Ireland, Italy, Latvia, Lithuania, Luxembourg, Moldova, Montenegro, Netherlands, Norway, Poland, Portugal, Romania, San Marino, Serbia, Slovak Republic, Slovenia, Spain, Sweden, Switzerland, the Republic of Macedonia, Turkey, Ukraine, and United Kingdom have ratified. Malta and Iceland have signed.

[54] See Art. 10, paras 1 and 3, and Art. 17 respectively.

(now the Steering Committee for Culture, Heritage and Landscape) which held its first meeting in April 2008.[55] The Committee has numerous functions, including the monitoring of other cultural heritage conventions, over twenty recommendations, and the Framework Convention on the Value of Cultural Heritage for Society (Faro Convention).[56] The explanatory report on the implementation of the ELC states that 'it transpires that it would be easier to achieve the objectives of the Convention if the representatives of contracting parties had the possibility of meeting regularly to devise joint-co-ordinated programmes and of jointly monitoring the application of the convention'.[57] Indeed the Draft ELC referred to such a 'Landscape Committee' comprised of states representatives, but this was omitted from the final text.[58]

Nevertheless, periodic conferences of the contracting parties have been held roughly every two years since the adoption of the Convention in 2000.[59] In addition, workshops for the implementation of the Convention take place more often than the conferences: a total of twenty workshops have been organized since 2000.[60] These provide a forum where NGOs, semi-state bodies, and a broad range of actors and stakeholders are accommodated and where host states and regions can showcase their landscapes and landscape initiatives, which represents an incentive for landscape protection in itself. For a number of years the workshops appeared to lack any clear vision and structure, and were characterized by lengthy conceptual interventions, coupled with practical examples of implementation at local levels, with a marked absence of relevant state departments.[61] This obviously influenced the choice of topic for the eighteenth workshop held in Armenia in 2016, entitled 'National Policies for the implementation of the European Landscape Convention: Challenges

[55] 1st CDPATEP Plenary Session, 28–29 April 2008, <https://www.coe.int/en/web/cdcpp-committee> accessed 30 January 2018.

[56] Framework Convention on the Value of Cultural Heritage for Society (opened for signature 27 October 2005, entered into force on 1 June 2011) CETS 199 (hereafter Faro Convention).

[57] Explanatory Report on the Implementation on the European Landscape Convention (council of Europe, 2000), available at <http://conventions.coe.int/treaty/en/Reports/Html/176.htm> accessed 30 January 2018.

[58] See Arts 84–91, Report on the Preliminary Draft European Landscape Convention, CG (4) 6, Part II. Strasbourg, 5 May 1997.

[59] See T-FLOR 1 (2001) 19, T-FLOR (2002) 27, T-FLOR (2004) 14, T-FLOR (2007) 14, CEP-CDPATEP (2009) 1, CEP-CDPATEP (2011), 18E CEP-CDCPP (2013) 12E, and CEP-CDCPP (2015) 34E.

[60] Workshop proceedings available at <http://www.coe.int/en/web/landscape/workshops> accessed 30 January 2018.

[61] This observation is based on personal attendance of these workshops, as well an analysis of workshop proceedings.

and Opportunities', which was aimed at national government departments with competence for landscape.[62]

An oft-cited best practice example of successful implementation of the ELC is the region of Catalonia. Based on the ELC's aims and objectives, Catalonia has developed a system of 'landscape catalogues', in which public participation is genuinely taken into account in the process of landscape assessment and policy formation (i.e. not just a box-ticking exercise).[63] These catalogues in turn inform land-use policy and planning (in the form of 'landscape directives'), which are then taken into consideration in planning applications and protected area designation.[64] The ELC's form of governance works well in the case of Catalonia—a relatively wealthy European region with a strong regional identity and political will on the part of the local government. This is the ideal example of how the ELC should work in practice and is understandable given the origins of the ELC: it was instigated by Mediterranean European regions and spearheaded by the Council of Europe's Congress of Local and Regional Authorities. The Convention is therefore suited for implementation at this level and with this model of governance in mind, combining strong regional identity, political will, and adequate resources. [65]

6.6 Problematizing the ELC from a Legal Perspective

The ELC has ignited an awareness of the importance of safeguarding landscape continent wide (and beyond) and goes a long way to effecting long-term changes through education, awareness-raising, and good landscape planning, but it lacks strength as a legal tool in itself. This is due not only to the overly broad definition of landscape provided in the text (which could be interpreted as 'environment', 'cultural heritage', or indeed 'economic development' by decision-makers), but also to the lack of a system of protection and procedural rights beyond public participation in the development of plans and policies. The lack of any criteria or list means that it is legally very difficult to prove

[62] Proceedings of the meetings are available at <http://www.coe.int/en/web/landscape/workshops> accessed 30 January 2018.

[63] <http://www.catpaisatge.net/eng/directrius.php> accessed 30 January 2018.

[64] The Landscape Act sets forth that Landscape Directives are provisions based on the landscape catalogues that define and legally integrate the proposed landscape quality goals, guidelines, and actions into partial land-use plans or land master plans approved by the Department of Land and Sustainability (DTES). The DTES defines landscape guidelines, with the assistance of the Landscape Observatory of Catalonia.

[65] Art. 4.

a breach of the Convention's obligations,[66] as it is presumed that local populations will actively engage in the formulation of policies and that this will work in favour of landscape protection and avoidance of disputes in the long term. Implementing the ELC is more subtle and focused on integrating landscape (and people's relationship with it) within landscape quality objectives, national spatial strategies, and planning processes. According to the explanatory report to the Convention, this requires starting from education and awareness raising to landscape character assessment and classification, to a range of other protection, management, and planning measures, the first of which is to recognize landscape in law as an expression of people's surroundings. This makes assessing the legal implementation, beyond a superficial comparative analysis of landscape laws, a somewhat complex task. First, the ELC and references to it rarely, if ever, play a role in legal proceedings. In none of the cases dealing with landscape under examination in this study was the ELC mentioned as a relevant treaty with binding obligations, neither by counsel nor by the judiciary. In the case law of the European Court of Human Rights examined in Chapter 9, for example, where other Council of Europe treaties dealing with cultural heritage were mentioned by the Court as important obligations allowing a state to impinge on other fundamental freedoms in the public interest,[67] not a single case to date has included reference to the ELC. Nor has the ELC been referenced by the judiciary in many high-profile landscape disputes in national courts.[68]

Second, the public participation conceived of in the Convention is restricted to participation in plans and policies, that is, in the landscape assessment, characterization, and valorization stage. While the ELC refers to the Aarhus Convention (on access to information, public participation, and access to justice) in its preamble, it makes no reference to access to justice or judicial review in its text. It can be seen that the emphasis of the Convention is on the pre-emptive and pro-active planning and development of landscape at local and regional level—as a territorial project, which is surely positive for improving overall landscape quality in Europe, but does not offer a solution with regard to solving disputes that arise at later stages in the planning

[66] A 'list of Landscapes of European significance' had been included in the Draft Landscape Convention but this was excluded from the final text, as it was felt to be contrary to the aims and objectives of the Convention.

[67] In particular, the European Convention on the Protection of the Architectural Heritage, see *Kozacioglu v Turkey*, Grand Chamber Decision 19/02/09. Application No. 2234/03, and *Bogdel v Lithuania*, Chamber Judgment 26 Nov 2013, Application No. 41248/06, para. 45.

[68] For example *Salafia v Minister for the Environment, Heritage and Local Government and Others (Tara and M3 Motorway)* [2006] IEHC 61; Supreme Administrative Court, Poland, II OSK 821/08 (Via Baltica bypasses) 16 September 2008.

process when the above-mentioned obligations have not been sufficiently provided for, and which may involve state-backed infrastructural or resource extraction projects in landscapes of high heritage value. Indeed, many people only become aware of significant landscape changes late in the planning process. William Logan notes that the aim of involving local communities in a genuine way is not always translated into practice, and that 'the insistence of the right of all voices to be heard does not necessarily imply the end goals of conciliation or reconciliation'.[69] Laurajane Smith argues that heritage programmes, when they try to include communities and society at large, tend to do so in 'assimilationist terms'.[70] Thus, people are invited to 'learn' about authorized versions of heritage. While the ELC outwardly appears to reject this approach of official or 'authorized' heritage discourse, it has the potential to fall into the same trap. While the explanatory report notes that landscape must become a mainstream political concern, since 'it plays an important role in the well-being of Europeans who are no longer prepared to tolerate the alteration of their surroundings by technical and economic development in which they have no say', the ELC nevertheless pays great attention to administrative arrangements, training for specialists in landscape appraisal and operations, the promotion of landscape specialists, and committees of experts.[71] In addition, public participation in landscape policies is not without its own challenges. As highlighted by some landscape architects in a recent volume on the implementation of the ELC in northern Europe, public engagement can often be reduced to the gathering of feedback from interest groups and politicians rather than trying to understand the use and values that residents place on the landscape.[72] This is also the finding of a research paper on public participation in landscape characterization and assessment in England, Norway, Slovakia, and Malta, which noted a 'prevailing gap between participation rhetoric on paper and participation at the operational level'.[73] In particular, it was found that public involvement is largely limited to consultation, with few efforts to ensure representativeness of participants.

[69] William S. Logan, 'Closing Pandora's Box. Human Rights Conundrums in Cultural Heritage Protection', in H. Silverman and D. F. Ruggels (eds), *Cultural Heritage and Human Rights* (Springer, 2007), 40.

[70] Laurajane Smith, *The Uses of Heritage* (Routledge, 2006), 44.

[71] Arts 4–8.

[72] Karsten Jorgensen, Morten Clemetsen et al. (eds), *Mainstreaming Landscape through the European Landscape Convention* (Routledge, 2016), 43.

[73] Elisabeth Conrad, Louis F. Cassar, Michael Jones, et al., 'Rhetoric and Reporting of Public Participation in Landscape Policy', *Journal of Environmental Policy and Planning* 13 (1) (2011), 23–47.

The approach of the ELC is arguably one of sustainable development and equitable landscape planning. Yet, as pointed out by Marc Antrop, landscapes change continuously in a more or less chaotic way as a reflection of society's social and economic needs at a given moment, and thus the concept of sustainable landscapes could be viewed as a utopian goal.[74] In addition, if landscape is 'perceived', then surely it can constitute a multitude of values and meanings for a multitude of people. Incorporating these disparate views in a meaningful way into landscape policies is a challenging task, one which is only attainable with sufficient resources and infrastructure to carry out such a process in an equitable manner, such as in the case of Catalonia. Landscape is a collective good and as such is about collective action, yet the collective dimension is left largely unexplored in the ELC and its supporting documentation. By contrast, the Framework Convention on the Value of Cultural Heritage for Society, which was adopted five years after the ELC and was somewhat inspired by it, defines a 'heritage community', as consisting 'of people who value specific aspects of cultural heritage which they wish, within the framework of public action, to sustain and transmit to future generations'.[75] This is significant because it defines a community on the basis of shared heritage values.

The preamble to the ELC states that the protection, management, and planning of landscape entail 'rights and responsibilities for everyone', and it is this aspect of the Convention that has been taken up by efforts at linking landscape to ideas of spatial justice, human rights, democracy,[76] and common goods.[77] The obligation exists in the ELC to provide for the right to participate, but there are no corresponding rights to access information or access justice when abuse of power occurs. The ELC is very much about the everyday and not the exceptional. It cannot be relied upon therefore to claim any real substantive rights or to access justice when participatory rights are not provided for, or when arbitrary or unjust decisions are made affecting landscape. This means that in order to ascertain the nature of the relationship between landscape and rights, it is human rights instruments and the case law of human rights courts that need to be analysed.

[74] Marc Antrop, Sustainable Landscapes: Contradiction, Fiction or Utopia, *Landscape and Urban Planning*, 75 (2006), 187–97.

[75] Art. 2(b).

[76] See also the resulting publication: Shelley Egoz, Jala Makhzoumi, and Gloria Pungetti (eds), *The Right to Landscape: Contesting Landscape and Human Rights* (Ashgate, 2011). See also, the proceedings from the International Conference, *Defining Landscape Democracy* (Oscarsborg, Norway, 3–5 June 2015).

[77] UNISCAPE, *Common Goods from a Landscape Perspective* (Faculty of Architecture, University of Florence, 16–17 January 2014).

Notwithstanding these limits, the lack of legal force should not undermine the enormously positive role and influence of the ELC on landscape discourse and society more broadly, and for the renewed activity taking places across Europe on the part of civil society organizations, communities and groups, and academia. In addition, the ELC has had some success in affecting change in planning laws throughout Europe, and has led to the development of landscape strategies and landscape character assessment in states parties. However, perhaps the greatest impact of the ELC lies in its power as a catalyst for landscape awareness—itself an objective of the Convention—and for [re]humanizing the concept of landscape itself.

6.7 On the Adoption of a Global Landscape Convention

In 2010, an expert meeting was convened by the Director General of UNESCO following a request by the IFLA to review the feasibility of adopting a global instrument on landscape protection.[78] The meeting was attended by twenty-three individuals from a variety of regions and fields (anthropologists, ecologists, geographers, landscape architects, planners, and lawyers) as well as representatives from a number of interested organizations (including the IFLA, IUCN, ICOMOS, UNESCO, and the Council of Europe). It appears from the report of the meeting that the ELC provided the wellspring for discussion. Its implementation over the first ten years was examined and its new conceptual approach was praised. It was noted how no such integrated instrument exists for landscape at the global level, and how an international landscape convention would 'capture an extraordinary but fragile renaissance that is taking place, as government authorities, civil society but also investors are beginning to appreciate the true value and complexity of the landscape'.[79] The meeting of experts discussed the challenges of such a convention, and concluded that a global convention was urgently needed. The proposal did not gain the support of UNESCO's Executive Council on that occasion, although there have been other developments in the field of cultural landscapes.[80]

[78] Expert meeting on 'The International Protection of Landscapes', Paris, UNESCO Headquarters, Room IV, 18 April 2011, Agenda.

[79] Ibid, at para. 7

[80] Namely, the UNESCO Recommendation on the Historic Urban Landscape (Chapter 6). A draft resolution was adopted in August 2011 and a revised Draft Recommendation was issued. The Recommendation states explicitly that it will 'not replace existing doctrines or conservation approaches; rather, it is an additional tool to integrate policies and practices of conservation of the built environment into the wider goals of urban development in respect of the inherited values

While the IFLA's proposals for a global landscape convention come from the desire to enhance awareness of landscape and its importance for well-being at the global level, it nevertheless poses certain problems if viewed in the context of international cultural heritage law. In order to be constructive and add something to the existing framework, an international landscape convention would need to address the roots of landscape deterioration and alteration caused by global policies, rather than rehash some of the principles of existing instruments. It is important to protect landscapes of outstanding universal value and other representative landscapes, but their protection, while providing examples of good practice, will not halt the processes that lead to landscape degradation overall. To echo paragraph 12 of the report, it is strongly suggested that a list not be included in any such Convention, since—aside from likely duplication with the already existing World Heritage List (and to a much lesser extent the Representative List of the Intangible Cultural Heritage of Humanity)—this would detract from the real challenges posed by landscape protection and enhancement—a complex process taking into account food production, land use and management, infrastructural projects, mining activities, and other large-scale development and resource extraction projects. Landscape is a reflection of a process, so it is a process that needs to be addressed in order to combat negative changes in the landscape. The relative success of the ELC can partly be traced to the fact that Europe shares many commonalities—politically, economically, and socially. Subsidiarity is a fundamental principle of the ELC, and indeed it has been the autonomous regions in Europe that have been most active in its implementation.

A global convention could see a state-oriented approach that may run the risk of being so broad so as not to have a meaningful impact, or of states adopting the approach of previous universal instruments and focusing only on a number of representative landscapes or landscape issues. Of course, 'landscape is a cultural entity that cannot be tied down to objective parameters that are valid for all; nor can it be defined exclusively according to rational parameters deriving from a universal logic'.[81] This is why an Annex noting regional differences and priorities would be constructive.

and traditions of different cultural contexts. This tool, which is a "soft-law" to be implemented by Member States on a voluntary basis.'

[81] Mariolina Besio, 'Conservation Planning: The Case of European Rural Landscapes', World Heritage Papers No. 7, *Cultural Landscapes; The Challenges of Conservation*, 11–12 November 2002, Ferrara, 60–7.

The Resolution adopted by the IFLA, attached in Annex III of the Report, lists a number of international instruments, most of which deal with historical, architectural, aesthetic, and cultural aspects of the landscape. This is understandable given that the IFLA is a federation of landscape architects, but in order to make a difference and add something to the existing framework, an international landscape convention would need to adopt a radical approach incorporating both the cultural and the ecological approaches to landscape (instruments such as the Convention on Plant Genetic Resources for Food and Agriculture (2004) are just as important) and combine this integration with democratic principles of governance and participation. Interestingly, the Report on the Feasibility of an International Landscape Convention mentions 'a right to landscape' twice, not envisaged to be enforceable, but rather as a recognition of people's right to a decent landscape and quality of life

In 2012, a meeting organized by UNESCO on the international protection of landscapes adopted the Florence Declaration on Landscape, which called upon intergovernmental agencies and secretariats responsible for United Nations programmes together with NGO to work towards an international mechanism.[82] Among other things, the Declaration reaffirms landscape as a common good. It also states that the 'right to landscape is a human necessity'.[83] If the emergence of calls for a right to landscape stem from the overemphasis on individual property rights (and the demise of public space through privatization, among other things), then further investigation into the nature of the relationship between landscape and human rights merits exploration (Chapters 8 and 9).

[82] Florence Declaration on Landscape, available at <http://iflaonline.org/archive-record/florence-declaration-on-landscape/> accessed 30 January 2018.
[83] Ibid.

7

Landscape Protection and EU Law

7.1 Introduction

Landscape protection is not singled out in EU law as a specific area of competence. However, given that landscape forms part of the definition of cultural heritage and more importantly, the environment, it is very much a subject of EU concern, particularly in the field of environmental impact assessment and procedural rights to access information, public participation, and access to justice in environmental matters. In addition, other policy areas such as agriculture have significantly influenced European landscapes. This chapter provides a critical overview of landscape protection in the EU. It begins by briefly outlining the impact of EU agricultural policy on European landscapes. It then moves on to ascertain the extent to which the cultural heritage dimension to landscape protection is considered within EU policy, and contrasts the lack of action in this area to the level of landscape protection within the realm of nature protection and habitats conservation. While the EU does not have specific competence in the field of culture, it nevertheless has a wide remit in the field of environmental protection, and it is here that the scope for the protection of landscapes is the widest. In particular, environmental impact assessment directives include the requirement to assess the effects of projects not only on environmental elements but also on cultural heritage and the landscape. In addition, while the European Landscape Convention (ELC) provides for public participation, EU law requires member states to legislate not only for public participation but also for access to justice and broader standing requirements in environmental matters. However, despite the influence of recent Council of Europe treaties on various EU policy documents, the conceptualization of landscape within the EU is still a rural scenic one, rather than one that connotes the various ways in which people interact with and relate to cultural landscape. Given that access to justice remains a problem for landscape matters not relating to environmental breaches but cultural ones, a greater role for the EU in cultural landscape protection is advocated.

7.2 The Impact of EU Agricultural Policy on European Landscapes

The EU's Common Agricultural Policy (CAP) has exerted perhaps the greatest impact on European landscapes compared to any other area of EU policy.[1] Fairclough points out that while the past impact of agriculture on the landscape is perceived as beneficial, 'the driving force behind the creation of beautiful landscapes, and of supposedly harmonious interactions with nature and bio-diversity, modern agriculture is popularly and widely seen as wholly destructive'.[2] This was due to the focus in the early years of agricultural policy being almost entirely on quantitative production and efficiency.[3] At the end of the 1980s and early 1990s, however, structural funds were reformed and more attention was paid to the side effects of productive agriculture.[4] A third phase for CAP was outlined in Agenda 2000, where agriculture was linked to rural development and issues such as the environment and to a lesser extent landscapes were considered, becoming access criteria for funds allotted to support agriculture.[5] These changes were driven by the same concerns behind the ELC: that CAP was encouraging over-production and over-industrialization, accelerating rates of change and loss of character in the landscape. The environmental part of the changes in the CAP agenda was significant but it was dominated by nature conservation; the cultural heritage dimension to the landscape was fairly minor.[6] Indeed, much of the literature dealing with CAP has focused

[1] Graham Fairclough, 'Europe's Landscape: Archaeology, Sustainability and Agriculture' in Graham Fairclough and Stephen Rippon (eds), *Europe's Cultural Landscape: Archaeologists and the Management of Change* (EAC, 2002), 6.

[2] Ibid.

[3] Council Regulation (EEC) No. 797/85 on improving the efficiency of agricultural structures, modified, is a good example of this approach.

[4] For example Council Regulation (EEC) 2092/91 of 24 June 1991 on organic production of agricultural products and indications referring thereto on agricultural products and foodstuffs; Council Regulation (EEC) No. 2328/91 of 15 July 1991 on improving the efficiency of agricultural structures, modified; Council Regulation (EEC) No. 2081/92 of 14 July 1992 on the protection of geographical indications and designations of origin for agricultural products and foodstuffs.

[5] See for example Council Regulation (EC) No. 1257/1999 of 17 May 1999 on support for rural development from the European Agricultural Guidance and Guarantee Fund.

[6] Fairclough, 'Europe's Landscape: Archaeology, Sustainability and Agriculture' in Graham Fairclough and Stephen Rippon (eds), Europe's Cultural Landscape: Archaeologists and the Management of Change (EAC, 2002), 1–12, 7. Jane Grenville (ed.), *Managing the Historic Rural Environment* (Routledge, 1999). F. Fischler, 'The European Union's rural development policy: protecting our heritage', in *Naturopa* 95/2001. David Stanners and Philippe Bordeau, *Europe's Environment: The Dobris Assessment* (European Environment Agency, 1995).

on maintaining the rural character of the landscape or 'countryside' and on alternative approaches to rural management and stewardship of the landscape from ecological perspectives.[7] Rural landscapes are obviously cultural landscapes, in the sense that they represent the interaction of people and agricultural custom and practice over time. However, other aspects such as historical sites, intangible and associative landscapes, or landscapes important for uses other than agriculture (such as, for example, rights of way on walking routes) lie beyond the scope of agricultural reforms.

7.3 Landscape, Cultural Heritage, and EU Law

The Treaty Establishing the European Community (Rome, 25 March 1957)[8] refers in its Article 151 to a 'common culture', which can be understood to mean 'shared' by more than one.[9] The Lisbon Treaty (TFEU) elaborates on this by providing that the 'Union shall contribute to the flowering of the cultures of the Member States, while respecting their national and regional diversity and at the same time bringing the common cultural heritage to the fore.'[10] The 'common' cultural heritage of Europe implies that there is an obligation not only to preserve the cultural heritage, but also to ensure a degree of public access.[11] Article 167 also refers to the 'dissemination of the culture and history of the European peoples', which points to the democratization of culture. This objective was recognized by the European Commission as far back as the 1970s and is linked to the idea of cultural rights enshrined in Article 27 of the Universal Declaration of Human Rights and Article 15 of the International Covenant on Economic, Social and Cultural Rights. The right to participate in cultural life has also been considered an aspect of citizenship.[12]

The developments made in the field of international cultural heritage law, particularly the ELC and the Faro Convention, have clearly influenced the thinking concerning cultural heritage in recent EU policy documents.

[7] Council Regulation (EEC) No. 2078/92 of 30 June 1992 on agricultural production methods compatible with the requirements of the protection of the environment and the maintenance of the countryside established a clear relationship between agriculture and landscape.

[8] European Union, *Treaty Establishing the European Community (Consolidated Version), Rome Treaty*, 25 March 1957, available at <https://ec.europa.eu/romania/sites/romania/files/tratatul_de_la_roma.pdf> accessed 30 January 2018.

[9] Rachael Craufurd Smith, *Culture and European Union Law* (Oxford University Press, 2004), 284.

[10] Art. 167 TFEU (ex Art. 151), para. 1.

[11] Craufurd Smith, *Culture and European Union Law* (n 9), 285.

[12] See Nick Stevenson (ed.), *Culture and Citizenship* (Sage, 2001).

In a Communication by the Commission to the Parliament entitled 'Towards an integrated approach to cultural heritage in the EU', it was recognized that 'Conservation is increasingly geared towards preserving and enhancing a whole cultural landscape rather than an isolated site, and is also becoming more people-centred.'[13] Cultural heritage is defined as 'a shared resource', and 'a common good' and it is acknowledged that, while heritage protection is primarily a matter for national, regional, and local authorities, the European Union has a role to play in line with the EU Treaties and in respect of the principle of subsidiarity.[14] The same document mentions 'development priorities such as the empowerment of civil society in local governance, conflict resolution and human rights promotion'.[15] Of significance here are the recent 'Conclusions on participatory governance of cultural heritage' adopted by the Council of the European Commission in 2014,[16] which aside from reiterating some of the points made by the Commission in the above-mentioned communication, as well as citing the Faro Convention as a point of reference, recognizes the importance of participatory governance in cultural heritage. It invites the member states and the Commission to co-operate on issues related to participatory governance and importantly for the present purposes, 'to enhance cooperation with international organisations such as the Council of Europe and UNESCO to promote a participatory approach to cultural heritage governance'.[17] This echoes Article 167(3) of the Treaty, which provides for co-operation with 'competent international organisations in the sphere of culture, in particular the Council of Europe'.

The role envisaged for the Commission in the field of cultural heritage is that of facilitator rather than standard-setter. The Commission is invited 'to promote evidenced based research on the impact of participatory approaches in cultural heritage policies' and 'to continue dialoguing with civil society organisations' in this regard.[18] Landscape is clearly considered within the scope of cultural heritage as conceived by the EU[19] and indeed, certain projects funded within the Seventh Framework Programme (FP7) deal with cultural

[13] European Commission, Communication from the Commission to the European Parliament, the Council, the European Economic and Social Committee and the Committee of Regions, *Towards an Integrated Approach to Cultural Heritage for Europe*, COM(2014) 477 final. Brussels, 22.7.2014, at 1.3.

[14] Ibid. [15] Ibid, at 2.3

[16] Council of the European Union, *Council Conclusions on Participatory Governance of Cultural Heritage* (2014/C 463/01) OJC 463, 23.12.2014, at 1-3.

[17] Ibid, at 26. [18] Ibid, at 27–8.

[19] Council of the European Union, *Draft Council Conclusions on Cultural Heritage as a Strategic Resource for a Sustainable Europe*, 8892/14 CULT 58, at 2.

landscapes.[20] Article 167 refers to incentive measures but excludes the possibility of the harmonization of laws and regulations of the member states in this area.[21] In addition, Article 167 states that action by the Union shall be aimed at encouraging co-operation between member states, as well as supporting their action in the 'conservation and safeguarding of cultural heritage of European significance'.[22] However, it is not clear what European significance means in this context—unlike the Natura 2000 Network, there is no common network of protected areas for cultural landscapes, and while projects dealing with cultural landscapes are supported and financed by the EU, and while CAP now contains measures for the maintenance of rural landscapes, the Union does not have any specific policy with respect to cultural landscape protection, per se.

7.4 Special Conservation Areas and the Natura 2000 Network

In contrast to cultural heritage, the environment is a specific area of competence for the EU and landscape is implicated in a number of environmental policies and directives: from special areas of conservation protected under the Natura 2000 Framework to environmental impact assessment directives and more recently, the Aarhus package.[23] Perhaps the legislation with the greatest conservation reach is Council Directive 92/43/EEC on the Conservation of natural habitats and of wild fauna and flora (more commonly known as the Habitats Directive), which complements the earlier Wild Birds Directive 79/409/EEC. The Wild Birds Directive was the first nature protection law to be adopted at European level. It protects all birds that are naturally occurring in Europe and aims to conserve key habitats of threatened, vulnerable, or rare species, such as the golden eagle, the spoonbill, the Cyprus warbler, and migratory birds in general.[24] The Habitats Directive extended protection beyond birds to rare, threatened, or endemic plants and animals, as well as habitat types such as heathlands, peatbogs, and coastal meadows, and therefore certain natural landscapes. The Directive

[20] For example, the HERCULES project on 'Sustainable Futures for Europe's Heritage in Cultural Landscapes. <http://www.hercules-landscapes.eu/> accessed 30 January 2018.

[21] Art. 167(5) TFEU. [22] Art. 167(2) TFEU.

[23] The decision to adopt the Aarhus Convention by the EU was made on 17 February 2005. See Decision 2005/370/EC. See also, COM (2003) 624, and OJ L 264, 25.9.2006, p. 13.

[24] Kerstin Sundseth and Peter Creed, *Natura 2000. Protecting Europe's Biodiversity* (European Commission, 2008), 15.

was a result of the obligations arising out of the Council of Europe's Berne Convention on the Conservation of Habitats and Wildlife in Europe, which was ratified by the EU in 1982.

The Natura 2000 Network was subsequently established to designate 'special areas of conservation' and 'special protection areas' across the European Union.[25] By 2008, over 25,000 sites had been included in the Network[26]—therefore affecting large tracts of the European landscape. In addition, the Network is not a system of strict nature reserves excluding all human activity. While it includes strictly protected nature reserves (including on privately owned land) it also includes much wider areas centred on people working together with nature. Under the Natura 2000 network, member states formally designate the relevant areas under national law in order to protect them from damaging activities. Under the Habitats Directive, specific assessment provisions have been created to help protect the EU's richest concentrations of biodiversity from threats posed by damaging plans and projects. The impact assessment provisions of Directive 92/43/EEC are found in Article 6(3), which provide that:

> Any plan or project not directly connected with or necessary to the management of the site but likely to have significant effect thereon, either individually or in combination with other plans or projects, shall be subject to appropriate assessment of its implications on the site in view of the site's conservation objectives. In light of the conclusions of the assessment [...] the competent authorities shall agree to plan the project only after having ascertained that it will not adversely affect the integrity of the site concerned and, if appropriate, after having obtained the opinion of the general public.

These provisions relate to the first step of a process governing plans or projects likely to affect sites making up the Natura 2000 network. In practice, the importance of the assessment provisions stems from the physical extent of the network and the network's role in ensuring the long-term status of the EU's biodiversity. The scope of the assessment here is both broader and narrower than Directive 85/337/EEC: broader because it refers to plans and encompasses all project types (instead of being limited to those listed in the annex) and narrower because it is solely concerned with impacts on nature. However, environmental impact assessment directives do include a cultural dimension within their scope of application.

[25] Art. 6, Habitats Directive 92/43/EEC.

[26] Sundseth and Creed (n 24), *Natura 2000. Protecting Europe's Biodiversity*, 21.

7.5 Landscape Protection and Environmental Impact Assessment

Environmental Impact Assessment (EIA) is a predictive tool of the late twentieth century that originated in the United States and is the product of many disciplines, particularly land-use planning and environmental sciences. It essentially amounts to a process of gathering information and using it in order to guide decisions likely to have an effect on the environment (which can include cultural heritage and the landscape). EIA is therefore preventative in purpose as it seeks to minimize problems from the outset, rather than addressing them once they emerge. The initial Directive 85/337/EEC of 27 June 1985 on the assessment of the effects of certain public and private projects on the environment has been amended four times, with the most recent amendment in 2014 (Directive 2014/52/EU of 16 April 2014) following an extensive review process.[27] The EIA Directive requires not only the consideration of environmental factors, including human health, land, soil, water, and air, but also material assets, *cultural heritage, and the landscape.*[28] The most recent amendment to the EIA Directive specifically mentions 'the protection and promotion of cultural heritage comprising urban historical sites and landscapes, which are an integral part of the cultural diversity that the Union is committed to respecting and promoting in accordance with Article 167(4) TFEU', as well as the fact that 'the definitions and principles developed in relevant Council of Europe Conventions, in particular the European Convention for the Protection of the Archaeological Heritage of 6 May 1969, the Convention for the Protection of the Architectural Heritage of Europe of 3 October 1985, the European Landscape Convention of 20 October 2000, the Framework Convention on the Value of Cultural Heritage for Society of 27 October 2005 can be useful'.[29] However, despite referencing these instruments, the concept of landscape itself appears narrowly construed to mean 'view' or scenery: 'In order to better preserve historical and cultural heritage and the landscape, it is important to address the *visual impact* of projects, namely the change in the *appearance or view* of the built or natural landscape

[27] Directive 2014/52/EU of 16 April 2014 (amending Directive 2011/92/EU on the assessment of the effects of certain public and private projects on the environment), OJ L 124, 25.4.2014, 1–18. Directive 2001/42/EC of 27 June 2001 on the assessment of the effects of certain plans and programmes on the environment and Directive 97/11/EC (amending Directive 85/337/EEC of 27 June 1985 on the assessment of the effects of certain public and private projects on the environment) OJ 1985 L 175/40, amended by Directive 97/11/EC. OJ 1997 L 73/5.

[28] OJ L 124, 25.4.2014, at 3(d).

[29] Ibid, at 16.

and urban areas, in environmental impact assessments' (emphasis added).[30] Landscape, as defined in the ELC and well within the scope of the definition of cultural heritage in the Faro Convention, accounts for more than just the 'appearance' of a place.[31] It also refers to the various relationships between people and place, as well as historical significance, and thus brings it closer to the notion of custom.

A key requirement of these directives is that of integrating prior assessment with the decision-making process. An assessment is obligatory for projects listed in Annex 1 of the Directive, deemed to have a significant effect on the environment due to their nature, size, or location. They include public or private projects such as, inter alia, long-distance railway lines, large airports, motorways, express roads, roads of four lanes or more, waste or water treatment plants, and other installations. Projects listed in Annex II are not automatically assessed and are subject to an EIA on a case-by-case basis. However, the Directive obliges all relevant national authorities, local authorities, and national courts to ensure that projects likely to have a significant effect on the environment (including the landscape) are subject to the assessment procedure.[32] All of the information gathered from the developer through consultation and assessment must be taken into account in the planning approval.[33] The decision regarding the project must be a reasoned one and must include 'a description, where necessary, of the main measures to avoid, reduce, and if possible, offset the major adverse effects'.[34] At this stage the EIA may raise issues of substantive compliance with other EU environmental legislation, such as effects on water quality or habitats and species. Non-compliance can take two forms: either failure to carry out—which can be challenged, and failure to properly carry out—which can lead to infringement proceedings by the Commission. The European Court of Justice has confirmed that under certain circumstances, an individual is entitled to invoke before a national court the provisions of the Directive in relation to a failure to properly carry out an EIA.[35] It is possible for the Commission to suspend the payment of EU funds where no EIA is undertaken for an EU-financed project. It is also possible for the Commission to seek interim relief, that is, to ask the European Court of Justice to halt a project being executed pending the

[30] OJ L 124, 25.4.2014, at.3, 16.

[31] Art. 2(a) of the Faro Convention defines cultural heritage as a 'group of resources inherited from the past which people identify, independently of ownership, as a reflection and expression of their constantly evolving values, beliefs, knowledge and traditions'. Landscape, as defined by the ELC, means an area, as perceived by people, whose character is the result of the action and interaction of natural and/or human factors. Art. 1(a).

[32] Art. 2. [33] Art. 8. [34] Art. 12.

[35] Case C-201/02, *Delena Wells* [2004] ECR I-723.

completion of an EIA. The first time the Commission resorted to this option was in 2007, in order to halt the construction of the Augustow and Wasilkow bypasses through the Rospuda Valley in Poland (protected under the Habitats Directive and Natura 2000 Network).[36] By contrast, in an Irish case concerning the failure to properly conduct an EIA in a cultural landscape of national, and arguably European and international, importance (the Tara-Skryne valley), infringement proceedings were initiated by the Commission but no further action was taken.[37] This was due to the lack of any other form of protection at European level for the cultural landscape in question, unlike the case of Rospuda Valley.

The two cases share many parallels: they both involved highly sensitive landscapes of European importance, which became the subject of state-approved road projects, supported by the local populations (who were not offered any alternatives). Both cases attracted widespread national and international condemnation; the EIA was flawed and the participatory process was lacking in both cases. The difference between the two cases, however, is that Rospuda was a designated 'natural' landscape, and benefitted from protection under the Natura 2000 Network. Tara, however, is an archaeological, historical, and associative cultural landscape, which was not protected under any European (or international) regime or framework. The needs of the local populations must undeniably be taken into consideration, as they are the ones living in the area and are entitled to adequate development. Yet, in both cases, the local populations were not offered any realistic alternatives, when in both cases alternatives existed. Tara was arguably the cultural landscape equivalent to the Rospuda natural landscape (this is substantiated by its subsequent inclusion on the Tentative List for World Heritage status).[38] Yet despite a similar international campaign and international pressure, ultimately, it did not benefit from any elevated level of protection beyond the procedural requirements of the EIA Directive. The Commission did receive a complaint,[39] and initiated infringement proceedings against Ireland.[40] It stated that it considered 'Ireland's approach to decisions involving the removal of historic structures

[36] Case C-193/07 *Commission v Republic of Poland* (Order of the President of the Court of 18 April 2007).

[37] Case C-50/09, *Commission v Ireland* (Judgment of the Court of 3 March 2011).

[38] The Royal Sites of Ireland: Cashel, Dún Ailinne, Hill of Uisneach, Rathcroghan Complex, and Tara Complex, submitted by Permanent Delegation of Ireland to the OECD and UNESCO <http://whc.unesco.org/en/tentativelists/5528/> accessed 30 January 2018.

[39] Meath Archaeological and Historical Society, Petition 546/2005 to the European Parliament Petitions Committee, supporting Petition No. 840/2004.

[40] IP/07/1524 Brussels, 17 October 2007, 'Commission to bring EIA case to Court of Justice'.

and archaeological monuments to be in contravention of the directive', but this did not prevent the motorway from proceeding.

During the 1990s, compliance with the EIA Directive became a touchstone issue in environmental controversies concerning major projects across the EU, particularly in member states undergoing a phase of rapid infrastructural development, such as Ireland, Spain, Portugal, and Greece. Among the environmental complaints submitted to the Commission and the European Parliament, the EIA Directive was the most cited EU instrument.[41] As a result of two reports carried out by the Commission on the implementation of the Directive,[42] as well as the developing case law of the Court of Justice and international developments, the Directive was amended in 1997, clarifying and reinforcing a number of key provisions such as those concerning the selection of individual projects to undergo EIA. In 1999 and 2001, the European Commission published a series of guidelines to assist practitioners and other stakeholders on several aspects of the Directive.[43] The influence of the Aarhus Convention resulted in the adoption of Directive 2003/35/EC, which amongst other things introduced provisions on public participation and access to justice in environmental matters.

7.6 Landscape Protection, EIA, and Access to Justice

While the ELC provides for public participation in the 'definition and implementation of landscape policies' as well as 'consultation' in 'identification and assessment', the Aarhus Convention on Access to Information, Public Participation and Access to Justice in Environmental Matters gives greater substance not only to the meaning of public participation but also the right to review procedures to challenge public decisions.[44] Notably, landscape is specifically mentioned within the definition of environment in Article 3.[45] Articles 6–8 of the Aarhus Convention identify three occasions for participation of the public: participation in decisions on specific activities; participation concerning plans, programmes, and policies; and

[41] For an account of early implementation of the Directive see Ludwig Kramer, *Focus on Environmental Law*. Vol. II, 1997, 240–57.

[42] COM (93) 28 of 2/4/93.

[43] Guidelines on the Assessment of Indirect and Cumulative Impacts as well as Impact Interactions (European Commission, 1999).

[44] Aarhus Convention on Access to Information, Public Participation and Access to Justice in Environmental Matters, Aarhus, 25 June 1998. 2161 UNTS 447. Entry into force 30 October 2001 <http://www.unece.org/env/pp/treatytext.htm/> accessed 30 January 2018.

[45] Art. 3(a).

participation during the preparation of executive regulations and/or generally applicable legally binding regulatory instruments. Furthermore, parties to the Convention must 'inform people of decisions taken on proposed activities of all kinds which are likely to affect them' as well as 'ensure that, when the final decision is taken on any proposed activity, the results of the public participation procedure are taken into consideration by the competent authorities'.[46] The 'public' in the Convention is given a broad meaning.[47] This is significant for landscape, as it involves not only the inhabitants or those directly affected by a planning decision, but also the wider public.[48] Accordingly, the Aarhus Convention entitles 'non-governmental organisations promoting environmental protection' as having a sufficient 'interest' to be entitled to access to a review procedure before a court of law.[49]

The European Union became party to the Aarhus Convention in May 2005.[50] Already in 1990 the European Commission introduced Directive 90/313/EEC on the Free Access to Information on the Environment.[51] On 24 October 2003 the Commission presented a Proposal for a Directive of the European Parliament and of the Council on access to justice in environmental matters.[52] This proposal was part of the Aarhus package, which also consisted of a proposal for a decision to ratify the Convention and another proposal for a regulation to apply the provisions of the Convention to EU institutions and bodies. In 2003, two Directives concerning the first and second pillars of the Convention were adopted: Directive 2003/4/EC of 28 February 2003 on public access to environmental information; and, Directive 2003/35/EC of 26 May 2003 providing for public participation and access to justice in respect of certain plans and programmes relating to the environment.[53] The

[46] Wiek Schrage, La Convention sur l'accès a l'information, la participation du public au processus décisionnel et l'accès a la justice en matière d'environnement', in La Convention d'Aarhus, *Revue juridique de l'environnement* 1999, édition spéciale, 5–7.

[47] Art. 4 states 'the 'public' means one or more natural or legal persons, and, in accordance with national legislation or practice, their associations, organizations, or groups. Art. 5: 'The public concerned' means the public affected or likely to be affected by, or having an interest in, the environmental decision-making; for the purposes of this definition, non-governmental organizations promoting environmental protection and meeting any requirements under national law shall be deemed to have an interest.

[48] Furthermore, public participation in the early stages of every landscape policy is a very ambitious objective. As noted by Luginbühl, although public participation is referred to in a number of texts, it is still a principle which is not strictly applied. See Council of Europe, *Landscape and Sustainable Development*, 2006, p. 48.

[49] Art. 5 (n 47).

[50] The decision on the conclusion of the Aarhus Convention by the EC was adopted on 17 February 2005. See Decision 2005/370/EC.

[51] [1990] OJ L158/56. [52] COM (2003) 624.

[53] Which amended, with regard to public participation and access to justice, Council Directive 85/337/EC of 27 June 1985 on the assessment of the effects of certain public and private projects

rest of the Aarhus package proposal was adopted on 6 September 2006 in the form of Regulation (EC) No. 1367/2006 on the application of the provisions of the Aarhus Convention to community institutions and bodies.[54] It entered into force on 28 September 2006 and became applicable on 17 July 2007. This means that the provisions of the Aarhus Convention are now binding on all member states. It is significant that the EIA Directives specifically refer to landscape and cultural heritage within the scope of environmental factors, and that a key requirement of these directives is integrating prior assessment with the decision-making process. This means that member states are bound legally to provide access to information, procedures for public participation, and possibilities for judicial redress for breaches involving landscape and cultural heritage. However, much will depend on the scope and definition of the latter within national law, as well as the nature of standing requirements in various jurisdictions. In Ireland, for example, standing requirements are quite strict, whereas in the Netherlands public interest proceedings are often entertained before national courts.[55]

The Charter of Fundamental Rights of the European Union provides for the right to information (Article 42), the right to be heard—essentially the right to participate (Article 41), and the right to an effective remedy and fair trial (Article 47). It also contains an article on environmental protection, providing that 'a high level of environmental protection and improvement of the quality of the environment must be integrated into the policies of the Union and ensured in accordance with the principle of sustainable development' (Article 37). Since the entry into force of the Lisbon Treaty in December 2009, the provisions of the Charter now have full effect for the member states. Yet before landscape and the cultural heritage can become a sufficient basis upon which to base a claim for judicial review, two things must happen, which can greatly facilitate, and indeed benefit from, international co-operation with UNESCO and the Council of Europe.

First, the concept of landscape and its interpretation within the context of environmental impact assessment must be developed. As it stands, the landscape component of an EIA has often been neglected—it is only *one* component for consideration among many others, such as soil, water, air quality,

on the environment (amended by 97/11/EC) and Directive 2001/42/EC of 27 June 2001 on the assessment of the effects of certain plans and programmes on the environment.

[54] OJ L 264, 25.9.2006, p. 13.

[55] B. van den Broek and L. Enneking, 'Public Interest Litigation in the Netherlands. A Multidimensional Take on the Promotion of Environmental Interests by Private Parties through the Courts', *Utrecht Law Review*, 10 (3) (2014), 77–90.

and archaeology, and as a result is hardly considered in the overall assessment.[56] As pointed out by Sas-Borjaska, in the opinion of many experts, landscape is the least important element of the environment because it is not countable and undergoes only subjective assessments, or visual impact assessments.[57] According to Holder, there are some serious doubts about the ability of environmental assessment to draw the public into decision-making about 'fairness' in any meaningful way because of the technical and scientific nature of the procedure, which works to exclude dialogue with the public, the result being that landscape and ethical problems are not taken into account.[58] Some components of EIA will be given more weight than others, particularly habitats and species protection, as they benefit from an enhanced level of protection under the Birds and Habitats Directives.[59] In addition, the latest elaboration of landscape within the consideration of EIA relegates it, yet again, to a scenic interpretation.

Second, although the EU has adopted the tenets of the Aarhus Convention (now part of EIA), and although landscape and cultural heritage fall within the definition of environment, without a special network of cultural landscapes of European significance, comparable to the Natura 2000 Network, many important cultural landscapes will be open to abuses of power in the name of the general interest of society, as decided by the member states.

The Faro Convention defines a heritage community as consisting 'of people who value specific aspects of cultural heritage which they wish, within the framework of public action, to sustain and transmit to future generations'. At present this includes participation, but not access to justice, when breaches of EIA concerning cultural landscapes occur.

7.7 A Greater Role for EU Law in Landscape Protection?

This chapter has illustrated that while the EU has no specific policy in relation to cultural landscapes, other areas of competence such as agriculture, and

[56] See, for example, Julie Martin Associates, *Landscape Character Assessment in Ireland: Audit and Evaluation* (Heritage Council, 2007), 66.

[57] Aleksandra Sas-Borjarska, 'Landscape Protection—the challenge for sustainable planning', 46th ISOCARP Congress 2010: <http://www.isocarp.net/Data/case_studies/1684.pdf>. Accessed 30 January 2018. Borjarska carried out the Landscape Impact Study for the alternative route through the Rospuda Valley.

[58] Jane Holder, 'Building Spatial Europe: An Environmental Justice Perspective', in Joanne Scott, *Environmental Protection—European Law and Governance* (Oxford University Press, 2009), 123.

[59] All projects are subject to an EIA. Furthermore, species and habitats are based on scientific criteria, not subjective or intangible values.

more importantly, environmental protection, do contain measures in favour of landscape protection. In particular, EU law on environmental impact assessment includes the consideration of the effects of certain projects not only on environmental elements but also on cultural heritage and the landscape. In addition, recent policy documents acknowledge that 'conservation is increasingly geared towards preserving and enhancing a whole cultural landscape rather than an isolated site, and is also becoming more people-centred'.[60] However, despite the influence of recent Council of Europe treaties on EU policy documents and the most recent amendment to the EIA Directive, the conceptualization of landscape is still a rural, scenic one—emphasizing natural values over cultural ones—rather than connoting the various ways in which people interact with and relate to landscapes (the cultural dimension). This is evidenced by the equation of landscape with 'view' in the recent EIA Directive, the emphasis on maintaining the rural, scenic quality of agricultural landscapes in the Common Agricultural Policy and on the emphasis placed on nature and habitats protection within EU environmental law. This confirms that a) cultural landscape policy is a matter of national member state competence; and b) it retains a scenic or preservationist meaning, rather than connoting a relationship (or use/practice) between people and a place over time. However, it is worth remembering that twenty-six EU member states have signed and ratified the ELC, which offers a broad scope for recognizing landscapes in law as a reflection of peoples' identity, and while the ELC provides for public participation, the EU ratified the Aarhus Convention and has already adopted secondary legislation implementing its provisions. This is extremely significant for landscape because a) the majority of landscape disputes arise at a later stage; and, b) landscape involves not only the inhabitants or those directly affected by the planning decision, it also involves the wider public (including NGOs). Accordingly, the Aarhus Convention also entitles 'non-governmental organisations promoting environmental protection' as having the 'sufficient interest' required to have access to a review procedure before a court of law.[61] This recognizes a collective dimension to environmental concerns, thus opening the door for public interest proceedings. Furthermore, if rights imply a claim by the beneficiary or holder of a right towards the addressee (state) to do something or refrain from doing

[60] European Commission, Communication from the Commission to the European Parliament, the Council, the European Economic and Social Committee and the Committee of Regions, *Towards an Integrated Approach to Cultural Heritage for Europe*, COM(2014) 477 final. Brussels, 22.7.2014, at 1.3

[61] See Art. 2, para. 5 and Art. 9, para. 2.

something, then access to justice is the logical culmination of the right to information and public participation. Nevertheless, it is national implementing measures that determine whether directives succeed in practice. A report on access to justice in member states shows that the 'sufficient interest' test at national level is still stringent.[62] Many national courts still strictly interpret 'sufficient interest' to mean the impairment of a right, and the applicants must be directly and personally affected by a plan or policy in question. Yet landscape is a collective good, and as such, damage or destruction cannot be measured in the same way as injury to person or property can.

Bearing this in mind, two areas of action could contribute to improving the protection and governance of landscapes at European level: first, future funds need to be directed at evidenced-based cultural landscape research including those disciplines and civil society organizations concerned not only with the *natural* but also the *cultural* dimension to landscape (conceived as both the historical dimension and the intangible dimension relating to use and practice).[63] Second, there needs to be some policy action in order to properly 'protect and promote the cultural heritage dimension of landscapes'.[64] Although cultural heritage is not perceived to be within the competence of the Union, it nevertheless falls within the area of environment and it is here that offers some scope for elaborating the content of landscape, both in relation to its significance within EIA, as well as in the creation of a possible network for cultural landscapes similar to the Natura 2000 Network. Importantly, the 'Conclusions on participatory governance of cultural heritage', adopted in 2014,[65] invite the member states and the Commission 'to enhance cooperation with international organisations such as the Council of Europe and UNESCO to promote a participatory approach to cultural heritage governance'.[66] This echoes Article 167(3) of the Treaty, which provides for co-operation with 'competent international organisations in the sphere of culture, in particular the Council of Europe'. The consideration of cultural landscapes is something that would complement the existing Natura 2000 Network, as well as the

[62] Esther Pozo Vera, *An inventory of EU Member States' Access to Justice in Environmental Matters* (Milieu, 2008).

[63] While cultural geography and anthropology are included within the HERCULES project on 'Sustainable Futures for Europe's Heritage in Cultural Landscapes, much of the project consortium is focused on natural sciences and the rural dimension to landscape <http://www.hercules-landscapes.eu/> accessed 8 May 2018.

[64] OJ L 124, 25.4.2014, at p. 3(16).

[65] Council of the European Union, *Council Conclusions on Participatory Governance of Cultural Heritage* (2014/C 463/01) OJC 463, 23.12.2014, at 2.3.

[66] Ibid.

World Heritage Convention and Council of Europe Treaties, while also being within the competence of the EU as outlined in Article 167. Action in this area could bolster the level of protection afforded to cultural landscapes across the member states, and provide clearer channels and standing for judicial review when abuse of power occurs.

8

Landscape and Human Rights

8.1 Defining Landscape-Related Rights

The reasons for exploring a human-rights approach to landscape protection are several. First, given the increasing assertion of a 'right to landscape',[1] the exact nature of the relationship between landscape and human rights merits further scrutiny. Second, human rights mechanisms are increasingly being used as a means for indirectly protecting the natural and cultural environment. This is due, in part, to the absence of other judicial fora for challenging governmental decisions affecting public spaces. Yet human rights are by nature limited by their focus on individual rights, whereas landscape is a collective good, and damage or harm to a landscape cannot be measured in terms of personal injury in the same way that the loss of property can. This poses two questions. First, is a human-rights approach suitable for landscape protection? And if so, is the current prevailing individual conceptualization of human rights a barrier to such an approach? In an attempt to answer these questions, the following two chapters endeavour to a) define the substantive rights associated with landscape protection; and b) examine the cases dealing with landscape in the jurisprudence of regional human rights courts. While there is no human right to landscape per se, landscape is implicated in human rights on a number of related levels: first, there exists a cultural rights dimension to landscape if we consider landscape as forming an integral part of cultural heritage, including practice and custom.[2] There is also a human rights dimension to landscape as expressed in the rights associated with environmental integrity.[3] Going beyond cultural rights and environmental protection, however, there are other rights associated with landscape protection,

[1] See Chapter 1 and Section 6.7.

[2] Landscape forms part of the definition of cultural heritage in a number of instruments, including the World Heritage Convention (Chapter 5) as well as certain human rights and environmental instruments discussed below.

[3] When it is a precondition for the fulfilment of other human rights and freedoms, such as health, private and family life, and sometimes, property.

such as the right to property (broadly interpreted to include customary rights or collective property) or the right to family and private life, although in practice these are often pitted against landscape protection rather than being in symbiosis with it.

The following two chapters are structured as follows. First, a commentary of the normative developments made at the universal level in relation to cultural rights and environmental rights is provided, and the relevance of these developments for the subject of landscape protection is explored. Second, the case law of the European Court of Human Rights and the Inter-American Court of Human Rights is examined to see whether a correlation exists between landscape related rights in standards and landscape related rights in practice. The aim is to concretize and define the limits and potential of a human rights approach to landscape protection, conceived broadly to include the relationship between people and landscape and not just the safeguarding of the physical space itself.

8.2 Landscape and Cultural Rights

> The concept of the cultural heritage covers all manifestations and messages of intellectual activity in our environment. These messages are passed on from generation to generation through learning and insights and are seen as 'mediated through' the built environment and landscape. Thus we have the idea that the physical elements of cultural heritage—that which has been traditionally viewed as comprising it—are in fact, the vehicles by which cultural heritage (in its intangible sense) is mediated to us. So the material culture is symbolic of cultural identity on a deeper level, a vessel of the intangible.[4]

As noted by Francesco Francioni, in so far as cultural heritage represents the sum of practices, knowledge, and representations that a community or group recognize as part of their history and identity, it is axiomatic that members of the group, individually and collectively, must be entitled to access, and enjoy such cultural heritage as a matter of right.[5] The right to culture was first recognized in the Universal Declaration of Human Rights (1948). Article 27(1) states that '[e]veryone has the right freely to participate in the cultural

[4] The Cultural Heritage—an Economic and Social Challenge (produced as a general text of the IVth European Conference of Ministers responsible for cultural heritage, Helsinki, 30-31 May (1995), 5 cited in Janet Blake, 'On Defining the Cultural Heritage', *International and Comparative Law Quarterly*, 49 (1) (2000), 68.

[5] Francesco Francioni, 'Culture, Heritage and Human Rights: An Introduction', in Francioni, and M. Scheinin, (eds), *Cultural Human Rights* (M. Nijhoff, 2008), 7.

life of the community, to enjoy the arts and to share in scientific advancement and its benefits', which clearly recognizes an individual right to culture. The International Covenant on Economic, Social and Cultural Rights (hereafter ICESCR) of 1966 reiterates this by providing that states parties 'recognise the right of everyone to take part in cultural life' (Article 15.1(a)).[6] This changes somewhat in the International Covenant on Civil and Political Rights (hereafter ICCPR) of the same year, which articulates cultural rights not as universal but as belonging to minorities: 'In those States in which ethnic, religious or linguistic minorities exist, persons belonging to such minorities shall not be denied the right, in community with other members of their group, to enjoy their own culture, to profess and practice their own religion, or to use their own language' (Article 27). A number of regional human rights treaties directly recognize the right to culture, including, *inter alia*, the 1969 American Convention on Human Rights (Article 26),[7] its 1988 Protocol of San Salvador (Article 14),[8] the 1981 African Charter on Human and Peoples' Rights (Article 22)–which also recognizes the right to the enjoyment of the cultural heritage of mankind[9]—as well as the host of declarations, recommendations, and conventions concerning the international protection of cultural heritage produced by UNESCO and the Council of Europe which refer to such a right in relation to cultural heritage and cultural diversity.[10] Some authors even argue the case for a right to cultural identity.[11]

[6] ICESCR, Art. 15 reads: 'The States parties to the present covenant recognize the right of everyone a) To take part in cultural life; b) To enjoy the benefits of scientific progress and its applications; c) To benefit from the protection of the moral and material interests from any scientific, literary or artistic production of which he or she is the author'.

[7] Article 26 obliges states parties to 'undertake measures, both internally and through international cooperation, especially those of an economic and technical nature, with a view to achieving progressively, by legislation or other appropriate means, the full realization of the rights implicit in the economic, social, educational, scientific, and cultural standards set forth in the Charter.'

[8] Article 14 comes under the heading 'Right to Benefits of Culture' and reiterates almost word for word the content of Art. 15 ICESCR, including that states parties recognize the right of everyone to take part in the cultural and artistic life of the community and to enjoy the benefits of scientific and technological progress.

[9] Art. 22(1): 'All peoples shall have the right to their economic, social and cultural development with due regard to their freedom and identity and in the equal enjoyment of the common heritage of mankind'.

[10] Taking the Council of Europe for example, see the European Social Charter (1961), the Convention on the Protection of the Architectural Heritage (1985), the Convention on the Protection of the Archaeological Heritage (1992), the Framework Convention for National Minorities (1994) and the Framework Convention on the Value of Cultural Heritage for Society (2005). UNESCO Declaration on the Principles of International Cultural Cooperation declares that 'each culture has a dignity and value which must be protected and preserved'.

[11] See Yvonne Donders, *Towards a Right to Cultural Identity?* (Intersentia, 2002). J. H. Burgers, 'The Function of Human Rights as Individual and Collective Rights', in Jan Berting et al. (eds), *Human Rights in a Pluralist World: Individuals and Collectivities* (Meckler, 1990), 63–74. Meyer-Bisch

Although the United Nations has stressed the indivisibility and interdependence of all human rights, in practice, cultural rights have received less attention and are generally less developed than other categories of human rights.[12] Few states have shown interest in adopting international standards in relation to cultural rights and up until recently, most did not consider that cultural rights might imply positive state obligations.[13] This is due to a number of reasons, but mostly due to the universal nature of human rights and the perceived exclusivity and ambiguousness of culture. In Europe, states were concerned that strengthening cultural rights might lead to tensions and instability in society, because granting communities certain rights might endanger the national unity.[14] European states also believed that the nature of cultural rights (and to a lesser extent economic and social rights) were fundamentally different to civil and political rights and thus required different treatment. While the latter could be granted immediately and implemented through legislation, the former were seen as largely aspirational and non–justiciable, and their implementation subject to progressive realization. In addition, culture was initially construed as an elitist concept—equivalent to the high arts—and was thus seen as something 'extra'.[15] Since the Cultural Turn, however, culture is generally considered in broad anthropological terms, as a way of life, a dynamic process instead of a collection of fixed objects.[16] International cultural heritage law and jurisprudence has begun to mirror this

(ed), 'Les droit culturels : Une catégorie sous-développée de droits de l'homme', *Revue internationale de droit comparé* (1994) 46.4, 1206–7. The UNESCO World Conference in Cultural Policies proclaimed in 1982 the 'right to cultural identity'.

[12] See, for example, Janusz Symonides, 'Cultural Rights: An Underdeveloped Category of Human Rights', *International Social Science Journal*, 50 (1998) 158, at 559.

[13] Asbjorn Eide, Catarina Krause, Allan Rosas et al. (eds), *Economic, Social and Cultural Rights: A Textbook* (Springer, 2001), 4–5.

[14] In 1994, when the CoE drafted an additional protocol for cultural rights, states opposed the inclusion of cultural identity for these reasons. CE Doc.CAHMIN (94) 35, December 1994, 11. Symonides recalls how the experience of the 1990s showed that the recognition of cultural rights to minorities is not a danger and a source of conflict but rather an important factor of peace and stability.

[15] According to Samba Cor Konate, one of the members of the Committee on Economic, Social and Cultural Rights, the drafters of the Covenant had a conception of cultural rights that was too limited and even incomplete because cultural activities were perceived as a luxury, something that could only be provided after other needs had been met. E/1993/22, paras 202–3.

[16] The term 'Cultural Turn' generally refers to developments in the humanities and social sciences involving a shift in emphasis towards meaning and culture rather than positivist epistemology. This shift occurred over a long period of time, but particularly since the 1970s. See Clifford Geertz, *The Interpretation of Cultures: Selected Essays* (Basic, 1973), Lynn Hunt, *The New Cultural History* (University of California Press, 1989), David Chaney, *The Cultural Turn: Scene-setting Essays on Contemporary Cultural History* (Routledge, 1994), Frederic Jameson, *The Cultural Turn: Selected Writings on the Post-Modern* (Verso, 1998).

development in recent years.[17] It must also be noted that the European view is not the only one. The African Commission on Human and Peoples' Rights, for example, has emphasized in a number of cases that economic, social, and cultural rights are as unequivocally justiciable as all other rights enshrined under the Charter.[18]

There has been no international instrument defining the precise content of cultural rights, but there have been attempts at creating a list. In 1995, the World Commission on Culture and Development presented its report 'Our Creative Diversity' to the UNESCO General Conference and the UN General Assembly.[19] The report recommended that the International Law Commission draft a list of cultural rights not currently protected by treaty law. It was envisaged that the list would then provide the basis for an international code of conduct on culture and that the Law Commission would examine the possibility of establishing an international office of an ombudsperson for cultural rights. It was envisaged that the office would handle individual and group complaints and negotiate peaceful means of settlement with the states involved. The report also suggested the possibility of establishing a court as part of the International Criminal Court, which would deal with violations of cultural rights.[20] Not surprisingly, all of the report's proposals, with the exception of the drafting of a list, were criticized by most UNESCO member states. As a result, UNESCO commissioned a report on cultural rights as provided for in existing instruments.[21] The working group established to prepare the report, known as the Fribourg Group, facilitated the work of the Council of Europe in a similar endeavour. Its task was to prepare a draft declaration on cultural rights for UNESCO, the aim being to consolidate existing cultural rights and highlight the cultural dimension to human

[17] UNESCO has moved away from the concepts of high culture only, to a more holistic approach that prompted work on intangible cultural heritage and traditional knowledge. At Council of Europe level, new instruments such as the ELC and Faro are emblematic of this shift, as they place emphasis on relationships between people and place rather than on places and objects per se.

[18] The normative content of economic, social and cultural rights has been elaborated in several decisions of the African Commission: *Social and Economic Rights Centre (SERAC) and Another v Nigeria* (2001) AHRLR 60 (ACHPR 2001); *Media Rights Agenda and Others v Nigeria* (2000) AHRLR 200 (ACHPR 1998); *Free Legal Assistance Group and Another v Zaire* (2000) AHRLR 74 (ACHPR 1995); *Purohit and Another v The Gambia* (2003) AHLR 96 (ACHPR 2003); *Union Interafricaine des Droits de l'Homme and Others v Angola* (2000) AHRLR 18 (ACHPR 1997); *International Pen and Others (on behalf of Saro-Wiwa) v Nigeria* (2000) AHRLR 212 (ACHPR 1998); *Malawi African Association and Others v Mauritania* (2000) AHRLR 149 (ACHPR 2000).

[19] UNESCO World Commission on Culture and Development, Our Creative Diversity (1995).

[20] UNESCO World Commission on Culture and Development, Our Creative Diversity (UNESCO, 1995), 281–4.

[21] Birgitta Leander, *Preliminary List of Cultural Rights* (UNESCO, 1996).

rights more generally, rather than create new ones. The draft declaration was presented to UNESCO's General Conference in 1996 but was not consequently adopted by the member states.

The European Convention on Human Rights and Fundamental Freedoms makes no explicit reference to culture in its text or protocols. In 1994, the ad-hoc Committee for the Protection of National Minorities of the Council of Europe (CAHMIN), drafted an additional protocol aimed at guaranteeing individual rights to culture (especially but not exclusively for persons belonging to minorities) with a view to the rights being justiciable in court.[22] The Committee considered several rights that were not included in the final text of the additional draft protocol. For example, the right to identity was rejected because it was considered too vague to be justiciable and because expressions of cultural identity were seen as already protected through the European Convention on Human Rights. Likewise, the right to freely choose one's own culture and the right to participate in cultural activities were excluded because they were considered to be covered by Articles 8 (private and family life), 9 (freedom of religion), and 10 (freedom of expression).[23] The protection of cultural and scientific heritage (including access to) was excluded because it was considered a positive obligation which would be financially burdensome on states. In addition, it was put forward by some that the protection of cultural heritage was more adequately covered by UNESCO instruments, and that it did not fall within the scope of the Convention as a new individual right.[24] Eventually the draft protocol was reduced to guaranteeing the right to a name and the freedom to use the language of one's choice, conditioned by clauses absolving states from any positive obligations. The work of the Committee was then shelved in 1996. Despite these stumbling blocks of the 1990s, in the last decade cultural rights have begun to gain more attention from scholars and the international community, and some positive developments have been made in terms of elaboration of their content. In 2007, the Observatory on Cultural Diversity and Human Rights launched the Fribourg Declaration on Cultural Rights, which is an updated form of the earlier work of the Fribourg Group.[25] In the context of the ICESCR, the recent adoption in 2008 of an optional protocol provides for the consideration of complaints

[22] CE Doc. CAHMIN (94) 33, November 1994, 3.CE Doc. CAHMIN (95) 22 Add., November 1995, 4. See, for further discussion, Ana Vrdoljak, 'Minorities, Cultural Rights and Intangible Heritage', *ESIL Research Forum on International Law Contemporary Issues*. Geneva 26–28 May 2005.

[23] CE Doc.CAHMIN (95) 21, September 1995, 5.

[24] Ibid.

[25] Text available at <http://hrlibrary.umn.edu/instree/Fribourg%20Declaration.pdf> accessed 30 January 2018.

by individuals in respect of rights enshrined in the Covenant.[26] The protocol allows individuals to seek justice for violations of their economic, social, and cultural rights at the international level for the first time, thus providing an international accountability mechanism for cultural rights. Furthermore, in 2009 the Human Rights Council established a mandate for an independent expert in the field of Cultural Rights.[27] Among other things, the expert's mandate is to identify best practice in the promotion of cultural rights, identify possible obstacles in their implementation, and work in co-operation with states in order to foster the promotion and protection of cultural rights.[28]

A significant development in the field of cultural rights has also been made at the Council of Europe level with the adoption of the Framework Convention on the Value of Cultural Heritage for Society (Faro), which recognizes that the 'rights relating to cultural heritage are inherent in the right to participate in cultural life, as defined in the Universal Declaration of Human Rights'.[29] Thus, the Convention views cultural heritage-related rights as part of cultural rights. The text also mentions, however, that none of the rights in the Convention should be interpreted so as to be enforceable.[30] State obligations are limited to the promotion and protection of the cultural heritage rather than its agents—individuals and communities—and it therefore falls short of being a human rights treaty.

This recent attention to cultural rights is to be welcomed, and is of relevance for landscape protection for a number of reasons. First, development detached from its cultural or social context reduces humankind to mere functionality, to what Leuprecht refers to as 'homo economicus'.[31] Cultural rights are essential for the dignity and well-being of the human spirit. Second, because the cultural sector cannot compete on the free market, it may require positive state support, and third, in Europe, states already have the material resources and institutional capacity to implement cultural rights, yet they are neglected and relegated to second-class status compared to civil and political rights.[32] Ben Boer even argues that 'taking away or abusing cultural

[26] Optional Protocol (GA resolution A/RES/63/117). The communications procedure already existed for complaints related to ICCPR Article 27, but Article 27 refers only to minorities, not to everyone.

[27] Resolution 10/23. Independent expert in the field of cultural rights, available at <http://ap.ohchr.org/documents/E/HRC/resolutions/A_HRC_RES_10_23.pdf> accessed 8 May 2018.

[28] See OHCHR, available at <http://www.ohchr.org/EN/Issues/CulturalRights/Pages/SRCulturalRightsIndex.aspx> accessed 8 May 2018.

[29] Art. 1(a). [30] Art. 6(c).

[31] Peter Leuprecht, 'Minority Rights Revisited: New Glimpses of an Old Issue', Philip Alston, *Peoples' Rights* (Oxford University Press, 2001), 122–3.

[32] See the European Social Charter 1961 (revised 1996, additional protocols 1988, 1991, 1995). C.A. Odinkalu, 'Analysis of Paralysis or Paralysis by Analysis' Implementing Economic, Social and

heritage violates the right to human dignity and freedom'.[33] Article 22 of the Universal Declaration of Human Rights recognizes this:

> Everyone, as a member of society, has the right to social security and is entitled to realization, through national effort and international co-operation and in accordance with the organization and resources of each state, of the economic, social and cultural rights indispensable for his dignity and the free development of his personality.

It should be borne in mind that landscape degradation and destruction often go hand in hand with the violation of other human rights and freedoms, and often stands as a symbol of underlying societal issues. But what cultural rights are implicated in landscape protection per se?

8.3 Defining Landscape in Cultural Rights Terms

Given that certain landscapes embody both physical cultural heritage and metaphysical associations, and that they are important for a sense of place and a sense of well-being, it is self-evident that culture and rights associated with culture would be implicated when discussing landscape protection, in particular when discussing the notion of landscape as cultural heritage or cultural landscapes. Indeed, the preamble to the European Landscape Convention (ELC) states in this regard that 'landscape contributes to the formation of *local cultures* and that it is a basic component of the European natural and *cultural heritage*, contributing to human *well-being* and consolidation of the European *identity* (emphasis added).[34] Faro provides for the recognition that 'everyone, alone or collectively, has the right to benefit from cultural heritage and contribute towards its enrichment'.[35] Cultural heritage in the Framework Convention is defined as: 'a group of resources inherited from the past which people identify, independently of ownership, as a reflection and expression of their constantly evolving values, beliefs, knowledge, and traditions. It includes all aspects of

Cultural Rights under the African Charter on Human and Peoples' Rights', *Human Rights Quarterly*, 23 (2001), 327–69.

[33] Ben Boer and Stefan Gruber, 'Heritage Discourses', in Kim Rubenstain and Brad Jessup (eds), *Environmental Discourses in International and Public Law* (Cambridge University Press, 2012), 375–98.

[34] Kathryn Last questions whether landscape can be used as a tool to foster 'European' identity because of its close links with nationalism. Kathryn Last, 'Heritage and Identity: the Challenge of Landscapes to the Culture/Nature Dichotomy', in Monica Sassatelli (ed.) *Landscape as Heritage: Negotiating European Cultural Identity* (EUI, 2006), 9–16.

[35] Art. 4(a).

the environment resulting from the interaction between people and places through time'.[36] The Framework Convention is positive for landscape protection because it requires states to conduct 'cultural heritage impact assessments' and to adopt 'mitigations strategies' when they plan the use of land or other processes of economic, political, social, and cultural development.[37] The Convention also promotes an 'integrated approach to policies concerning cultural, biological, geological and landscape diversity to achieve a balance between these elements',[38] and encourages democratic participation in the identification, preservation, and protection of the cultural heritage. However, as mentioned above, neither the ELC nor the Framework Convention are human rights treaties.

Before discussing the cultural rights associated with landscape protection, the definition of culture for the purpose of articulating rights must be briefly addressed. There are numerous definitions of culture. Rodolfo Stavenhagen outlines three principle conceptions of culture, which roughly correspond to the understanding of culture in the literature and work of the UN.[39] I will borrow substantially from him for the purposes of outlining them. The first is 'culture as capital', that is, the conception of culture as the accumulated material heritage of humankind in its entirety, or of a particular human group, including monuments and artefacts. According to this position, the right to culture would imply the equal right of access by individuals to this cultural capital. The second conception of culture is 'culture as process'; the process of artistic and scientific creation'. From this perspective, the right to culture means the right of individuals to freely create their cultural works with no restrictions and the right of all persons to enjoy free access to these creations (museums, libraries, concerts, theatre, etc.). Cultural policies are therefore directed to further the position of the individual cultural creator in society (the artist, writer, performer), who in realty, symbolizes the freedoms of thought and expression, which has been one of the motivating forces of struggles for human rights throughout history. The third conception of culture to which Stavenhagen draws our attention is 'culture as a total way of life', the view of culture which means the sum total of the material and spiritual activities and products of a given social group which distinguished it from other similar groups. This third conception of culture as 'a total way of life' is essentially the right to cultural identity, that is, the right of every cultural group to maintain and develop its own specific culture, and to access that culture

[36] Art. 2(a). [37] Art. 8(a). [38] Art. 8(b).

[39] Rodolfo Stavenhagen, 'Cultural Rights: A Social Science Perspective', in Asbjørn Eide, Catarina Krause, and Allan Rosas (eds), *Economic, Social and Cultural Rights: A Textbook* (n 13), 87–90.

without discrimination. For this reason, a collective approach is often called for when referring to cultural rights, since some of these rights can only be enjoyed by individuals in community with others and such a community must have the possibility to preserve, protect, and develop its common culture. 'Beneficiaries of these rights may be individuals but their content evaporates without the preservation and the collective rights of groups'.[40] Other prominent scholars largely concur with Stavenhagen on the three conceptions of culture for a legal understanding of cultural rights.[41]

In relation to landscape protection, the first and the third of Stavenhagen's conceptions of culture are relevant: the first would apply to landscapes in the material sense, as physical immovable heritage, and would correspond to the right to access and to have this heritage safeguarded. The third, culture as a total way of life, would correspond mainly to the right of indigenous peoples and certain minorities to their own culture, which often manifests itself in a way of life associated with the use of land resources. At universal level, the rights implicated in cultural heritage (and thus cultural landscape) protection are covered by the far-reaching provision on the 'right to participate in cultural life', first enshrined in the Universal Declaration of Human Rights (Article 27), and then ICESCR (Article 15 1(a)) and ICCPR (Article 27). Therefore, this provision will be analysed in most detail in this discussion, particularly as regards protection of and access to cultural heritage. In order to shed more light on the nature and scope of the right 'of everyone to take part in cultural life' (ICESCR Article 15 1(a)), it is worth examining the long awaited General Comment No. 21 on the subject.[42] In General Comment No. 21, the Committee on Economic, Social and Cultural Rights expanded on the normative content of the right, as well as the meaning of culture and each component of Article 15 1(a) for the purposes of its implementation. In relation to the normative content:

> The right to take part in cultural life can be characterized as a freedom. In order for this right to be ensured, it requires from the State party both abstention (i.e., non-interference with the exercise of cultural practices and with access to cultural goods and services) and positive action (ensuring preconditions for participation,

[40] Ibid, at 93.

[41] Roger O'Keefe, 'The Right to take part in Cultural Life under Article 15 of the ICESCR', *ICLQ* 47 (1998), 904–32, at 905; Elsa Stamatoploulou, *Cultural Rights in International Law. Article 27 of the Universal Declaration of Human Rights and Beyond* (M. Nijhoff, 2007), 109. Alexandra Xanthaki, *Indigenous Rights and United Nations Standards: Self-Determination, Culture and Land* (Cambridge University Press, 2009), 204–5.

[42] Committee on Economic, Social and Cultural Rights, General Comment No.21, E/C.12/GC/21, 21 December 2009. The Limburg Principles and the Maastricht Guidelines provided the most authoritative interpretation of cultural rights previously.

facilitation and promotion of cultural life, and access to and preservation of cultural goods).[43]

On the meaning of 'cultural life':

The Committee considers that culture, for the purpose of implementing article 15 (1) (a), encompasses, inter alia, [...] natural and man-made environments, [...] through which individuals, groups of individuals and communities express their humanity and the meaning they give to their existence, and build their world view representing their encounter with the external forces affecting their lives. Culture shapes and mirrors the values of well-being and the economic, social and political life of individuals, groups of individuals and communities.[44]

The meaning of 'to participate' or 'to take part'

There are, among others, three interrelated main components of the right to participate or take part in cultural life: (a) participation in, (b) access to, and (c) contribution to cultural life.[45]

Under the specific legal obligations relating to Article 15 1(a), 'states are under the duty to respect and protect cultural heritage in all its forms, in times of war and peace'. 'Such obligations include the care, preservation and restoration of historical sites, monuments, [...], among others'.[46] Furthermore, the Covenant imposes on states parties the 'specific and continuing' obligation to take 'deliberate and concrete measures aimed at the full implementation' of the right, and regressive measures are not permitted.[47]

It can be garnered from General Comment 21 and previous discussions on the content of Article 15 that the right to participate in cultural life entails two forms of state obligations: negative, in the form of abstention from conduct that would destroy or damage cultural goods and spaces, and positive, in the form of ensuring preconditions for participation, access, and preservation. States are called upon to preserve the physical state of the cultural heritage and its deliberate destruction is viewed upon gravely.[48] Landscapes are clearly considered as part of the concept of culture within the scope of the right to participate in cultural life, as the duty to protect 'natural and man-made environments' is an aspect of the state's obligations

[43] Committee on Economic, Social and Cultural Rights, General Comment No.21, E/C.12/GC/21, 21 December 2009, para. 6.

[44] Ibid, at para. 13. [45] Ibid, at para.15. [46] Ibid, at para. 50(a).

[47] Ibid, at paras 45 and 46.

[48] E/1991/23, para.79; E/1992/23, paras 310, 312; E/1993/22, para. 186. See, in relation to Iraq's destruction of the cultural heritage of religious communities and minorities, E/1995/22, para. 136.

under Article 15.[49] The nature of state's duties under Article 15 are both to safeguard the cultural heritage for the promotion of cultural identity of its own citizens, and at the same time protect elements of the cultural heritage for the benefit of all humanity. Accordingly, a state may be under the obligation to make cultural heritage situated in its territory accessible to international researchers.[50] Problems may arise, however, when competing claims are made on cultural rights grounds. For example, the right of access may not always go hand in hand with the preservation of a cultural landscape. This tension was evident when the Committee on Economic, Social and Cultural Rights sought clarification from Colombia regarding its ban on archaeological excavations,[51] which according to the Colombian representative was designed not to ban excavations but to protect the country's cultural heritage and safeguard sites which were places of worship for indigenous people, who regarded archaeological excavations as an affront to their cultural identity.[52] In this instance, the Committee allowed the state's margin of appreciation.[53]

From a thorough reading of General Comment 21 and the state reports of the ICESCR, it can be concluded that for the purposes of Article 15 1(a), it is predominantly the anthropological concept of culture that is referred to.[54] While the Article is broad, culture in its material sense cannot be protected per se. According to Groni, the right to take part in cultural life should not be misinterpreted as an instrument to protect cultural property or cultural heritage for its own sake.[55] However, cultural heritage can be covered by the right to the extent that this heritage as materialized is essential for the identity of individuals and groups or establish a relationship to the human person.

In one of the few cases where land-related questions arose in the context of the ICESCR, it was not within the context of Article 15 1(a) but

[49] See Committee on Economic, Social and Cultural Rights, General Comment No.21, E/C.12/GC/21, 21 December 2009, para. 13, and the Revised Guidelines regarding the Form and Contents of Reports to be submitted by States Parties under Arts 16 and 17 of the International Covenant on Economic, Social and Cultural Rights, E/1991/23, para. 1 (f).

[50] E/1992/23, para. 313. [51] E/1992/23, para. 313. [52] Ibid, at para. 315.

[53] 'Margin of appreciation' is the term used to describe a certain level of discretion in a state's implementation of the European Convention on Human Rights, particularly as regards practical differences in domestic laws. One of its functions is to balance individual rights with national interests, and in this regard, it permits some derogation from the Convention's obligations.

[54] Christian Groni, Committee on Economic, Social and Cultural Rights, Day of General Discussion. Right to take part in Cultural Life (Art. 15 (1) (a) of the Covenant), 9 May 2008, E/C.12/40/3. Stamatopoulou believes that the anthropological paradigm—namely culture as a way of life—while useful in the context of UNESCO's work—is too vague on which to base actual rights and obligations. See Elsa Stamatopoulou, *Cultural Rights in International Law. Article 27 of the Universal Declaration of Human Rights and Beyond* (M. Nijhoff, 2007), 5.

[55] Groni, Committee on Economic, Social and Cultural Rights, Day of General Discussion. Right to take part in cultural life (n 54), 7.

under Articles 16 and 17.[56] The Committee expressed its concerns about the Government of the Solomon Islands' plans to privatize communal land with a view to making it accessible for commercial use and urban development. It recalled that approximately 90% of the land in the Solomon Islands was held under customary land tenure, meaning that the land belongs to the community as a whole rather than to individuals. The Committee considered that the envisaged privatization of land under customary tenure would undermine the foundations of Solomon Islands society and lead to the dispossession of the majority of people, thereby depriving them of their basic source of income. Here, it was the relationship between customary land tenure and society that was held important, the customary tenure being essentially 'a way of life' of the islanders. Thus the protection of the landscape from commercial use and urban development was indirectly advocated due to concerns for societal well-being and economic survival.

8.4 Landscape and Cultural Rights: Whose Rights?

If we take the two conceptions of culture relevant for landscape protection—culture as capital, and culture as a total way of life—the first view implies rights for the individual or the state, or humanity. That is, the right of individuals to cultural development or the right of access; the rights of states to protect their 'national' culture (which is more of an obligation, and in any case, human rights exist to protect the individual or groups against the state); and the rights of humanity to protect the culture of humankind. Indeed, UNESCO has established the concept of the 'common heritage of humanity' which is 'recognised and affirmed for the benefit of humanity', as discussed earlier. However, humanity, although entitled to the protection of such heritage, appears too vague to be established as a rights-holder per se. General Comment No. 21 affirms that for the purposes of Article 15 1(a) the term 'everyone'

> may denote the individual or the collective; in other words, cultural rights may be exercised by a person (a) as an individual, (b) in association with others, or (c) within a community or group, as such.[57]

This reiterated what the UN Commission stated in Resolution 2002: 'States have the primary responsibility for the protection of the full enjoyment of cultural rights by everyone.'[58] Despite the extension of cultural rights to

[56] E/2000/22, para. 203 concerning the Solomon Islands. [57] Ibid, at para. 9.

[58] Commission on Human Rights Resolution 2002/06, *Promotion of the enjoyment of the cultural rights of everyone and respect for different cultural identities*, 22 April 2002.

'everyone', Wilhelm points out that the state approach towards cultural rights has been mainly individual, because states consider a collective approach too dangerous for the stability of society.[59] In this way cultural identity (in Europe) has been reduced to forms of expression, such as language and religion, and cultural rights have been equated to education and artistic creation. Wilhelm pleads instead for a more collective dimension comparable to the recent developments in the field of rights of minorities and indigenous peoples, where a broader more collective perspective of culture has been adopted.[60] In the context of culture as artefact, the Committee has applied Article 15 almost exclusively as an individual right, a right of each citizen to take part in cultural activities. Yet, when culture in its anthropological sense is referred to, it has almost always been applied as a group right. I would agree with O'Keefe that there is no reason as to why Article 15 1(a) cannot be applied as both, that is, collective regarding the material cultural heritage, as well as regarding culture as a way of life.[61] Indeed, the new optional protocol to the ICESCR, previously mentioned, allows for complaints of violations from both individuals, individuals in association with others, and groups.

In relation to cultural heritage and landscape—whether conceived of access to or protection of—an individual approach is hard to conceive of. First, landscape is a cultural entity that cannot be tied down to objective parameters that are valid for all; nor can it be defined exclusively according to rational parameters deriving from a universal logic.[62] Second, the tight nexus between landscape and custom, or landscape and place, is necessarily linked to the creation of group identity—whether regional, national, or even European.[63] For these reasons, landscape can be interpreted as a collective good closely associated with cultural identity. Although this has exclusively been applied to indigenous groups or minorities; I would submit that equally it can be applied to a group formed on the basis of common values. A 'heritage community', as defined by the Framework Convention on the Value of Cultural Heritage for Society, 'consists of people who value specific aspects of cultural

[59] M. Wilhelm, 'L'Entendue des Droits à l'Identité a la Lumière des Droits Autochtones', in Patrice Meyer-Bisch (ed), *Les Droits Culturels, une catégorie sous-développée de droits de l'homme, Actes du VIIIe Colloque interdisciplinaire sure les droits de l'homme* (Éditions Universitaires, 1993), 226–31.

[60] Ibid, at 236–37.

[61] Roger O' Keefe, 'The Right to Take Part in Cultural Life under Article 15 of the ICESCR', *ICLQ*, 47 (4) (1998), 917.

[62] World Heritage Centre, *Cultural Landscapes: the Challenges of Conservation*, World Heritage 2002, Shared Legacy, Common Responsibility; Associated Workshops, 11–12 November 2002 (Ferrara), World Heritage Papers 7, 59.

[63] See, for example, Wendy J. Darby, *Landscape and Identity: Geographies of a Nation and Class in England* (2000). Simon Schama, *Landscape and Memory* (Berg, 1995), Pamela J. Stewart and Andrew Strathern, *Landscape, Memory and History. Anthropological Perspectives* (Pluto, 2003).

heritage which they wish, within the framework of public action, to sustain and transmit to future generations'.[64] Fourth, forms of participation in public decision-making are difficult to conceive as other than group rights. And lastly, in the case of destruction or damage to a landscape, for arguments sake, it is difficult to identify individual victims.[65] Landscape, unlike property, belongs to a community as a whole, and its destruction or degradation affects physical and mental well-being which cannot be measured in terms of personal injury, damage to property, or monetary loss. An exception to this narrow conceptualization of cultural rights can be evidenced in the jurisprudence dealing with the cultural rights of indigenous peoples.

As illustrated by some landscape theorists and cultural geographers, the term 'landscape' re-emerged in Europe at a time of major social, cultural, and economic upheaval—brought about by the dispossession of the peasant classes, the end of communal land tenure, mass migration to cities, and the Industrial Revolution. The visual and imagined landscape became almost a substitute for the loss of a real connection with the land and 'an aesthetic value replaced a use and dependency value'.[66] Many indigenous peoples still have a use and dependency value with the land, a relationship more akin to Olwig's 'substantive nature of landscape'.[67] It is this use and dependency which differentiates the rights associated with landscape in some indigenous contexts, in addition to the spiritual and religious significance attached to certain places.[68] In the case of *Buzzacott v Hill* (Federal Court of Australia) for example, a motion was made to strike out proceedings, on behalf of the Arabunna people, instituted against the Commonwealth, the Minister for Foreign Affairs and Trade, and the Minister for Environment, because they did not apply to place the traditional landscape of the Arabunna people on the UNESCO World Heritage List.[69] They claimed that such a failure constituted genocide. Their argument was that the resulting mining and related activities would threaten the Arabunna people's traditional way of life, and sought an order compelling the government to protect the land and damages by proceeding with a World Heritage application, not a criminal

[64] Art. 3(b).

[65] I refer to 'destruction' or 'damage' here to imply where there are adverse cultural, historical, or environmental values attached to a landscape that have been watered down or omitted in impact assessments.

[66] See the theory of Dennis Cosgrove, cited in Chapter 2.

[67] See Chapter 2.

[68] It is a widely held view that land rights form part of indigenous peoples' right to self-determination. See, for example, J. Castellino, 'Conceptual Difficulties and the Right to Indigenous Self-Determination', in N. Ghanea and A. Xanthaki (eds), *Minorities, Peoples and Self-Determination* (M. Nijhoff, 2005), 55–74.

[69] Judgment of 1 September 2000, reproduced in ILM, 2000, 20.

prosecution. The strike-out motion was referred by a judge to a full court sitting in Adelaide, but adjourned by that court to be handled by the Federal Court with another appeal (*Nulyarimma v Thompson*). The Court recognized the crime of genocide as a peremptory norm of international *jus cogens,* but dismissed the claim because Australia had not passed legislation defining it as a criminal offense under domestic law. The Court also reiterated that in any case the notion of cultural genocide was omitted from the definition of Genocide in the Convention. Despite the outcome, the very application on the basis of cultural genocide illustrates the inseparable way in which the aboriginal people in this case viewed land, law, and culture.

The special relationship between indigenous people and landscape was confirmed by the UN Human Rights Committee in General Comment No. 23.[70] Non-binding instruments, such as the General Assembly's Declaration on the Rights of Persons belonging to Minorities and the Declaration on the Rights of Indigenous Peoples, also contain specific cultural rights relating to land.[71] In addition, ILO Convention No. 169 concerning Indigenous and Tribal Peoples in Independent Countries contains numerous references to the lands and resources of indigenous peoples.[72] Although the relationship between indigenous peoples and landscape is equally relevant in the context of environmental rights, it will be discussed here because land-related rights have often been articulated in terms of cultural integrity in the context of Article 27 ICCPR, which provides:

> In those states in which ethnic, religious or linguistic minorities exist, persons belonging to such minorities shall not be denied the rights, in community with the other members of their group, to enjoy their own culture, to profess and practice their own religion, or to use their own language.

In General Comment No. 23 on Article 27 ICCPR, the Human Rights Committee interpreted Article 27 in a broad manner: 'Culture manifests

[70] UN Doc. CPPR/C/21/Rev.1/Add.5, para. 7. 'With regard to the exercise of the cultural rights protected under article 27, the Committee observes that culture manifests itself in many forms, including a particular way of life associated with the use of land resources, especially in the case of indigenous peoples. That right may include such traditional activities as fishing or hunting and the right to live in reserves protected by law. The enjoyment of those rights may require positive legal measures of protection and measures to ensure the effective participation of members of minority communities in decisions which affect them.'

[71] In particular Art. 2.1 of the Declaration on the Rights of Persons belonging to National or Ethnic, Religious and Linguistic Minorities, UN Doc. A/RES/47/135 or Art. 8 of the UN Declaration on the Rights of Indigenous Peoples, UN Doc. A/61/L.67.

[72] Art. 15 provides the right to the use management and conservation of their resources. Art. 2 provides for participation of peoples. Art. 4 provides for safeguarding measures for the environment of such peoples with their freely expressed wishes. Art. 6 provides that the state must consult and Art. 7 also provides for participation in EIA. Right to a remedy is provided in Art. 12.

itself in many forms, including a particular way of life associated with the use of land resources, especially in the case of indigenous peoples.'[73] Indeed, the case law of the Human Rights Committee under the Optional Protocol of the Covenant has reflected this interpretation of Article 27, especially in relation to a) the use of land and resources in a way that respects the culture of a minority or indigenous group; b) the possible limitations of such rights by other development concerns in the area; and, c) the requirement of free, prior, and informed consultation by the state with the group affected by the decision.

The use of cultural rights for the protection of indigenous landscapes is evident in a number of cases before the Inter-American Court (see Chapter 9) and Commission which referred to Article 27. In a case dealt with by the UN Human Rights Committee, *LLamari Lansman et al v Finland*,[74] Sami herdsmen claimed that stone quarrying on their ancestral lands obstructed their traditional livelihoods and interfered with their cultural rights. The Human Rights Committee maintained that economic and social activities may be addressed under Article 27 ICCPR if the activities concerned form part of a minority's culture. The state is therefore obliged to ensure that any form of economic development which it engages in does not interfere with its duties to protect the cultural rights of minorities. Although the Committee concluded that there was no violation of Article 27 in this case, its interpretation of the article highlights the fact that states do not have unlimited freedom to pursue economic development without consideration of cultural rights (of minorities).

Article 27 also played a role in a number of cases before the Inter-American Court and Commission. In its 1985 decision concerning the Yanomami of Brazil, the Inter-American Commission invoked Article 27 of the ICCPR and held that 'international law in its present state [...] recognizes the right of ethnic groups to special protection on their use of their own language, for the practice of their own religion, and in general, for all those characteristics necessary for the protection of their cultural identity'.[75] The Commission viewed a series of incursions into Yanomami lands as a threat not only to the Yanomami's physical well-being, but also to their culture and traditions. Notably, the Commission cited Article 27 even though Brazil was not party to the Covenant. Likewise in the case of the *Miskito Indians v Nicaragua*,[76] the

[73] General Comment No. 23, CCPR/C/21/Rev.1/Add.5.

[74] *Lansman et al v Finland*, communication No. 511/1992, UN GAOR, 52nd Session, UN doc. CCPR/C/52D/511/1992, 8 November 1994.

[75] Case No. 7615 (Brazil), Inter-Am. Commission Res. No. 12/85 (March 1985), Annual Report of the Inter-American Commission on Human Rights, 1984-1985, O.A.S. Doc. OEA/Ser.L/V/II.66, doc. 10, rev.1 at 24, 31.

[76] *Miskito Indians v Nicaragua*, Case 7964, 'Miskito Report'.

Inter-American Commission cited Nicaragua's obligations under Article 27 of the Covenant and found that the special legal protections accorded to Miskito for the preservation of their cultural identity should extend to 'the aspects linked to productive organisation, which includes, among other things, the issue of ancestral and communal lands.' This is noteworthy, since Article 27 has had influence beyond the UN system into a regional human rights court.

The traditional lands of many indigenous peoples have been reduced or occupied, without their consent, by timber, mining, and oil companies, at the expense of their culture and the protection of the environment.[77] This represents a continuous form of repression and dispossession under the guise of 'development', and is reminiscent of the *terra nullius* doctrine which was used by states to legitimatize colonization, declared by the ICJ as far back as 1975 as 'erroneously and invalidly applied'.[78] A landmark case for the recognition of indigenous land rights the world over was *Mabo v Queensland*,[79] which concerned a claim by members of the Meriam people to rights in land in the Murray islands in the Torres Strait. The Australian High Court held that when the Imperial Crown acquired sovereignty over the islands in 1879, the land rights of the indigenous peoples had not been extinguished. The Canadian Supreme Court also affirmed in *Delgamuukw v The Queen*[80] that native title is a legal interest in the land itself and can compete with other types of proprietary interest. As stated by Lokan:

> 'by defining native title rights primarily at the level of community, native title doctrine reinforces the community's identity. [...] This is a marked departure from the individual basis of common law property rights in most other countries.'[81]

However, there are limitations to the right, and native title cannot necessarily prevail over other individual rights, or in cases where the public has the right to access places such as parks, reserves, and beaches. Furthermore, problems of proof often arise in disputes over indigenous lands, the passage of time being one. The Finnish State, for example, insists that lands claimed by Sami are public lands belonging to the state:

> From a legal perspective, it would be inappropriate to have the question of titles of the Sami to the land resolved by means of instituting court proceedings. The

[77] Concluding Observations of the Committee on Economic, Social and Cultural Rights, Columbia, UN Doc.E/C.12/1/Add.74 of 30 November2001, paras 11 and 12.

[78] *Western Sahara* Case, ICJ Reports (1975), 12.

[79] *Mabo v Queensland*, No. 2 (1992) 107 A.L.R. 1.

[80] *Delgamuukw* Case [1997] 3 S.C.R. 1010, 153 D.L.R. (4th) 193, [1998] 1 C.N.L.R 14, 37 ILM 268.

[81] Andrew Lokan, 'From Recognition to Reconciliation: The Functions of Aboriginal Rights Law', *Melbourne University Law Review*, 23 (1999), 89.

outcome of the proceedings could involve uncertainties relating to questions of evidence. Instead, adequate historical research based on archives could provide a sound basis for political decision-making.[82]

However, for the purposes of access and use for traditional practices, whether they be economic or spiritual,[83] indigenous peoples and minorities enjoy a level of protection under Article 27 ICCPR, which may include the protection of their landscape from culturally or ecologically destructive interventions.

8.5 Landscape and Environmental Rights

The link between environmental protection and human rights was first explicitly recognized in the Stockholm Declaration, adopted by the United Nations Conference on the Human Environment in 1972, the preamble of which states that protection of the environment is 'essential [...] to the enjoyment of basic human rights—even the right to life itself'. Principle 1 of the declaration proclaims:

> Man has the fundamental right to freedom, equality and adequate conditions of life, in an environment of a quality that permits a life of dignity and well-being, and he bears a solemn responsibility to protect and improve the environment for present and future generations.

Although these provisions do not directly recognize the right to a healthy environment as such, they establish a link between well-recognized rights and the quality of the environment. Environmental quality is presented as a pre-requisite for achieving 'adequate conditions for life'. The Stockholm Declaration thus builds on some earlier language contained in the ICESCR, which recognizes the individual's right to the 'continuous improvement of living conditions'[84] as well as to the 'enjoyment of the highest attainable standard of physical and mental health',[85] and commits states to protecting the right to health by positive measures.[86] The above provision also recalls the preamble to the ELC, which acknowledges that landscape contributes to

[82] Committee on Economic, Social and Cultural Rights, Implementation of the ICESCR, Finland, UN Doc. E/C.12/FIN/5 of 8 February 2006, para. 69.

[83] For example, Protocol 3 to the accession agreement governing the entry of Sweden and Finland to the European Community recognizes that reindeer herding has a fundamental place in Sami culture.

[84] Art. 11, ICESCR. [85] Art. 12, para. 1. [86] Art. 12, para. 2(b).

'human well-being'.[87] If we conceive of landscape as the public space, then the right to a healthy environment could be read in the right to a quality landscape. As stated, the concept of well-being involves several aspects of the human relationship with the outside world and with oneself, which are not easy to separate: a material dimension, associated with the satisfaction of physical and biological needs, and a spiritual dimension, associated with the satisfaction of psychological and emotional aspirations: well-being is, as Yves Luginbühl puts it, 'being well disposed in mind and body'.[88] The Stockholm Declaration was formulated in more solemn terms, as a commitment *erga omnes* to the protection of an international public good, rather than a reciprocal obligation between states, thus recalling the language of human rights treaties. It also introduced the concept of inter generational responsibility to protect and improve the environment.

This language changed somewhat in the 1992 Rio Declaration on Environment and Development, which states instead that '[h]uman beings are at the centre of concerns for sustainable development. They are entitled to a healthy and productive life in harmony with nature' (Principle 1), which puts forward an anthropocentric rationale for environmental protection. It is no coincidence that the adoption of the World Heritage Convention in 1972 coincided with the Stockholm Declaration, and that twenty years later, in 1992, the inclusion of the category of cultural landscapes within the scope of the Convention coincided with the adoption of the Rio Declaration. The primary purpose of the above provision is to articulate an anthropogenic rationale for environmental protection and sustainable development. Likewise, the purpose of including cultural landscapes within the scope of the World Heritage Convention was to give recognition to the people in the landscape and the importance of their role in sustaining traditional practices in relative harmony with nature. The approach of the Rio Declaration diverges somewhat from that of Stockholm; the emphasis on 'productive life' in the Rio Declaration reflects the apprehensions of developing countries fearing that environmental protection could take precedence over economic development, and can be contrasted with the 'solemn responsibly to protect' in the former. Marc Pallemaerts notes that the Rio Declaration effectively watered down the human rights dimension of environmental protection and that while it fails to clearly affirm the right to a healthy environment, it expressly recognizes the right to development, albeit not explicitly as an

[87] Preamble, ELC and its explanatory report in English.

[88] *Landscape and Sustainable Development: Challenges of the European Landscape Convention* (Council of Europe Publishing, 2006), 32.

individual right.[89] The UN Declaration on the Rights of Indigenous Peoples, adopted by the General Assembly in September 2007, provides for protection of the environment through people; its preamble acknowledges that respect for indigenous knowledge, cultures and traditional practices contributes to sustainable and equitable development and proper management of the environment.[90] The non-binding Bizkaia Declaration on the Right to the Environment states that 'everyone has the right, individually or in association with others, to enjoy a healthy and ecologically balanced environment [... which ...] may be exercised before public bodies and private entities, whatever their legal status under national and international law'.[91] 'The Declaration can be seen as a contribution to the ongoing debate concerning the recognition and the progressive development of a human right to a healthy and ecologically balanced environment.' [92]

Environmental rights are provided in a number of regional human rights treaties. The African Charter on Human and Peoples' Rights[93] contains several direct references to environmental rights. Article 21 provides that 'All peoples shall freely dispose of their wealth and natural resources' and that this right 'shall be exercised in the exclusive interest of the people'. Article 24 states that 'All peoples shall have the right to a general satisfactory environment favourable to their development.' The Additional Protocol to the American Convention on Human Rights also refers to the right to live in a healthy environment, as well as to the protection, preservation and improvement of the environment.[94] An important step in developing environmental rights was made in 1998 with the adoption of the Aarhus Convention on Access to Information, Public Participation in Decision-making, and Access to Justice in Environmental matters.[95] Described by former UN Secretary General Kofi Annan as 'the most ambitious venture in environmental democracy undertaken under the auspices of the United Nations',[96] the Aarhus Convention

[89] Marc Pallemaerts, 'Introduction', in Marc Pallemaerts and Maguelonne Dejeant-Pons, *Human Rights and the Environment* (Council of Europe, 2002), 13.

[90] UN General Assembly, United Nations Declaration on the Rights of Indigenous Peoples: resolution / adopted by the General Assembly, 2 October 2007, A/RES/61/295.

[91] Declaration on the Right to the Environment, adopted by the International Seminar held in Bilbao, Spain, on 13 February 1999 under the auspices of UNESCO and the UN High Commissioner for Human Rights. UNESCO Doc. 30c/INF11 1999.

[92] Ibid. at para. 2.

[93] Banjul Charter on Human and Peoples Rights, O.A.U. Doc. CAB/LEG/67/3/Rev.5 Art. 24.

[94] Art. 11. OAS Treaty Series No. 69 (1988) in Basic Documents pertaining to Human Rights in the Inter-American System OEA/Ser L V/II.82 Doc 6 Rev 1, at 67 (1992).

[95] Convention on Access to Information, Public Participation and Access to Justice in Environmental Matters, Aarhus, 25 June 1998. 2161 UNTS 447. Entry into force 30 October 2001.

[96] Jeremy Wates, 'NGOs and the Aarhus Convention', in Tullio Treves et al. (eds), *Civil Society, International Courts and Compliance Bodies* (Asser, 2005), 167.

rests on the three pillars of Principle 10 of the Rio Declaration; that is, access to environmental information,[97] which allows citizens to take advantage of the second and third participatory rights—public participation in decision making,[98] and access to justice in environmental issues.[99] The Aarhus Convention is also noteworthy for the way in which it highlights the importance of civil society engagement, and the role of NGOs is formalized in the operation of the Convention itself.[100]

Principle 10 of the Rio Declaration on Environment and Development provides:

> Environmental issues are best handled with the participation of all concerned citizens, at the relevant level. At the national level, each individual shall have appropriate access to information concerning the environment that is held by public authorities, including information on hazardous materials and activities in their communities, and the opportunity to participate in decision-making processes. States shall facilitate and encourage public awareness and participation by making information widely available. Effective access to judicial and administrative proceedings, including redress and remedy, shall be provided.[101]

There are generally three ways in which human rights and environmental protection intersect. The first is the use of human rights guarantees when their enjoyment is threatened by environmental harm. This is an anthropocentric approach which seeks to ensure that the environment does not deteriorate to the point where the right to life, health, family, and private life, and culture are seriously impaired.[102] Protection of the environment in these cases is instrumental—it is not an end in and of itself.[103] This approach has been

[97] Arts 4 and 5.

[98] Arts 6 (specific activities), 7 (concerning environmental plans and policies), and 8 (during the legislative and administrative process).

[99] Art. 9.

[100] Decision 1/7, Report of the First Meeting of the Parties to the Convention on Access to Information, Public Participation in Decision-Making and Access to Justice in Environmental Matters, UN Doc. ECE/MP.PP/2/Add.8 (2002): 'communications may be brought before the Committee by one or more members of the public concerning a Party's compliance with the Convention.'

[101] Already in 1982, the World Charter for Nature provided that 'all persons, in accordance with their national legislation, shall have the opportunity to participate, individually or with others, in the formulation of decisions of direct concern to their environment, and shall access to means of redress when their environment has suffered damage or degradation'.

[102] Many claims in favour of landscape protection have been made on the basis of health concerns, a case in point being the proposed airport extension at Ampugnano, Siena. See *Studio dei Valori Ambientali dell' Area in Prossimata dell' Aeroporto Commerciale di Ampugnano*, Relazione technica, V. D' Oriano, Firenze, Aprile 2009, kindy supplied to the author by Avv. D Oriano.

[103] This was stated by Judge Weeramantry in a separate opinion on the *Gabcikovo-Nagymaros* Case (Hungary-Slovakia), ICJ, Judgment of 25 September 1997.

applied to the vast majority of cases before human rights courts, and while it can be useful in addressing imminent pollution, Dinah Shelton argues that it is ultimately deficient because it does not address threats to non-human species or to ecological processes.[104] Nor is it a suitable approach for landscape protection (unless the plan or policy in question not only destroys the landscape, but poses severe health risks). The second way in which human rights and environmental protection intersect is the use, within environmental treaties, of human rights guarantees in drafting international instruments, rights such as information and participation (which may be used to garner information about the natural and cultural environment), or the right to freedom of association for members of non-governmental organizations. However, the short-term effectiveness of compliance mechanisms in this type of approach can be questioned. A third approach aims to incorporate the environmental agenda fully within human rights by formulating a new human right to an environment that is not only safe for humans but one that is ecologically sound and sustainable in the long term.

Shelton makes the convincing argument that, without a substantive element, environmental considerations will remain susceptible to restriction for the sake of other, socio-economic objectives, such as ensuring continued 'development' or 'saving jobs'.[105] Shelton argues that a right to a healthy environment, should it exist, would be balanced against other social interests on an equal basis.[106] If there existed a right to environment and a right to development, the same juridical balancing of interests would be required. Law often responds to social problems by restraining the exercise of power and establishing agreed norms of public conduct. Viewed from this perspective, formulations of rights reflect emerging social values.

At national level, some courts have begun to broaden standing requirements to allow legal redress for violations of environmental rights without necessarily requiring individual injury to health or property, because one major motive for guaranteeing environmental rights is to prevent injury from occurring.[107] A progressive provision included in the Ecuadorian Constitution in 2008, for example, declares nature a legal person.[108] The Constitution states

[104] Dinah Shelton, 'Environmental Rights', in Phillip Alston, *Peoples' Rights* (OUP, 2001), 188.

[105] Ibid, at 192.

[106] Ibid and Dinah Shelton, 'Human Rights and Environment, Past, Present and Future Linkages and the Value of a Declaration', High Level Expert Meeting on the New Future of Human Rights and environment: Moving the Global Agenda Forward, Nairobi, 30 November–1 December 2009 (UNEP and OHCR).

[107] In the case *Montana Environmental Information Centre v Department of Environmental Quality*, 296 Mont. 207, 988, P.2d 1236 (1999).

[108] Constitutión Política de la República de Ecuador (new Arts 71–4, 2008) <https://www.oas.org/juridico/pdfs/mesicic4_ecu_const.pdf> accessed 30 January 2018.

that 'the government has the duty to protect nature on behalf of all the inhabitants of Ecuador present and future' and that 'nature has the right to integral respect for its existence and for the maintenance and regeneration of its life cycles, structure, functions and evolutionary processes'.[109] Furthermore, 'all persons, communities, peoples and nations may call upon the public authorities to enforce the rights of nature'.[110] This is essentially a provision to enable standing on behalf of nature (although as noted by some scholars, the absence of specific criteria for who may sue on the environment's behalf creates fundamental uncertainty about the justiciability of the amendments, and casts doubt on the constitution's ability to serve as a real source of rights).[111]

Norway recently included a progressive amendment to its Constitution in 2014, which, although not recognizing nature as a legal entity, nevertheless recognizes that every person 'has a right to an environment that is conducive to health and to a natural environment whose productivity and diversity are maintained. Natural resources should be managed on the basis of comprehensive long-term considerations whereby this right will be safeguarded for future generations as well.'[112] Interestingly, this provision has just been tested in a climate action suit brought by Greenpeace against the Norwegian state for its granting of oil drilling licences in the Arctic.[113] The plaintiffs argued that Norway's Ministry of Petroleum and Energy violated the Norwegian Constitution (Article 112) and petitioned for a ban on oil and gas licences for deep-sea extraction from sites in the Barents Sea. The Oslo District Court ruled in favour of the government on 4 January 2018, and the applicants are seeking an appeal, arguing that the court's interpretation of Article 112 was excessively narrow.

Perhaps the most progressive initiative to date concerning environmental rights came in 2017, when the New Zealand government passed into law a deed granting the Whanganui River legal personhood.[114] The river's transformation from property to person arguably pushes the boundaries of environmental rights even further and opens up possibilities for other natural entities to be granted legal agency. While the Ecuadorian Constitution

[109] Art. 71. [110] Art. 71.

[111] Mary E. Whittemore, 'The Problem of Enforcing Nature's Rights under Ecuador's Constitution: Why the 2008 Environmental Amendments Have No Bite', *Pacific Rim Law & Policy Journal*, 20 (3) 659–91.

[112] Art. 112.

[113] Case No. 16-166674TVI-OTIR/06, judgment <https://www.domstol.no/no/Enkelt-domstol/Oslo--tingrett/> accessed 30 January 2018.

[114] Te Awa Tupua (Whanganui River) Claims Settlement Bill 129-2, Parliament of New Zealand <https://www.parliament.nz/en/pb/bills-and-laws/bills-proposed-laws/document/00DBHOH_BILL68939_1/te-awa-tupua-whanganui-river-claims-settlement-bill> accessed 30 January 2018.

granted legal personhood to nature, and while many constitutions recognize environmental rights to varying degrees, granting a specific river such status is a more concrete action, with definite consequences for any planning decisions involving the Whanganui River in the future. It will be interesting to see what effect this will have in practice.

8.6 What Rights to Landscape?

In light of the normative content of cultural rights and the rights implicated in environmental protection, what is the nature of landscape related rights from a substantive viewpoint? The environmental dimension is severely limited by the absence of rights to environmental protection and the anthropocentric nature of human rights law. Given the broad scope of the right to take part in cultural life, it could be argued that there does exist a cultural right to landscape, provided that the landscape in question is essential for the identity of a particular group or forms a relationship to the human person. However, the practical implications of this can be problematic. Firstly, most of the jurisprudence on the right to take part in cultural life stems not from the state reports on the implementation of Article 15 ICESCR, but from the Human Rights Committee in the context of Article 27 ICCPR. This is likely due to the lack, until recently, of a complaints mechanism under the ICESCR, and to the fact that landscape is more of a collective good, and does not fit well with the individual conception of culture as artefact; rather, it fits as culture in an anthropological sense, as a way of life, and thus has been applied almost exclusively to indigenous peoples and minorities.[115] Second, the indigenous landscape is still characterized by a use and dependency value, often tied to a specific territory. Thus, access to the landscape in the indigenous context becomes a customary right—not a universal one.[116] In ascertaining whether a cultural right to landscape exists therefore, the answer is a tentative yes, but in practice only in relation to

[115] Wilhelm points out that when culture artefact is referred to, it is almost always dealt with as an individual right. When culture in an anthropological sense, it is almost always applied to minorities and indigenous people. M. Wilhelm, 'L'Entendue des Droits a l'Identité a la Lumière des Droits Autochtones', Patrice Meyer-Bisch (ed), *Les Droits Culturels, une catégorie sous-développée de droits de l'homme, Actes du VIIIe Colloque interdisciplinaire sure les droits de l'homme* (Éditions Universitaires, 1993), 226–31.

[116] During the 1966 Commission Drafting Group, a representative of the indigenous communities of the Pacific expressed the position of indigenous communities as the following: 'First of all, it must be legally accepted that we are the first settlers, first dwellers or proprietors of our land. Second, we are a collective group who were imposed upon by uninvited external forces who disrupted the normal march of history'. Statement of Kekula P. Bray-Crawford of Hawaii, 21Oct–1 Nov 1996.

indigenous peoples and minorities. The cultural rights implied in the right to participate in cultural life in Article 15 1(a) ICESCR that are relevant in the context of landscape protection are mainly participatory; that is, the right of access and the right to participate meaningfully in decisions on cultural policies through democratic institutions. If the participative process takes into consideration the aspirations of groups and communities, as well as expert information on environment and cultural heritage, then the state should form its policies on the basis of consultation. The problem with purely participatory provisions is that there is a presumption that a participatory approach will be fair to all the parties concerned. This is not necessarily the case. The 'democratic' interest may run the risk of being interpreted to mean 'development' when often the short-term benefits outweigh the long-term effects and 'official' or 'authorized' narratives may exclude the cultural rights of certain groups and communities.[117]

However, the recent optional protocol to the ICESCR provides for the consideration of complaints by 'individuals', 'individuals in association with others', and 'groups' in respect of rights enshrined in the Covenant.[118] This offers some promise for expanding the interpretation of intangible cultural rights to non-indigenous, non-minority persons. I would agree with Roger O'Keefe that there is no reason as to why Article 15 1(a) cannot be applied as both an individual and a group right.[119] In light of the complaints procedure for cultural rights under the ICESCR, individuals and associations have the opportunity to challenge the decision-making process, and this ought not be restricted to indigenous and minorities.

[117] Laurajane Smith, *The Uses of Heritage* (Routledge, 2006).

[118] Optional Protocol (GA resolution A/RES/63/117). The communications procedure already existed for complaints related to ICCPR Art. 27, but Art. 27 refers only to minorities, not to everyone.

[119] Roger O'Keefe, 'The Right to Take Part in Cultural Life under Article 15 of the ICESCR', *ICLQ*, 47 (4) (1998), 904–23, at 917.

9

Landscape in Human Rights Case Law

9.1 Landscape in Regional Human Rights Systems

The European Convention on Human Rights and Fundamental Freedoms (ECHR)[1] makes no reference to any right to the environment or cultural heritage in its text or protocols. In an early decision, the European Commission on Human Rights stated that 'no right to nature preservation is as such included amongst the rights and freedoms guaranteed by the Convention'.[2] In 2005, the Council of Europe issued a 'Manual on Human Rights and the Environment' which states that the 'Convention is not designed to provide general protection of the environment as such and does not expressly guarantee a right to a sound, quiet, and healthy environment.'[3] Nevertheless, the Commission stated in the *Fredin* case that the 'interest of preserving nature is commonly recognised in all Contracting Parties as being of great importance in present-day society' and the Court in the same case recognized that 'in today's society the protection of the environment is an increasingly important consideration'.[4] Although environmental protection is not guaranteed under the Convention, the case law has tailored itself to include protection of the environment under certain circumstances, namely when it has a direct impact on the effective enjoyment of other individual rights and freedoms, such as

[1] Council of Europe, *European Convention for the Protection of Human Rights and Fundamental Freedoms, as amended by Protocols Nos. 11 and 14*, 4 November 1950, ETS 5.

[2] *X and Y v Germany*, Application no. 7407/76, Decisions and Reports 5, 161. However, the Commission stated in the *Fredin* case that the 'interest of preserving nature is commonly recognised in all Contracting Parties as being of great importance in present-day society'. It should also be recalled that the Court in the same case recognised for its part that 'in today's society the protection of the environment is an increasingly important consideration'. App. No. 46117/99. Judgment of 10 November 2004.

[3] Council of Europe Committee of Experts for the Development of Human Rights', Final Activity Report on Human Rights and the Environment', 10 November 2005, DH-DEV(2005)06 rev, 10.

[4] *Fredin v Sweden*, App. No. 18928/01. Judgment of 22 January 1991.

the right to family and private life and the right to property,[5] or as a legitimate restriction of those rights in upholding the 'general interest'. If we apply this to landscape, the first of these two approaches rests on tenuous grounds because in order to invoke any of the rights in the context of the environment, applicants have to show a breach of one of the rights guaranteed in the Convention to 'individuals'. This means being individually directly or indirectly impaired by the measure in question. The Convention does not allow for an *actio popularis*. The narrow approach of the Court in matters of the environment and indeed cultural heritage means that the question of landscape protection has mostly entered the realm of Strasbourg jurisprudence in the second of the above: the upholding of restrictions on individual rights in the general interest of society. These cases are dealt with in the section below. By contrast, the American Convention on Human Rights does contain explicit provisions relating to the environment. Article 11 of the Additional Protocol to the Convention (Protocol of San Salvador) refers to the right to live in a healthy environment, as well as to the protection, preservation, and improvement of the environment.[6] Article 14 of the Protocol of San Salvador provides for the 'right to the benefits of culture', which is similar in normative content to the right to participate in cultural life discussed in detail in Chapter 8.

Given the lack of a specific mention of landscape or cultural heritage in both of the regional human rights treaties under examination, what 'substantive' rights are involved in cases dealing with landscape in human rights courts? Rights to landscape may include rights of access (for example, to rights of way on public or private lands); usufruct rights (rights to fish, hunt, graze, or conduct other subsistence farming activities on public or private land); rights to enjoy sacred sites on public or private land (this is most evident in the case of indigenous communities and certain minorities); rights to participate in planning decisions affecting the local landscape; and rights to a healthy environment. The latter implies the right not to have landscape damaged to the extent that it will harm human health or well-being; environmental protection per se is not well-established in human rights systems. The level of recognition of the aforementioned rights to landscape varies from jurisdiction to jurisdiction. However, international human rights law supersedes national law for those states that have signed and ratified the relevant human rights treaties, with the exception of permitted derogations, and it provides

[5] See *Guerra and Others v Italy*, App. No. 14967/89 of 19 February 1998; *Taskin et al. v Turkey*, App. No. 46117/99 of 10 November 2004; *Oneryildiz v Turkey*, App. No. 48939/99, 30 November 2004.

[6] Art. 11. OAS Treaty Series No. 69 (1988) in Basic Documents pertaining to Human Rights in the Inter-American System OEA/Ser L V/II.82 Doc 6 Rev 1 at 67 (1992).

an insight into the practice of various states through an analysis of its case law. For the purposes of the present analysis, therefore, the case law of the two major standard-setting regional human rights courts will be examined.

If the content of rights to landscape includes mainly use and access, then it is those cases involving the limitation on use or access to landscapes that require attention. In addition, cases involving the challenge to development or construction in landscapes are also addressed, as these are often based on the premise that such development will preclude the access and enjoyment of the landscape in question. While the rights to landscape can be considered mostly as cultural rights, or customary rights, and in some instances also, environmental rights, the human rights invoked or involved indirectly in cases dealing with landscape are not at all obvious at first glance, and may include the right to property (in a broad sense to include custom or other rights), the right to family and private life, or other rights. The lack of explicit rights to landscape makes this a necessary fact. It must also be noted that the word 'landscape' itself is not always used in the following cases. In cases where the term 'landscape' is specifically mentioned, it is interesting to see its narrow association with preservation rather than use.

9.2 Landscape in the European Court of Human Rights

The ECHR and Fundamental Freedoms makes no reference to cultural heritage or the environment in its text or protocols. However, rights *to* landscape (envisaged as either the right to use or access a landscape, or as 'landscape protection') can be indirectly achieved through the Convention in a number of ways. First, the protection of other rights guaranteed in the Convention might require the safeguarding of an environment of quality. This represents an indirect form of landscape rights. Second, the right to property might entail more than mere private ownership and include other usufructuary or customary rights, such as in the case of indigenous peoples. Third, the 'general interest in a democratic society' permits restrictions on the exercise of some rights and freedoms, such as the private right to property or those contained in Articles 8, 9, 10, and 11 of the Convention[7] in favour of upholding the rights of others to access or enjoy landscapes of value. The question of landscape protection has mostly entered the realm of Strasbourg jurisprudence in this way: the upholding

[7] Maguellone Déjeant-Pons, L'insertion du droit de l'homme à l'environnement dans le systèmes régionaux de protection des droits de l'homme, *Revue universelle des droits de l'homme* (1991), vol. 3, No. 1, 461.

of restrictions on individual rights in the 'general interest of society'. The cases dealing with landscape protection analysed below are grouped into these three categories, starting with the most common scenario.

Landscape protection versus other human rights and freedoms

In most cases of the European Court of Human Rights (ECtHR) dealing with landscape, landscape 'protection' (as part of environmental, cultural heritage and town planning measures) comes into conflict with other human rights and is, in fact, the reason for the alleged violation. Such cases usually concern complaints by persons of restrictions on the use of their property, where the Court (and formerly the Commission when it existed) have held that these restrictions have been justified for the protection of the environment or cultural heritage, and as such necessary in the 'general interest', or for the 'protection of the rights and freedoms of others'. An early example of this was evident in the case of *Herrick v the United Kingdom* (1985), which involved a restriction on the use of a bunker owned by the applicant on the island of Jersey.[8] The restrictive measure involved the refusal of an official permit to authorize her owning it as a summer residence. The Commission decided that the decision of the local authority was justified on the grounds of the 'general interest' to safeguard a landscape of particular interest, a green zone reputed to be one of the most outstanding features on Jersey. [9] In upholding the restriction, the Commission stated that 'planning controls are necessary and desirable in order to preserve areas of outstanding natural beauty for the enjoyment of both the inhabitants of Jersey and visitors to the island'.[10]

In its Grand Chamber judgment in *Kozacioglu v Turkey*, the Court held that failure to take special architectural or historical characteristics of a listed building into account when assessing compensation for expropriation amounted to a violation of Article 1 Protocol No. 1, because it had placed a disproportionate burden on the applicant. Nevertheless, it went on to underline the importance of the protection of cultural heritage when assessing the legitimate aim of the interference.[11] 'Finding it natural that the margin of appreciation available to the legislature in implementing social and economic policies should be a wide one, the Court will respect the legislature's judgment as to what is 'in the public interest' unless that judgment is manifestly

[8] Application No. 11185/84, DR 42, 275.

[9] See Article 8 of the European Convention on Human Rights and Art. 1 of the First Protocol. European Commission's Decision on Admissibility of 13 March 1985, DR 42, 280.

[10] Ibid.

[11] *Kozacioglu v Turkey*, Grand Chamber Decision 19/02/09. Application No. 2234/03.

without reasonable foundation. [...] This is equally true, *mutatis mutandis*, for the protection of the environment or of a country's historical or cultural heritage.'[12] In this respect, the Court further stated that 'the conservation of the cultural heritage and, where appropriate, its sustainable use, have as their aim, in addition to the maintenance of a certain quality of life, the preservation of the historical, cultural, and artistic roots of a region and its inhabitants. As such, they are an essential value, the protection and promotion of which are incumbent on the public authorities.'[13] The Court referred to the European Convention on the Protection of the Architectural Heritage (Granada) and the obligations upon states to protect the cultural heritage of European importance in this regard.[14] This was reiterated by the Court almost verbatim in *Bogdel v Lithuania*, which concerned the privatization and consequent expropriation by the state of a plot of land that had been earmarked for World Heritage status.[15] The domestic proceedings had originally been taken by the Trakai residents themselves, who were concerned that the plot of land had been misappropriated by the applicants, who intended to enlarge their property on territory designated as a heritage site. The Court reiterated its relevant case law to that effect and concluded that the state's interference with the applicants' property rights was in the 'public interest' within the meaning of Article 1 Protocol No. 1.[16]

In relation to natural heritage sites, the Court has stressed on a number of occasions the importance of protecting the environment over property rights.[17] Particularly noteworthy is the case of *Depalle v France*, which concerned the protection of coastal zones for public use and enjoyment.[18] In this instance, the Court held that the state's interference with the applicant's right to property had pursued a legitimate aim in the general interest: to promote unrestricted public access to the shore. The Court recognized the state's wide discretion in issues concerning 'regional planning and environmental conservation policies where the community's general interest was pre-eminent'.[19] In these cases, rights *to* landscape (conceived as right to the protection of environmental and cultural spaces) are viewed by the Court as a paramount concern, and well within the scope of the state's margin of appreciation to override other individual rights and freedoms. In a way, they represent the triumph of public rights to landscape protection over private rights to property.

[12] Ibid, at 53. [13] Ibid, at 54. [14] Ibid, at paras 30 and 54.

[15] *Bogdel v Lithuania*, Chamber Judgment 26 Nov 2013. Application No. 41248/06, para 45.

[16] Ibid, at paras 60–2.

[17] *Hamer v Belgium* 21861/03 (ECHR 2007-XIII, *Turgut and Others v Turkey*, 1411/03, para. 90, 8 July 2008.

[18] *Depalle v France*, Grand Chamber Judgment 29 March 2010. Application No. 34044/02.

[19] Ibid.

Conversely, in the case of *Sud Fondi et autres v Italie*,[20] where applicants alleged a violation of their right to property for a decision that was made by the authorities of Bari essentially to preserve the landscape, the Court declared a violation of Article 1 Protocol No. 1. The case dealt with the controversial towers that were constructed along the coast of Bari in 1995, known locally as 'Punta Perrotti'. The application was made by the three construction firms who had received planning permission by local authorities in 1992, even though their construction was in violation of national law at the time, namely Law No. 431 of 1985 (Galasso Law) which prohibited the granting of planning permission in sites of natural interest, including coastal zones. In 1996, the State prosecutor initiated an inquiry into the legality of the building complex and a year later, ordered the seizure of the complex and opened a criminal suit against the directors of the three construction firms. The applicants appealed the measure to the Court of Cassation, which annulled the decision and ordered the restitution of the complex to the contractors, as the site had not breached any prohibition in the town plan. Then two years later, in 1999, the Bari Court declared the complex of buildings illegal (as they did not conform with national Law No. 431 of 1985). However, given the difficulty in reconciling national and regional legislation, the Court acquitted the accused of any intention or fault. The Court also ordered the confiscation of the complex and their acquisition to the patrimony of the Council of Bari. The *Ministro dei beni culturali* subsequently ordered a ban on all construction in the coastal zone adjacent to Bari, including Punta Perotti, on account of its outstanding natural interest.[21] This measure was then annulled by the regional administrative court the following year. The State Prosecutor appealed the annulment and demanded conviction of the accused. In 2000, the Court of Appeal revoked the decision of the Court of First Instance and deemed the granting of planning permission legal in the absence of a ban on construction in Punta Perotti at the time of the project's approval.[22] Consequently the Court of Appeal acquitted the accused and revoked the confiscation of the complex and lands. Finally, in 2001, the Court of Cassation quashed the Court of Appeal's decision and upheld the illegality of the project in light of landscape restrictions.[23] The Court noted that the regional law concerning the protection of landscape had not yet entered into force at the time of approval, but that the national landscape law was in force. The applicants then

[20] *Sud Fondi et autres v Italie* Application no. 75909/01. Decision of 20/01/09. For a thorough discussion of the case see commentary by Elena Sciso, 'Punta Perotti: ancora una condanna per una confisca da parte della Corte europea dei diritti dell'uomo.' *Rivista di Diritto Internazionale*, vol. XCII (2009) 487–96.

[21] Ibid. [22] Ibid. [23] Ibid.

took the case to Strasbourg, alleging a violation of their rights under Article 7 (no punishment without law) and Article 1 Protocol 1 (right to property) of the Convention. Although the Court held that there had been a violation of their rights under both Articles, it nevertheless maintained that the initial authorization of planning permission should not have been granted by the local Bari administration, noting the 'inertia' of the authorities charged with 'safeguarding the environment'. Notably the Court stated:

> Le fait que la même municipalité qui avait délivré les permis illégitimes soit devenue propriétaire des terrains ne revêt aucune importance particulière : le patrimoine est en effet celui de la *collectivité* des habitants de la ville, et non pas celui des administrateurs responsables de la procédure administrative incriminée. Au demeurant, les circonstances de la cause montrent en l'espèce « que la position de l'individu face au pouvoir n'a pas été certes celle d'un particulier écrasé par un État Léviathan mais, plutôt, celle d'un particulier qui a conclu un accord *contra legem* (n'étant, ontologiquement, un accord *contra legem* rien d'autre que la rencontre entre une demande visée à obtenir quelque chose d'interdit et une réponse positive à cette demande) avec un secteur déterminé de l'État, qui a opéré au mépris de la loi et des intérêts de la *collectivité*. [...] comme l'auraient reconnu les juridictions nationales.[24] (emphasis added)

The Court also stated that Article 1 Protocol 1 not only covers 'biens actuels' but also 'heritage values', and declared paradoxical that the Comune of Bari (which national judges had declared responsible for having issued the illegal planning permission in the first place) should then become the owner of the confiscated lands. The Court also declared disproportionate the measures adopted by the Bari authorities in safeguarding the environmental-landscape equilibrium of the area of Punta Perotti, and suggested that this could have been achieved by ordering the demolition of the towers (which it did in 2006) and cancelling the previous planning permission, not confiscating the entire area, 85% of which was not built upon.[25] The Italian state was ordered to pay very substantial compensation to the three companies involved. As pointed out by Elena Sciso, there is a problem with the coherence as to

[24] Ibid, at para. 134. This roughly translates as follows: The fact that the same municipality that issued the illegal permits became the owner of the land is of no particular importance: the heritage is indeed that of the community of the inhabitants of the city, and not of the administrators responsible for the administrative procedure complained of. Moreover, the circumstances of the case show 'that the position of the individual in the face of power was certainly not that of a private person crushed by a Leviathan state but rather, that of an individual who entered into an agreement *contra legem* (meaning nothing more than a confluence of a request to obtain something illegal and a positive response to that request) with a specific sector of the state, which operated in violation of the law and the interests of the community. [...] as the national courts have acknowledged'. (author's translation)

[25] Ibid, at paras 138 and 141.

whether legal confiscation amounts to criminal or administrative sanction. The difference between the two is substantial.[26]

The towers were demolished in 2006—an act welcomed by the inhabitants of Bari and environmental and heritage organizations nationwide.[27] Yet if the planning process had been transparent and had provided for public participation from the outset—taking into consideration 'the collectivity'—the disastrous chain of events could have been avoided altogether; from the spoiling of the landscape of Punta Perotti to demolition of the towers, from the lengthy court cases culminating in Strasbourg, to large-scale compensation and waste of public funds. What is important about this case is that, although the Court issued a violation of Article 1, Protocol No. 1, it nevertheless underlined that heritage belongs to the 'collectivity' of the city's inhabitants and not the administrators, and that they should not have issued planning permission for the towers in the first place. This highlights the contradiction inherent in the notion of property.

Landscape preservation versus landscape use

The second type of landscape cases to come before the ECtHR involves claims brought by ethnic minorities, such as Roma or Irish Travellers, concerning their use and access to landscapes for dwelling purposes. Here rights *to* landscape are in a way the object of the applicants' claim, but this approach often comes into conflict with established landscape protection measures, thereby creating two different forms of landscape rights in direct conflict with one another: landscape preservation versus landscape use. The conflict was evident in a number of cases before the Court. In the case of *Chapman v the United Kingdom*,[28] for example, the applicant alleged that planning and enforcement measures against her occupation of caravans violated her right to respect for her home and private and family life (Article 8). She complained that the restrictions also entailed an interference with the peaceful enjoyment of her possessions (Article 1, Protocol 1) and that she suffered discrimination contrary to Article 14 of the Convention. The land in question was a designated 'Landscape Conservation Area' within a

[26] Elena Sciso, 'Punta Perotti: ancora una condanna per una confisca da parte della Corte europea dei diritti dell'uomo.' *Rivista di Diritto Internazionale*, vol. XCII (2009) 487–496.

[27] See, for example, Nicola Brescia, 'Demolire Punta Perotti un obligo per la città'. *La Repubblica*, 5/02/2009. <http://www.repubblica.it/2009/01/sezioni/ambiente/punta-perotti-condanna/punta-perotti-condanna/punta-perotti-condanna.html> accessed 8 May 2018.

[28] *Chapman v the United Kingdom*. Grand Chamber Judgment 18 January 2001. Application No. 27238/95.

Green Belt zone. The applicant sought planning permission and was refused on the grounds that the occupation of her land was 'detrimental to the rural character' of the area.[29] The Court found that the interferences did not constitute a violation of her rights under the Convention and that the decision of the local authorities was 'necessary in a democratic society'.[30] A similar ruling was reached in the case of *Buckley v the United Kingdom*,[31] whereby the applicant, also from the Roma community, was refused planning permission for three caravans on the grounds that the planned use of the land would detract from the 'rural and open quality' of the landscape. In the dissenting opinion of Judge Pettiti, he stated that the government's approach in this case was to give 'priority to protection of the landscape over respect for family life', thereby reversing the ranking of fundamental freedoms under Article 8.[32]

In these cases, we see a similar line of reasoning by the court as in the first type of cases above, even though the upholding of restrictions in the 'general interest' may not necessarily respect the interest of those of a different cultural or ethnic identity. The saying that landscape 'belongs to everybody' becomes problematic here, because it evidently is not everybody's landscape. The ECHR does not include a specific provision on the protection of culture or cultural identity, and the term culture is not mentioned in the text. The provisions that do touch upon aspects of cultural identity[33] have not generally been applied to cultural heritage or land use, but rather to issues relating to religious freedom, education, and language.[34] For minority groups such as the Roma, travelling is an essential part of their culture; they do not seek to gain property rights on areas of land, but rather use it for a time before moving on, and in this way the conceptualization of landscape—as opposed to land—should be in harmony rather than conflict with their rights to enjoy their way of life. The right to access one's culture is problematic for the Roma, because they do not have the same historical links or customary entitlement to the land as, for example, indigenous groups may have.

[29] Ibid. [30] Ibid.

[31] *Buckley v United Kingdom*, Judgment 29 September 1996. Application No. 20348/92.

[32] Dissenting Opinion of Judge Petiti, European Court of Human Rights judgment in the case of *Buckley v the United Kingdom*, Application No. 20348/92.

[33] Namely Art. 8 on respect for private life and family life; Art. 9 on freedom of thought, conscience and religion; Art. 10 on freedom of expression, Art. 11 on freedom of assembly and association, and Art. 2 Protocol 1 on the right to education.

[34] Council of Europe, Cultural rights in the case law of the European Court of Human Rights (Council of Europe, 2017) at: <http://www.echr.coe.int/Documents/Research_report_cultural_rights_ENG.pdf> accessed 30 January 2018.

Landscape protection in its own right?

The third way in which the subject of landscape protection has come before the ECtHR is when it has been the object of the applicants' claim. Some of these cases involve indigenous peoples' claims, and focus on the right to use certain lands or protect them from destructive development, rather than to acquire title in the lands in question. In relation to indigenous land rights, however, the European Court has adopted a conservative stance. First, many cases involving indigenous rights to landscape have been dismissed by the Court for procedural issues (for example, *Könkäma and 38 other Saami villages v Sweden; Hingitaq 53 and others v Denmark*).[35] Second, in cases that have been admitted, the burden to prove ancestral occupation or customary use is often onerous. For example, in an early case before the European Commission, *G and E v Norway*, two Sami applicants claimed that the construction of a hydroelectric dam authorized by Norway violated their property rights because the work caused the loss of part of what they considered to be their traditional lands.[36] According to the Commission, the applicants could not provide sufficient proof of their precise connection with the flooded land, and were not entitled to compensation. Indeed the Commission appeared quite resistant to the idea that 'traditional use' of the land by the Sami (for hunting, fishing, and reindeer grazing) could be interpreted as 'possession' within the meaning of the Convention. This refers to the wording of Article 1 Protocol No. 1 on the right to property: 'Every natural or legal person is entitled to the peaceful enjoyment of his possessions.' However, it was prepared to admit that the dam could affect their traditional way of life in the area in a way that triggered the application of Article 8 (right to family and private life). Interestingly, the Commission later reversed its view on possession by stating in relation to another case that Sami hunting and fishing rights could be 'regarded as possessions within the meaning of Article 1 Protocol 1 of the Convention'.[37] In another case involving a right to landscape made under Article 1, Protocol No. 1, *Handolsdalen Sami Village v Sweden*,[38] the Court was asked to rule on the admissibility of winter grazing. The case was brought because the Sami applicants had lost their case in Swedish courts to have their traditional winter grazing rights recognized on

[35] *Konkäma and 38 Sami villages v Sweden*, Application No. 27033/95, Decision 25/11/ 1996. *Hingitaq 53 and Others v Denmark*, Application No. 18584/04, Decision 12/01/2006.

[36] *G. and E. v Norway*, Application No. 9278/81 & 9415/81 (joined). Decision of 03/10/1983.

[37] *Konkäma and 38 Sami villages v Sweden*, Application No. 27033/95, Decision 25/11/ 1996, at 85.

[38] *Handölsdalen Sami Village and Others v Sweden*, Application No. 39013/14. Judgment of 30 March 2010.

land belonging to private parties. The applicants argued that this violated their rights under Article 1, Protocol No. 1. However, the Court found that the right to access private property for the purposes of reindeer grazing had no basis in law and was inadmissible. In her dissenting opinion, Judge Ziemele referred to the developments in international law concerning indigenous rights, particularly the 2007 UN Declaration on the Rights of Indigenous Peoples, and challenged the Court's decision.[39] Other authors have criticized the ECtHR for its conservative approach to indigenous land rights cases.[40] This stands in contrast to the approach of the Inter-American Court and Commission, which have elaborated a significant case law recognizing indigenous customary rights to lands despite lack of title (discussed in 9.3).

Attempts have also been made to take the issue of landscape protection to the Court outside the indigenous context. The case of *Kyrtatos v Greece*,[41] for example, concerned the illegal construction of a tourist development in a wetland of Ayios. In 1993, the applicants and the Greek Society for the Protection of the Environment and Cultural Heritage applied to the Council of State for judicial review of illegal building permits. Their main argument was that these were illegal because there was a wetland in the area concerned and, under a constitutional provision protecting the environment, no buildings could be erected in an important natural habitat for various protected species. Their application was successful; however, on 21 April 1997 a special committee of the Council of State found that the authorities had failed to enforce its decisions: they had not demolished the two buildings erected near the applicants' property and had continued issuing building permits in respect of the area. The applicants complained, under Article 6 (right to a fair hearing within a reasonable time) and 8 (right to respect for private and family life) for the authorities' failure to enforce the Council of State's decisions annulling the building permits. They complained that the destruction of the scenically beautiful and ecologically important wetland adversely affected their lives, even though it posed no danger to health. The Court ruled that although the building permits and consequent destruction resulted in a violation of the law, the applicants had not shown how the alleged damage to the environment had directly affected their rights under the Convention. The Court did not accept that the interference with the conditions of wildlife

[39] Ibid, Partly Dissenting Opinion of Judge Ziemele, at paras 2 and 3.

[40] See, for example, Ghislan Otis and Aurélie Laurent, 'Indigenous Land Claims in Europe: The European Court of Human Rights and the Decolonization of Property', *Arctic Review on Law and Politics*, 4 (2) 156–80.

[41] *Kyrtatos v Greece* [2003] ECHR 242. Application No. 41666/98.

in the area constituted an attack on the applicants' private or family life.[42] There had accordingly been no violation of that provision. The Court reaffirmed in this regard that 'neither Article 8 nor any of the other Articles of the Convention are specifically designed to provide general protection of the environment as such.'[43] Representative actions seeking to challenge the law in the abstract are not accepted by the ECtHR.[44] As the Commission pointed out, 'the applicant cannot complain as a representative for people in general, because the Convention does not permit such an *actio popularis*. The Commission is only required to examine the applicant's complaints that he himself was the victim of a violation.'[45] Thus the ECtHR's approach to standing is quite narrow.

Article 34 of the Convention requires that the applicants be victims of an alleged violation and prove that they are directly affected by the matter complained of. Even in the case of associations and NGOs, they must prove that they are themselves in some way affected. Clear violations of the rule of law cannot be remedied if the applicant is not sufficiently affected or if no direct link between the alleged victim and the violation can be proven. As pointed out by Christian Schall, the substantive law available in the ECHR is not ideal for public interest proceedings.[46] The strict approach of the Court in matters of the environment precludes a challenge on landscape grounds because a) environmental integrity is not seen as a value per se for the community affected or society as a whole but rather as a criterion to measure the negative impact on a person's life, property, private and family life; and, b) the individualistic approach followed by the Court excludes the admissibility of public interest proceedings on environmental or heritage grounds, unless the applicants can show a direct impact of the activities complained of in relation to their individual rights. Thus resources that are more widely shared (such as landscapes) cannot be protected by the ECtHR, even if the applicants, as in *Kyrtatos*, have a special interest in that particular part of the environment. Interestingly, in *Kyrtatos*, the procedural element of the case was upheld by the Court in so far as a violation of Article 6(1) (right to a fair hearing within a reasonable time) was found.[47] Indeed, in a number of cases the Court has

[42] Ibid, at 53. [43] Ibid, at 52.

[44] Persons, non-governmental organizations, or groups are allowed to bring a case if they can prove they are victims of a violation of one of the rights enshrined in the Convention (Article 34).

[45] *X Association v Sweden* (1982) 28 DR 204, 206.

[46] Christian Schall, 'Public Interest Litigation Concerning Environmental Matters before Human Rights Courts: A Promising Future Concept?' *Journal of Environmental Law* 20:3 (2008), 428.

[47] The violation concerned the length of civil proceedings they had instituted against their neighbour, whom they accused of trespassing on their property, and also the length of administrative proceedings concerning the threatened demolition of the applicants' house.

issued a violation of the procedural aspect of the case when it involved environmental issues.[48] It is notable that in the case of *Taskin*, the Court took both principle 10 of the Rio Declaration and the three pillars of the Aarhus Convention into account when it assessed the relevant law.[49] It assessed the substantive rights only briefly and went on to examine the procedural rights guaranteed to the relevant Turkish citizens. Thus, it appears that the ECtHR is willing to have regard to the general principles of Aarhus in its jurisprudence concerning Article 8. However, the Court does not seem willing to accept the implications of Aarhus more generally, and particularly in relation to NGOs, to broaden *locus standi* in its own procedure.[50]

What the aforementioned cases illustrate is that the ECtHR is rather conservative in the realm of rights to landscape, except when those rights entail landscape protection or preservation in the 'general interest of society'. This implies two facts: first, landscape protection, as decided by local authorities, is considered important enough and within the state's margin of appreciation to override other rights and freedoms. Yet this is still a negative form of protection, meaning that landscape preservation was not the aim of the applicants, but the problem. Second, non-traditional forms of property rights, such as rights of use or access, are not seriously considered by the Court, neither in the case of minorities nor indigenous peoples. This represents both a scenic, preservationist approach to landscape as well as a narrow conceptualization of property. Of course, part of the reason is due to the lack of specific mention of the natural or cultural environment in the Convention, in addition to the fact that the right to property does not have collective but rather individual connotations and is restricted to the enjoyment of one's possessions, despite the Commission's pronouncement that it can also include hunting and fishing rights.[51] The approach of the ECtHR will now be contrasted with the approach of the Inter-American Court in cases concerning the landscape of indigenous peoples.

[48] *Zander v Sweden*, App. No. 14282/88, 25 November 1993; *Okyay v Turkey*, Application. No. 36220/97 43 Eur. Ct. H. R. Rep 788, 2006. In *Taskin v Turkey* the Court held that it may examine the decision making process of the government to ensure that the interests of the individuals concerned were taken into consideration. It noted that the public should have access to the conclusions of investigations and studies carried out by the government, which would enable them to assess the danger to which they are exposed.

[49] *Taskin and Others v Turkey*, Application. No. 46119/99.

[50] See also, an earlier case of *Asselbourg and Greenpeace v Luxembourg*, Application No. 29121/95, ECtHR 29 June 1999.

[51] *Könkäma and 38 other Saami villages v Sweden; Hingitaq 53 and others v Denmark* (n 35), at 85.

9.3 Landscape in the Inter-American Court of Human Rights

The case law of the Inter-American Court of Human Rights is significantly more progressive than its European counterpart in matters of landscape. This is due to a number of reasons. First, most of the cases dealing with the rights to access or use lands, or to have them protected from destructive development, are based on claims by indigenous peoples. Due to the resource-rich nature of many traditionally owned or occupied lands, especially in the Amazon region, conflicts often arise as a result of logging, mining, and hydroelectric projects approved by the state. As noted by the UN Committee on Economic, Social and Cultural Rights, the traditional lands of many indigenous peoples have been reduced or occupied, without their consent, by timber, mining, and oil companies, at the expense of their culture and the balance of the ecosystem.[52] This represents a continuous form of repression and dispossession under the guise of development.

Challenges to development in communal lands

Many cases concerning rights to landscape in the Inter-American system concern legal challenges to the granting of logging or mining concessions on communal or ancestral lands, where a community lacks proper title but has traditionally occupied the area. In these cases, the interventions by large-scale agro-forestry projects would have a severe impact on the communities' way of life. For example, in the case of *Awas Tingni v Nicaragua*, a Korean corporation was granted concessions by Nicaragua to commence logging in the communal lands of the Awas Tingni community.[53] The community tried to prevent the government from proceeding, first through negotiations and then by resorting to the judiciary. The case was eventually brought before the Inter-American Commission on Human Rights and then the Inter-American Court of Human Rights. In a landmark decision, the Inter-American Court held that the international human right to property, particularly as affirmed in the American Convention on Human Rights, includes the right of indigenous peoples to the protection of their customary land and resource tenure. The Court held that Nicaragua violated the property rights of the Awas Tingni

[52] Concluding Observations of the Committee on Economic, Social and Cultural Rights Columbia, UN Doc.E/C.12/1/Add.74 of 30 November2001, paras 11 and 12.

[53] *The Mayagna (Sumo) Awas Tingni Community v Nicaragua*, Judgment of 31/08/ 2001, Inter-Am. Ct. H.R., (Ser. C) No. 79 (2001).

community by granting a foreign company logging concessions within the community's traditional lands and by failing to otherwise provide adequate recognition and protection of the community's customary tenure. As pointed out by James Anaya, this was the first legally binding decision by an international tribunal to uphold the collective land rights of indigenous peoples in face of the state's failure to do so.[54] Likewise, in *Maya Indigenous Community of Toledo v Belize*, the Inter-American Commission found that Belize had violated the Mayan communities' right to use and enjoy their property by granting concessions to third parties to exploit natural resources within Mayan lands without informed consent.[55] The Commission noted that indigenous peoples' right to property is based on international law and does not depend on domestic recognition of property interests. The Commission broadly defined indigenous property rights as not limited 'exclusively by entitlements within a state's formal legal regime, but also include that the indigenous communal property that arises from and is grounded in indigenous custom and tradition', and further underscored 'the distinct nature of the right to property as it applies to indigenous people, whereby the land traditionally used and occupied by these communities plays a central role in their physical, cultural and spiritual vitality'.[56]

Landscape and other human rights

The second form of indigenous landscape cases to come before the Inter-American system concern the protection of other rights guaranteed in the Convention (for example, the right to life) that indirectly require the safeguarding of the landscape. Indeed, as early as 1985, in the case of *Yanomami v Brazil*, the Inter-American Commission established a link between environmental quality and the right to life in response to a petition brought on behalf of the Yanomami of Brazil.[57] The petition alleged that the government violated the rights of the Yanomami by constructing a highway through their territory and authorizing the exploitation of the territory's resources. These actions led to the influx of non-indigenous people who brought diseases that remained untreated due to lack of medical care. The Commission found that

[54] James Anaya and Claudio Grossman, 'The Case of Awas Tingni v Nicaragua: A New Step in International Law of Indigenous Peoples', *AJICL*, 19 (1) (2002), 1–15.

[55] *Maya Indigenous Communities of Toledo District v Belize*, Case 12.053, IACtHR Report 40/04 (2004), at 153, 194.

[56] Ibid, at 155.

[57] *Yanomami Case*, Case 7615, Inter-Am. C.H.R. Res. No. 12/85, OEA/Ser.L/V/II.66, doc. 10, rev. 1, 24 (1985).

the government had violated a host of rights including the right to life, liberty, and personal security, as well as the right of residence and movement, and the right to health and well-being. In the more recent case of *Moiwana Community v Suriname*,[58] the Inter-American Court dismissed Suriname's argument that the right to property of an indigenous community was time-barred. It concluded that in cases where the state is directly responsible for the original displacement of the population and does not provide for their safe return, the right to claim collective property is not lost.[59] The village of Moiwana remained abandoned after a 1986 attack by government forces, who killed thirty-nine unarmed members of the community, including women and children. The community's property was destroyed and survivors were forced to flee. Throughout the case, particular emphasis was placed on the special relationship between the N'djuka and their land, and the consequent violation of rights arising out of their displacement. According to an expert witness, 'land is for the N'djuka people an embodiment of their collective identity; it also serves as a repository of their cultural history, as well as the primary source of their subsistence'.[60] In its decision, the Court linked the forced displacement of the community from its traditional lands with, inter alia, the violation of the right to personal integrity (Article 5) and the right to private property (Article 21). The Court recalled that 'in case of indigenous communities that have occupied their ancestral lands with their customary practices—but lack of a formal property title—the possession of the land should be sufficient to obtain the official recognition of the property and to obtain subsequent registration.'[61]

Landscape preservation versus landscape use

The third type of landscape case to present itself before the Inter-American Court concerns the aforementioned conflict involving landscape preservation versus landscape use. In a decision in 2010, the Inter-American Court ruled against Paraguay for failing to guarantee the communal right to property of the Xákmok Kásek Indigenous community.[62] The community began proceedings as far back as 1990 with the aim of recovering their ancestral lands. In 2008, the government declared 12,450 hectares of the Salazar estate a Protected Wildlife Area under private ownership (Decree 11804/08), without consulting the community members or considering their territorial

[58] *Moiwana Community v Suriname* (IACrtHR) Judgment of 15 June 2005, Series C No. 124.
[59] Ibid, at paras 128–35. [60] Ibid, at para. 80(e). [61] Ibid, at para. 131.
[62] *Case of Xákmok Kásek Indigenous Community v Paraguay*, IACtHR Series C No. 214.

claim, despite the fact that 4,175 hectares of the estate overlapped with lands claimed since 1990. In its decision, the Inter-American Court found that throughout these years of struggle, the Xákmok Kásek community suffered significant restrictions on the use of their land by the private owners of the estate. These restrictions intensified in recent years, as the community found its traditional subsistence activities and movement around the lands increasingly limited. Hunting was banned and the private owners hired guards to monitor activities, so that gathering food and fishing became impossible.[63] The Inter-American Court found that Paraguay had violated the communal right to property, the right to life, the right to personal integrity, and the rights of the child. Notably, the Court reiterated its consideration in previous decisions that the 'close relationship of indigenous peoples to their traditional lands and the natural resources relevant to their culture that are found there, as well as the intangible elements resulting from them, must be safeguarded under Article 21 of the American Convention'.[64] The Court repeated that for indigenous communities, 'their relationship with the land is not merely a matter of possession and production, but rather a material and spiritual element that they must enjoy fully, even in order to preserve their cultural legacy and transmit it to future generations'.[65] It also noted that the concept of property in the indigenous context can have a collective meaning, in the sense that possession is not focused on individuals but on the group and its community, and that while this concept of property does not necessarily correspond to the classic concept of property, it nevertheless deserves equal protection under the Convention.[66] Notably, the Court stated that 'failing to recognise the specific versions of the right to use and enjoyment of property would be equivalent to maintaining that there is only one way of using and enjoying property and this, in turn, would make the protection granted by Article 21 meaningless for millions of individuals'.[67] The significance of this ruling for the recognition of the landscape rights of indigenous peoples cannot be underestimated. The Court has firmly acknowledged that the concept of property entails several aspects, and not solely the fact of abstract title.

[63] Ibid, at paras 74 and 75.

[64] See para. 85, where specific reference was made to: the *Case of the Yakye Axa Indigenous Community v Paraguay*, Judgment of 17 June 2005, Series C No. 125, para. 137; the *Case of the Sawhoyamaxa Indigenous Community v Paraguay*, Judgment of 28 November 2007, Series C No. 172, para. 118; and the *Case of the Saramaka People v Suriname*, Judgment of 29 March 2006, Series C No. 146, para. 88.

[65] See para. 86. The Court already stated this in the case of the *Mayagna (Sumo) Awas Tingni Community v Nicaragua*, Judgment of 31 August 2001, Series C No. 79, para. 149.

[66] Ibid, at paras 86 and 87.

[67] Ibid, at para. 87.

This essentially represents a right to landscape or a right to property as originally conceived, before the term evolved to connote mere title or ownership of the land in question, rather than the identification of the individual with the land through custom.[68]

Landscape protection in its own right?

However, while all of the above cases concerned the rights of indigenous peoples, in *Metropolitan Nature Reserve v Panama*,[69] the applicant filed a petition to the Inter-American Commission on behalf of all the citizens of Panama. He alleged that the construction of a public highway through the Metropolitan Nature Reserve violated the Panamanian citizens' rights to property, in so far as the Nature Reserve was designated as a protected area of environmental, scientific, and cultural value for Panamanian people by law. The Inter-American Commission concluded that the petition was inadmissible, as it was overly broad and the applicant had failed to identify victims. This approach of the Commission can be contrasted with the cases above concerning indigenous rights to communal lands. In the former cases, the right to property was construed by the Court and Commission to include the customary right of indigenous communities to access and use the lands they had occupied but without title. Apart from the central role these lands play in the 'cultural and spiritual vitality' of indigenous peoples, there is still very much a use and dependency value. In the latter case, however, the issue concerned a nature reserve of environmental and cultural value for the 'citizens' of Panama, and not for one particular group. The difference between the former cases and the latter is emblematic of the problem that exists when articulating landscape protection in human rights language. In the Inter-American system, a collective approach—and a broader interpretation of property—is adopted, but only in relation to indigenous peoples. When it involves a case dealing with a nature reserve or public space, the approach is very different. This is the same in the European context, where the narrow conceptualization of rights and the required level of standing preclude the admission of public interest proceedings in landscape matters, even if the area is protected by law and has significance for the citizens of the state.

[68] For a discussion on the origins of property, see Nicole Graham, *Lawscape: Property, Environment, Law* (Routledge, 2010), 26.

[69] *Metropolitan Nature Reserve v Panama*, Case 11.533, Report no 88/03, IACtHR, OEA/SerL/V/II.118 Doc 70 Rev 2 at 524 (2003).

9.4 The ECtHR and the IACHR Compared

A number of overall observations can be drawn from the above examination of the case law. This first notable feature is that the protection of landscape has been deemed by the ECtHR as an important enough issue to override private property rights. Yet landscape here has played a purely 'negative' role, in the sense of its interpretation as a legitimate restriction on other rights in the name of 'general' or 'public' interest; the question of landscape protection was rarely the purpose of the applicants' claims. The second notable feature of these cases is that the general interest is that decided by the state. In *Herrick*, it was the 'rural' and 'scenic' quality that was to be preserved, which was essentially upholding an aesthetic interpretation of landscape, an 'official' landscape. Tensions between the majority and the minority culture were seen in cases involving the Roma community, where their cultural rights—argued in the context of the peaceful enjoyment of their possessions—were suppressed in favour of the general interest in preserving the landscape of the majority. In the case of *Buckley v the United Kingdom*, for example, where the applicant was refused planning permission for three caravans on the grounds that the planned use of the land would detract from the rural and open quality of the landscape, Judge Pettiti stated that the government's approach in the case was to give 'priority to protection of the landscape over respect for family life', thereby reversing the ranking of fundamental freedoms under Article 8, Protocol No. 1. Third, in one instance where landscape protection (the protection of a wetland) *was* the purpose of the applicants' claim before the ECtHR—and it was argued in the context of Article 8—the Court found that the applicants could not show how their rights were individually impaired by the measure in question. Thus, the ECtHR adopts a narrow approach to the question of standing and is not a likely forum for the 'positive' protection of landscape.

This can be contrasted with the approach of the Inter-American system, where in relation to indigenous communities, the right to property has been interpreted broadly to include customary rights to ancestral lands. This broad interpretation includes a collective, customary, and intangible dimension that is linked to a way of life. There is also a strong cultural element in these cases which is absent in the case law of the European system. However, this collective approach has only been applied in relation to indigenous and tribal people. When it involved a case dealing with a nature reserve or public space, the approach is very different. This highlights a dichotomy that exists between indigenous landscape and non-indigenous or 'Western' landscape; the former is interpreted in light of a use and dependency value, often combined with cultural links with the land, while the latter is often equated solely with aesthetic or environmental values. However, this can be a false dichotomy, as beyond the use and dependency value, both indigenous and non-indigenous cultures may share customary or associative relationships with the land.

9.5 Collective Rights and Public Spaces

In the context of the jurisprudence on landscape and human rights, the question of individual and collective rights becomes integral. Ronald Garet proposes three equally important components of the human being in relation to rights: a) personhood, namely the individual good; b) communality, namely the group good; and, c) sociality, the common good.[70] Human rights primarily protects the integrity of personhood, or the individual good. Human rights can also protect the group good in cases of minorities and indigenous peoples. The last component, sociality, or the common good, however, is the object mostly decided by the state, but is rarely the object of a challenge before human rights courts due to narrow standing requirements and the individual conceptualization of human rights. Recent communitarian critique of political liberalism has lamented the current individualism of rights. According to George Pavlakos, this critique suggests that rights are products of collective action.[71] Far from corresponding to universal claims of individuals, as neoliberal theory teaches us, their content derives from the values of particular collectives or communities. Pavlakos puts forward the thesis that the communitarian critique of human rights, if marshalled properly, essentially amounts to a passage from rights as private reasons to rights as pubic reasons. Rights preserve their justificatory role as motives for action even after their transformation to public reasons. 'In fact, it is especially then that they retain this power' he claims.[72] Some authors argue against the notion of collective rights, arguing that they pose a danger to and have the potential to undermine other substantive fundamental rights.[73] There is also the argument that NGOs and civil society organizations are not necessarily representative of the common

[70] Ronald Garet, 'Communality and Existence: The Rights of Groups' (1993) 56 *Southern California Law Review* 1001–1050.

[71] George Pavlakos, 'Non-Individualism and Rights', in Koen De Feyter and George Pavlakos (eds), *The Tension between Group Rights and Human Rights. A Multidisciplinary Approach* (Hart, 2008), 147.

[72] Ibid, at 148.

[73] Jack Donnelly, 'Third Generation Rights', in C. Brolmann et al. (eds), *Peoples and Minorities in International Law* (Brill, 1993), 119–50.

good, that their 'glory is not democratic legitimacy, but the ability to be a pressure group'.[74] It is not that simple, however. First, in relation to the environment, nature cannot speak for itself and thus requires parties to act on its behalf. Second, to ascribe to national democracies the full virtues of representativeness ignores the fact that in many states, democracy is a weak concept. Third, there is increasing acknowledgement of the social empowerment of communities and groups to take part in the deliberative process leading to environmental decisions affecting their lives (as evidenced at the normative level by the ELC as well as a host of other non-binding texts), and to access justice when abuse of power has occurred (as in the Aarhus Convention). There is at the same time a movement towards a greater realization of collective or group rights in documents such as the United Nations Declaration on the Rights of Indigenous Peoples,[75] the ILO Convention on Indigenous and Tribal Peoples (No. 169),[76] and the African Charter on Human and Peoples' Rights, which recognizes rights of the family and rights of peoples.

In relation to cultural heritage, Francesco Francioni notes that 'at the level of collective rights, cultural heritage may have important implications for the right to development, understood both as economic development induced by a rational and sustainable use of a state's cultural patrimony, and human and cultural development sustained by a society's sense of identity and continuity with its past'.[77] Proponents of collective rights generally argue that the individualistic approach of human rights based on the principles of equality and non-discrimination no longer meets the current global issues relating to development and the environment, and the needs of communities. As noted by Yvonne Donders, the criticism is that the codification of human rights has focused too much on an individualistic outlook of the world and human nature.[78] Although there seems to be a widespread verbal consensus on the

[74] Kenneth Anderson, 'The Ottawa Convention Banning Landmines: The Role of International Non-Governmental Organisations and the Idea of International Civil Society', *European Journal of International Law* 11 (91) (2000), 118. See also, the proceedings of the Fiesole Workshop, Tullio Treves et al. (eds), *Civil Society, International Courts and Compliance Bodies* (Asser, 2005), 57–61.

[75] UN General Assembly, *United Nations Declaration on the Rights of Indigenous Peoples: resolution adopted by the General Assembly*, 2 October 2007, A/RES/61/295 available at <http://www.unhcr.org/refworld/docid/471355a82.html> accessed 30 January 2018.

[76] Convention (No. 169) Concerning Indigenous and Tribal Peoples in Independent Countries, 72 ILO Official Bulletin 59; 28 ILM (1989), 1382, Art. 1(1)(b).

[77] Francesco Francioni, 'Culture, Heritage and Human Rights: An Introduction', in Francioni Francioni and Martin Scheinin (eds), *Cultural Human Rights* (M. Nijhoff, 2008), 8. This might relate to participation in decision making regarding cultural landscape policies. Development as innovation rather than as tradition, which could engender a tension.

[78] Yvonne Donders, *Towards a Right to Cultural Identity* (Intersentia, 2002), 94.

indivisibility of all human rights, in practice the social and cultural dimension of human rights is seriously neglected.[79] Of course, it is unlikely that a broad *actio poularis* would be permitted before the ECtHR. Even if standing requirements were widened within the scope of Article 34—which already allows for applications by associations and groups—the lack of any substantive right to culture or environmental protection under the Convention makes an application on the basis of landscape very difficult—unless argued in the context of other fundamental rights such as property, or family and private life, and even then, it is not straightforward.

[79] Peter Leuprecht, 'Minority Rights Revisited: New Glimpses of an Old Issue', in Philip Alston (ed.), *Peoples' Rights* (Oxford University Press, 2001), 122.

10

Conclusions

This book has explored the various avenues—institutional, substantive, and procedural—for the protection of landscape in international law. It has shown that the term 'landscape' has evolved from being conceptually tied to nature and aesthetics to a much broader, dynamic concept, emphasizing the human dimension of landscape and the symbiotic relationship between people and place over time. I have argued that this brings landscape closer to its early origins, to what Kenneth Olwig terms the 'substantive nature' of landscape. In international law, landscape can mean one or a combination of three things: a) it can be a culturally significant landscape with associative importance articulated in terms of memory, identity and a sense of place; b) it can be a naturally significant landscape, important both for the ecosystems that inhabit it as well as for the respite it offers to humans; and, c) it can be an ordinary, lived-in landscape and have significance for the way of life of its inhabitants. Emphasis in the first and second kind of landscape is on their heritage value, whether natural or cultural, whereas in the third kind, landscape is implicated in terms of democracy and spatial justice. In all cases, landscape can be conceived as public space, or a common good. It was also evidenced in the preceding chapters that protection refers not only to the safeguarding of landscapes themselves, but also and perhaps more importantly, to the safeguarding of the relationships between people and the places that matter to them. Importantly, protection does not mean the freezing of certain areas, a preposterous notion, but rather the sensitive consideration of development in places that have special significance for people. Four main conclusions will now be advanced in relation to the role of international law in landscape protection. These relate to a) state obligations regarding landscape protection; b) the influence of the World Heritage Convention and the European Landscape Convention; c) the substantive and procedural nature of landscape rights; and, d) the role of EU law.

The first overall conclusion of this book is that there exists an emergent landscape law which places an obligation on states to protect landscapes of 'outstanding universal value', as well as to implement policies aimed at landscape protection, management, and planning, including of ordinary landscapes where people live and work. This is evidenced by the international treaty movement (World Heritage Convention, ELC, ICESCR, Faro) explored in Chapters 4, 5, and 6. It is also evidenced in an indirect way through the case law of the human rights courts (Chapter 9) where in almost all of the cases, the Court upheld measures by the state authorities which impinged upon individual rights to property in favour of the 'general interest' in protecting the landscape. Thus, it would seem that landscape protection was deemed of such importance that it should necessarily impinge upon the rights of individuals relating to property or investment.It was shown how the ELC and the World Heritage Convention, while both recognizing the human dimension to landscape, differ considerably from one another in terms of their scope, objectives, and operational structure. In contrast to the World Heritage Convention, the ELC avoids the list-like approach and advocates the management and rehabilitation of landscapes, as well as their conservation. A 'List of Landscapes of European Significance' had been included in the Draft ELC, but was excluded from the final draft, as it was felt to be contrary to the aims and objectives of the Convention. Given the democratic rationale of the ELC, it is understandable that a list approach was avoided. However, not having a list may be viewed as both a blessing and a curse: a blessing in so far as it provides for a broader, more diverse understanding of landscape as a dynamic concept, but a curse because, in attempting to be as inclusive and dynamic as possible, it runs the risk of being legally unenforceable and faces more challenges in terms of quality control. In the case of the World Heritage Convention, for example, the mere fact of inscription on the World Heritage List has helped to protect a number of landscapes from harmful development.[1] At the same time, however, the categorization of a landscape as World Heritage is not unproblematic, and can be perceived as undemocratic for the people who live in World Heritage landscapes, as illustrated by the cases of Dresden and Montichiello discussed in Chapter 5.

This is where the approach of the ELC diverges from the World Heritage Convention and leads us to our second overall conclusion: central to this emerging international landscape law is the right to participate in the definition

[1] See Chapter 5.

and implementation of landscape policies. This right of public participation is enshrined not only in the ELC, but also in the Faro Convention, and the Aarhus Convention on Access to Information, Public Participation and Access to Justice in Environmental Matters, as well EIA Directives. Combined, these instruments apply to landscape, cultural heritage, and the environment and collectively imply that people have rights in relation to the planning and development of landscapes. It is this radical idea of placing people at the centre of landscape policies that has contributed to the positive reception of the ELC and its extra-legal influence, as well as the broader discussions taking place on landscape democracy. While the World Heritage Convention has received substantial criticism for lack of democratic accountability and issues of representativeness, by contrast, the ELC has provided the wellspring for landscape-related activity in academia, civil society organizations, and local and regional authorities across Europe and beyond.[2] States parties have begun adopting landscape strategies, which although not legal instruments, offer some guidance for future planning at national level with due consideration of landscape. In 2010, IFLA called for an international landscape convention, and in 2012, a meeting organized by UNESCO on the international protection of landscapes adopted the Florence Declaration on Landscape, which called upon intergovernmental agencies and secretariats responsible for United Nations programmes together with non-governmental organizations to work towards an international instrument for landscape protection. Among other things, the Declaration reaffirmed landscape as a common good, and the right to landscape as a human necessity.[3] In addition, the ELC has recently been amended to include non-European countries who wish to share the Convention's principles. The ELC has thus contributed to the awareness of the importance of landscape protection continent wide (and beyond) and goes along way to affecting long-term changes through bottom-up processes. Its most marked reach therefore has been societal rather than strictly 'legal'.

Since the adoption of the ELC, landscape protection is increasingly articulated in rights terms,[4] yet the extent and nature of rights envisaged in the 'right to landscape' are not clear. Ultimately, it amounts to what kind of landscape one perceives, and as outlined in Chapters 5, 6, 8, and 9, landscape can

[2] See, for example, the intellectual activity mentioned in Chapter 1 (Introduction), as well as the Networks established for the implementation of the European Landscape Convention (UNISCAPE: <http://www.uniscape.eu/> and CIVILSCAPE: <http://european.landscape-forum.eu/>) accessed 8 May 2018.

[3] Florence Declaration on the International Protection of Landscapes: <http://whc.unesco.org/en/news/943/> accessed 30 January 2018.

[4] Ibid.

be perceived in myriad different ways. Is it the right to access landscapes? Or the right to have them protected from destructive development? Or is the 'right to landscape' ultimately related to custom? Surely, it can be all of these things. While linking landscape with human rights provides the language for articulating the importance of landscape to people, it poses some limits with regard to justiciability, and it inevitably raises questions concerning not only the substantive nature of the 'right to landscape' but also who the holders of that right might be. While international cultural heritage instruments increasingly advocate a human rights approach when dealing with heritage and landscape, they still rest to a large extent on the sovereignty of the state and ultimately decisions concerning landscape are made by the state or its agents. In the case of the World Heritage Convention, for example, it is the state that must nominate a site to the tentative list. Cultural heritage instruments are not intended to grant individuals and groups rights that might be justiciable in a court of law. Yet what happens when a landscape is under threat by the very state charged with its protection? In a case discussed in Chapter 8, when a community attempted to use the World Heritage Convention to prevent a state from granting mining rights and therefore protect a landscape, the case was dismissed.[5] Humankind has been propounded as *titulaire* of rights relating to World Heritage, but this more ephemeral rightsholder cannot and should not override the rights of local inhabitants. On the other hand, landscape as conceived in the ELC is too broad to be associated with any substantive right per se, even though it does bring landscape closer in line with its earlier meaning and recognizes the important function of landscape for identity and human well-being.

The landscape approach is appealing to many sectors of society because it incorporates heritage, human rights, and the environment under one conceptual umbrella and provides a vocabulary to discuss these issues in holistic terms across borders and property divisions. However, claims for rights to landscape, while based on real issues of concern—and sometimes on genuine violations of national law—are not a viable means of accessing justice for land rights violations or for preventing destructive development in local landscapes.[6] This is due to two reasons: first, in most of the cases where landscape protection has been dealt with by regional human rights courts, it usually plays a 'negative' role, in the sense of its interpretation as a legitimate restriction on other rights, especially the right to property.[7] In these cases,

[5] *Buzzacott v Hill* (Federal Court of Australia), Judgment of 1 September 2000, reproduced in ILM, 2000, 20.

[6] Amy Strecker, 'The Law is at Fault? Landscape and Agency in International Law', in Ed Wall and Tim Waterman (eds), *Landscape and Agency* (Ashgate, 2017), 52–65.

[7] See the cases discussed in Chapter 9.

particularly in the European context, landscape is pitted against property, still retains a scenic connotation, and is not associated with use and dependency. Second, when applicants have argued for landscape protection, as illustrated in Chapter 9, the lack of a specific vocabulary of environmental or cultural rights means that they must argue on the basis of other rights, such as the right to the enjoyment of property, but property is narrowly defined in the European context and cases are often dismissed on inadmissibility grounds due to the lack of locus standi or identifiable victims.[8] Human rights are by nature limited by their focus on individual rights.[9] Yet, landscape is a collective good, and as such, cannot be measured in terms of personal injury in the same way that the loss of property can.

An exception to this rule is the interpretation in the Inter-American context of the rights to culture and, in particular, the right to property in the case of indigenous peoples. In relation to culture, the UN Human Rights Committee has confirmed that states do not have unlimited freedom to pursue economic development without consideration of cultural rights (of minorities) in relation to landscapes. In the cases dealing with indigenous peoples' land rights violations, the Inter-American Court has held that the international human right to property, particularly as affirmed in the American Convention on Human Rights, includes the right of indigenous peoples to the protection of their customary land and resource tenure. The Court has stated that for indigenous communities, 'their relationship with the land is not merely a matter of possession and production, but rather a material and spiritual element that they must enjoy fully, even in order to preserve their cultural legacy and transmit it to future generations'.[10] More recently, in 2010, the Court has expanded on this interpretation and noted that the concept of property in the indigenous context can have a collective meaning, in the sense that possession is not focused on individuals but on the group and its community, and that while this concept of property does not necessarily correspond to the classic concept of property, it nevertheless deserves equal protection under the Convention.[11] The Court has thus acknowledged that the concept of

[8] For example, *Konkäma and 38 Sami villages v. Sweden*, Application No. 27033/95, Decision 25/11/ 1996. *Hingitaq 53 and Others v Denmark*, Application No. 18584/04, Decision 12/01/ 2006, *and E. v. Norway*, Application No. 9278/81 & 9415/81 (joined). Decision of 03/10/1983. In *Handölsdalen Sami Village and Others v Sweden*, the Court found that the right to access private property for the purposes of reindeer grazing had no basis in law and was inadmissible. Application No. 39013/14. Judgment of 30 March 2010.,

[9] Francesco Francioni, 'Human Rights in an Environmental Horizon', *EJIL*, 21(1) (2010), 41–55.

[10] *Case of the Mayagna (Sumo) Awas Tingni Community v Nicaragua*, Judgment of 31 August 2001, Series C No. 79, para. 149.

[11] *Case of Xákmok Kásek Indigenous Community v Paraguay*, IACtHR Series C No. 214, paras 86 and 87.

property entails several aspects, and not solely the fact of abstract title. This essentially represents a 'right to landscape' or a right to property as originally conceived, when land had significance greater than the sum of its economic production value and was also an important component of identity.

The third conclusion of this analysis, therefore, is that a 'right to landscape' does exist in international law, but only in relation to indigenous peoples and minorities. This right is not explicitly stated in landscape terms, but rather derives from the rights to culture and property. Interestingly, the substantive nature of this right is closely linked to custom, in essence, to the origins of landscape as recovered by Kenneth Olwig. As outlined in Chapter 1, Olwig showed how the elements of territory and community, community justice, body politic, and custom were inherently embedded in early landscape (or the Norse conception of *landskapr*).[12] Yet despite the progressive judicial activism on the part of the Inter-American Court, this broad interpretation of property to include custom applies only to the case of indigenous peoples, which means that it does not apply to rural communities sharing similar lifestyles as indigenous peoples and others who may also lack title in traditionally occupied lands. This is certainly the case in the Caribbean, for example, where a variety of ethnic minorities are not recognized as indigenous and therefore cannot access the same vocabulary of rights. In addition, as already mentioned, the ECtHR has adopted a rather conservative stance towards property to date.

Given the limits of property for landscape protection outside the indigenous context, it seems that cultural rights offer the most tangible link for expressing landscape protection in human rights terms. While the right to property may necessitate dwelling, occupation, or traditional ownership (even where it is interpreted as custom), culture can connote various relationships between people and place as well as customary links. In the long-awaited General Comment 21 on the normative content of Article 15 1(a), the Committee on Economic, Social and Cultural Rights considers that culture, for the purposes of implementing Article 15 1(a) encompasses, inter alia, 'natural and manmade environments [...] through which individuals, groups of individuals and communities express their humanity and the meaning they give to their existence'. Thus landscapes can be considered as part of the concept of culture within the scope of the right to participate in cultural life, as the duty to protect 'natural and manmade environments' is an aspect of the state's obligations under Article 15 1(a). While cultural heritage cannot be protected for its own sake, it can be covered by the right to

[12] Kenneth Olwig, 'Recovering the Substantive Nature of Landscape', *Annals of the Association of American Geographers*, 86 (1996), 630–653, 631.

the extent that this culture as materialized is essential for the identity of individuals and groups or establishes a relationship to the human person. This implicates landscape on a number of levels and does not restrict the scope of this right to cultural landscapes of indigenous peoples and minorities. The recent adoption in 2008 of an optional protocol to the ICESCR provides for the consideration of complaints by individuals, individuals in association with others, and groups in respect of the rights enshrined in the Covenant. Another positive initiative in the field of cultural rights was the adoption, at regional level, of Faro. As mentioned in Chapter 8, Faro recognizes that 'the rights relating to cultural heritage are inherent in the right to participate in cultural life, as defined in the Universal Declaration of Human Rights'. It also recognizes that 'everyone, alone or collectively, has the right to benefit from cultural heritage and contribute towards its enrichment'. A 'heritage community', as defined by the Framework Convention, consists of 'people who value specific aspects of cultural heritage which they wish, within the framework of public action, to sustain and transmit to future generations'. This idea of a community, formed not on the basis of ethnic affiliation or belonging to a particular place, is highly progressive. It offers the possibility for collective action not only based on these shared characteristics but also on broader spectrums of identity, epistemic background, or a combination thereof. Importantly, it bases value on broad terms, beyond having or owning, to sustaining and transmitting 'within the framework of public action'. While the cultural right to landscape is predominantly a participatory right, it could be argued that 'public action' includes the right to challenge decisions as well as contribute to them.

The last overall conclusion of this book relates to the EU context. While cultural heritage is not a specific area of competence for the EU, the environment is, and landscape and the cultural heritage form part of the definition and scope of environmental protection. In particular, the Aarhus Convention was deemed noteworthy for the way in which it highlights the importance of civil society engagement, and the way in which the role of NGOs is formalized in the operation of the Convention itself. Articles 6–8 of the Aarhus Convention identify three occasions for participation of the public: participation in decisions on specific activities; participation concerning plans, programmes, and policies; and, participation during the preparation of executive regulations and/or generally applicable legally binding regulatory instruments. Furthermore, parties to the Convention must 'inform people of decisions taken on proposed activities of all kinds which are likely to affect them' as well as 'ensure that, in the decision due account is taken of the outcome of the public participation'. The 'public' in the Convention is given a broad meaning. Notably, it entitles not only 'those affected or likely to be affected by', but also those 'having an interest in the environmental decision-making procedures referred to', including 'non-governmental organisations promoting environmental protection' as having the 'sufficient interest' required to have access to a review procedure before a court of law (Article 2(5)). This is extremely significant for landscape, because it recognizes a collective dimension to environmental concerns, thus opening the door for public-interest proceedings. Since the EU adopted the Aarhus Convention and incorporated the Aarhus package into EIA legislation, its provisions are binding on member states.

Notably, EIA includes the consideration of the effects of certain projects not only on environmental elements but also on cultural heritage and the landscape. In addition, recent policy documents acknowledge that 'conservation is increasingly geared towards preserving and enhancing a whole cultural landscape rather than an isolated site, and is also becoming more people-centred'.[13] However, despite the influence of recent Council of Europe treaties on EU policy documents, the conceptualization of landscape is still a rural, scenic one—emphasizing natural values over cultural ones—rather than connoting the various ways in which people interact with and relate to landscapes. This is evidenced by the equation of landscape with 'view' in the recent EIA Directive, the emphasis on maintaining the rural scenic quality of agricultural landscapes in the CAP, and on the emphasis placed on nature and habitats protection within EU environmental law. Interestingly, this mirrors the case law of the ECtHR dealing with landscape issues, which also confirms that cultural landscape policy is a matter of national competence, and still retains a rural, scenic, or preservationist meaning.

In conclusion, although state practice is lagging behind the normative developments made in the field of international landscape protection, landscape has contributed positively to the corpus of international cultural heritage law and indeed has emerged as a nascent field of international law in its own right. First, the category of cultural landscapes within the World Heritage Convention recognizes the importance of people in the management of World Heritage sites and proved influential in the developments leading to a more people-centred approach to landscape protection, further developed in the ELC. Taken together, these developments

[13] European Commission, Communication from the Commission to the European Parliament, the Council, the European Economic and Social Committee and the Committee of Regions, *Towards an Integrated Approach to Cultural Heritage for Europe*, COM(2014) 477 final. Brussels, 22.7.2014, at 1.3

constitute a turning point in the protection and governance, not only of landscape, but of heritage more broadly, to the point where a 'landscape approach' has become synonymous with involving people in heritage and environmental governance. Communities across the globe are facing increasing changes in their landscapes due to global policies, which in turn requires global solutions. Landscape law is an important contributing factor in generating awareness of place in this regard, and claims for landscape rights are one symptom of how other concepts (especially property) are deemed to have failed in their social responsibility. Yet landscape cannot operate on a par with the right to property, even if, as Olwig points out, its original meaning connoted notions of justice, custom, and community. What it can do, however, is act as an umbrella term, integrating environmental and cultural values in what I have termed 'public space', and raise awareness of the non-proprietary interests in land outside of private property and ownership—which are diverse. Landscape represents, not abstract beauty standards, but the rich and diverse relationships that people have with places that matter to them. Adrian Phillips once stated that 'landscape is more likely to concern the man in the street or the woman in the field, than is biodiversity'[14] which is why landscape, as an integrating tool for sustainable development, has potential. Landscape is the visual result of our treatment of the earth and it is this powerful perception that engenders a demand amongst people for better quality landscapes. People see and feel the landscape. It is thus a powerful symbol that can be used as a tool to better the natural and cultural environment for communities and individuals everywhere.

[14] Adrian Phillips, 'Practical Considerations for the Implementation of the European Landscape Convention', IUCN, *Landscape Conservation Law: Present Trends and Perspectives in International and Comparative Law*, (IUCN, 2000), 18.

References

Agius, Emanuel and Busuttil, Salvino, *Future Generations in International Law* (Earthscan, 1998).

Aitchison, John. 'Cultural Landscapes in Europe: A Geographical Perspective', in Bernd Von Droste, et al. (eds), *Cultural Landscapes of Universal Value* (Gustav Fischer Verlag, 1995), 272–88.

Almqvist, Jessica, *Human Rights, Culture, and the Rule of Law* (Hart, 2005).

Alston, Phillip, *Peoples' Rights* (Oxford University Press, 2001).

Anaya, James, *Indigenous People in International Law* (Oxford University Press, 2004).

Anaya, James and Grossman, Claudio, 'The Case of Awas Tingni v Nicaragua: A New Step in the International Law of Indigenous Peoples', *AJICL*, 19 (1) (2002), 1–15.

Anderson, Benedict, *Imagined Communities: Reflections on the Origins and Spread of Nationalism* (Verso, 1983).

Anderson, Kenneth, 'The Ottowa Convention Banning Landmines: The Role of International Non-Governmental Organisations and the Idea of International Civil Society', *EJIL*, 11 (1) (2000), 91–120.

Andrews, Malcolm, *Landscape and Western Art* (Oxford University Press, 1999).

Añon Feliu, Carmen, *Culture and Nature: International Legislative Texts Referring to the Safeguard of Natural and Cultural Heritage* (Olschki, 2003).

Antrop, Marc, 'Why Landscapes of the Past are Important for the Future', *Landscape and Urban Planning*, 70 (2005), 21–34.

Antrop, Marc, 'Sustainable Landscapes: Contradiction, Fiction or Utopia.' *Landscape and Urban Planning*, 75 (2006), 187–197.

Armstrong, David, *Handbook of International Law* (Routledge, 2009).

Atapattu, Sumudu A., *Emerging Principles of International Environmental Law* (Transnational Publishers, 2006).

Baker, Alan and Biger, Gideon (eds), *Ideology and Landscape in Historical Perspective* (Cambridge University Press, 2006).

Barbati, Carla, 'Il paesaggio come realta ético-culturale', *Aedon Revista di Arte e Diritto*, 2 (2007), 1127–45.

Barsh, Russel L., 'How Do You Patent a Landscape? The Perils of Dichotomizing Cultural and Intellectual Property', *International Journal of Cultural Property*, 8 (1999), 14–47.

Baslar, Kemal, *The Concept of the Common Heritage of Mankind in International Law* (Martinus Nijhoff, 1998).

Bederman, David J., *International Law in Antiquity* (Cambridge University Press, 2009).

Bell, Catherine and Paterson, Robert K. (eds), *Protection of First Nations Cultural Heritage: Laws, Policy and Reform* (UBC Press, 2009).

Bender, Barbara (ed.), *Landscape Politics and Perspectives* (Berg, 1993).

Bender, Barbara, 'Stonehenge—Contested Landscapes', in Bender, Barbara (ed.), *Landscape Politics and Perspectives* (Berg, 1993), 245–80.

Bernie, Patricia E. and Alan E. Boyle, *International Law and the Environment* (Oxford University Press, 2002).

Berting, Jan (ed.), *Human Rights in a Pluralist World* (Meckler, 1990).

Besio, Mariolina, 'Conservation Planning: The Case of European Rural Landscapes', World Heritage Papers No. 7, Cultural Landscapes; The Challenges of Conservation, 11–12 November 2002, Ferrara, 60–7.

Betlem, Gerrit, 'Standing for Ecosystems—Going Dutch', *Cambridge Law Journal* 54 (1) (1995), 153–70.

Bianchi, A., 'Human Rights and the Magic of Jus Cogens', *EJIL*, 19 (3) (2008), 491–508.

Birnie, Patricia, Boyle, Alan, and Redgwell, Catherine (eds), *International Law and the Environment* (Oxford University Press, 2009).

Blackstone, William, *Commentaries on the Laws of England.* Books 1 and 2 (edited by Wilfred Prest) (Oxford University Press, 2016).

Blake, Janet, 'On Defining the Cultural Heritage', *ICLQ*, 49 (2000), 61–85.

Blankenship, J., *Reading Landscape: Mid-Century Modernism and the Landscape Idea* (UMass, 2011).

Boccardi, Giovanni and Killian, Jaroslav, 'Report: Reinforced Monitoring Mission to the Dresden Elbe Valley World Heritage Property Germany', February 2008.

Bodansky, Daniel, 'The Legitimacy of International Governance: A Coming Challenge for International Environmental Law?', *ASIL*, 93 (1999), 596–624.

Boer, Ben, and Gruber, Stefan, 'Heritage Discourses and Intergenerational Justice', in Kim Rubenstain and Brad Jessup (eds), *Environmental Discourses in International and Public Law* (Cambridge University Press, 2012), 375–98.

Boisson de Chazour, Laurence, 'Treaty Law-Making and Non-Treaty Law Making: The Evolution Structure of the International Legal Order', in Rudiger Wolfrum and Volker Roben (eds), *Development of International Law in Treaty Making* (Springer, 2005), 463–480.

Bonnel, Victoria.E., Hunt, Lynn, and Biernacki, Richard, *Beyond the Cultural Turn: New Directions in the Study of Society and Culture* (University of California Press, 1999).

Bonnici, Ugo M., *An Introduction to Cultural Heritage Law* (Midsea Books, 2008).

Borelli, Silvia and Lenzerini, Federico, *Cultural Heritage, Cultural Rights and Cultural Diversity. New Developments in International Law* (Martinus Nijhoff Publications, 2012).

Boukhari, Sophie, 'Beyond the Monuments: A Living Heritage', *UNESCO Sources*, No. 80, June 1996.

Boyle, Alan E., The Gabčíkovo-Nagymaros Case: New Law in Old Bottles' (1997) *Yearbook of International Environmental Law*, vol. 8, 13–20.

Boyle, Alan E., and Anderson, Michael, *Human Rights Approaches to Environmental Protection* (Oxford University Press, 1996).

Boyle, James, 'The Second Enclosure Movement and the Construction of the Public Domain', in James Boyle (ed.), *Collected Papers: Duke Conference on the Public Domain* (Center for the Public Domain, 2003), 33–74.

Breathnach, Edel, *Tara: A Selected Bibliography, Discovery Programme Reports 3* (Royal Irish Academy, 1995).

Brewer, John and Staves, Susan (eds), *Early Modern Conceptions of Property* (Routledge, 1996).

Bright, Susan and Dewar, John (eds), *Land Law: Themes and Perspectives* (Oxford University Press, 1998).

Brolmann, C. et al. (eds), *Peoples and Minorities in International Law* (Martinus Nijhoff, 1993).

Brown, Lester R., *World Without Borders: The Interdependence of Nations* (Foreign Policy Association, 1972).

Brown, M.F., 'Heritage Trouble: Recent Work on the Protection of Intangible Cultural Heritage', *IJCP*, (2005), 12: 40–61.

Brownlie, Ian, *Principles of Public International Law* (Oxford University Press, 2008).

Brown Weiss, Edith, *In Fairness to Future Generations: International Law, Common Patrimony and Intergenerational Equity* (Transnational Publishers, 1989).

Brown Weiss, Edith, 'Our Rights and Obligations to Future Generations', *American Journal of International Law*, 84 (1990), 198–207.

Brown Weiss, Edith, 'The Rise or Fall of International Law?' *Fordham Law Review*, 69 (2000), 345–72.

Bruntland Commission, *Report of the World Commission on Environment and Development* (United Nations, 1987).

Brus, Marcel, 'Bridging the Gap between State Sovereignty and International Governance: The Authority of Law', in Gerard Kreijen (ed.), *State, Sovereignty and International Governance* (Oxford University Press, 2004), 2–24.

Buijs, Arjen E., Pedroli, Bas, and Luginbühl, Yves,, 'From Hiking through Farmland to Farming in a Leisure Landscape: Changing Social Perceptions of the European Landscape', *Landscape Ecology*, 21 (2006), 375–89.

Burgers, Herman J., 'The Function of Human Rights as Individual and Collective Rights', in Jan Berting (ed.) *Human Rights in a Pluralist World* (Meckler, 1990), 63–74.

Buttimer, Anne and Wallin, Luke (eds), *Nature and Identity in Cross-Cultural Perspective* (Kluwer, 1999).

Buzzini, Gionata P. and Condorelli, Luigi, 'Article 11, List of World Heritage in Danger and Deletion of a Property from the World Heritage List', in Francesco Francioni and Federico Lenzerini (eds), *The 1972 World Heritage Convention: A Commentary* (Oxford University Press, 2008175–99.

Calcatinge, Alexandru, *The Need for a Cultural Landscape Theory: An Architect's Approach* (LIT Verlag, 2012).

Caldwell, Lynton K., 'Rights of Ownership or Rights of Land Use? The Need for a New Conceptual Basis for Land Use Policy', *William and Mary Law Review*, 15 (1974), 766–75.

Cameron, C., 'The Strengths and Weaknesses of the World Heritage Convention', *Nature and Resources*, 28 (1992), 1–11.

Cançado, Trindade A. A. *International Law for Humankind. Towards a New Jus Gentium* (Martinus Nijhoff, 2010).

Carducci, Guido, 'Articles 4-7, National and International Protection of Cultural Heritage', Francesco Francioni and Federico Lenzerini (eds), *The 1972 World Heritage Convention: A Commentary* (Oxford University Press, 2008).

Carman, John, *Against Cultural Property: Archaeology, Heritage and Ownership* (Duckworth, 2005).

Carozza, Paolo G.,'Subsidiarity as a Structural Principle of International Human Rights Law', *AJIL*, 97 (2003), 38–79.

Carpentieri, Paolo, 'La Nozione Giuridica di Paesaggio', *Revista Trimestrale di Diritto Pubblico*, 2 (2004), 363.

Cassals, Neus T., *Group Rights as Human Rights. A Liberal Approach to Multiculturalism* (Springer, 2006).

Cassese, Antonio, *International Law* (Oxford University Press, 2005).

Cassese, Antonio, *The Human Dimension of International Law* (Oxford University Press, 2008).

Castellino, Joshua, 'Conceptual Difficulties and the Right to Indigenous Self-Determination', in Nazila Ghanea and Alexandra Xanthaki (eds), *Minorities, Peoples and Self-Determination* (M. Nijhoff Publishers, 2005), 55–74.

Chaney, David C., *The Cultural Turn: Scene Setting Essays on Contemporary Cultural History* (Routledge, 1994).

Chinkin, Christine M., *Third Parties in International Law* (Clarendon Press, 1993).

Christie, Edward, *Finding Solutions for Environmental Conflicts* (Elgar Publishing, 2008).

Cicero, *The Republic and the Laws*, Translation Niall Rudd (Oxford University Press, 1998).

Cleere, Henry, 'The Uneasy Bedfellows: Universality and Cultural Heritage', in Robert Layton, Julian Thomas, and Peter G. Stone (eds), *Destruction and Conservation of Cultural Property* (Routledge, 2001), 22–9.

Clark, Kenneth, *Landscape into Art* (Murray, 1949).

Claval, Paul, 'Changing Conceptions of Heritage and Landscape', in Niamh Moore and Yvonne Whelan (eds), *Heritage, Memory and the Politics of Identity* (Routledge, 2007) 85–93

Conrad, E., Cassar, L.F., Jones, M. et al. (eds), 'Rhetoric and Reporting of Public Participation in Landscape Policy', *Journal of Environmental Policy and Planning*, 13 (1) (2011), 23–47.

Cordonnier Segger, Marie-Claire and Gehring, Markus W., *Sustainable Development in World Trade Law* (Kluwer, 2005).

Cosgrove, Daniel and Daniels, Stephen, *The Iconography of Landscape. Essays on Symbolic Representation, Design, Use of Past Environments* (Cambridge University Press, 1998).

Cosgrove, Dennis, *Social Formation and Symbolic Landscape* (University of Wisconsin Press, 1998).

Cosgrove, Dennis, 'Landscape and the European Sense of Sight Eyeing Nature', in Kay Anderson and Mona Domosh et al. (eds), *Handbook of Cultural Geography* (Sage Publications, 2002), 249–68.

Council of Europe, *Heritage and Beyond* (Council of Europe Publishing, 2009).
Council of Europe, *Paysage et Développement Durable, les Enjeux de la Convention Européenne du Paysage* (Council of Europe Publishing, 2006).
Council of Europe, *Manual on Human Rights and the Environment* (Council of Europe Publishing, 2006).
Council of Europe, Explanatory Report to the European Landscape Convention (Council of Europe, 2000).
Council of Europe, Proceedings of the Council of Europe Celebration of the 10th Anniversary of the European Landscape Convention (Council of Europe, 2012).
Council of Europe, Landscape Facets, Reflections and Proposals for the Implementation of the European Landscape Convention (Council of Europe, 2012).
Council of Europe, Explanatory Report to the Council of Europe Framework Convention on the Value of Cultural Heritage to Society (Council of Europe, 2005).
Council of Europe, Presentation to the Framework Convention on the Value of Cultural *Heritage for Society* (Council of Europe, 2005).
Craik, Neil, *The International Law of Environmental Impact Assessment: Process, Substance and Integration* (Cambridge University Press, 2008).
Craufurd Smith, Rachael, *Culture and European Union Law* (Oxford University Press, 2004).
Cullen, Holly and Morrow, Karen, 'International Civil Society in International Law: The Growth of NGO Participation', *Non-State Actors and International Law,* 1 (2001), 7–39.
Dailoo, S.I. and Pannekoek, F., 'Nature and Culture: A New World Heritage Context', *IJCP*, 15 (2008), 25–47.
Darby, Wendy J., *Landscape and Identity: Geographies of a Nation and Class in England* (Berg, 2000).
De Feyter, Koen and Pavlakos, George., *The Tension between Group Rights and Human Rights. A Multidisciplinary Approach* (Hart Publishing, 2008).
Deimann, Sven and Dyssli, Bernard (eds), *Environmental Rights. Law, Litigation & Access to Justice* (Cameron May, 1995).
Dejeant-Pons, Maguelonne, 'L'insertion du droit de l'homme a l'environnement dans le systèmes régionaux de protection des droits de l'homme', 3 (1) (1991), *Revue universelle des droits de l'homme,* 461–70.
Dejeant-Pons, Maguelonne, 'La dimension territoriale du développement durable. Les travaux du Conseil de l'Europe en matière d'aménagement du territoire et de paysage', in Michel Prieur (ed.), *Pour un droit commun de l'environnement* (Dalloz, 2007), 1005–81.
Dejeant-Pons, Maguelonne and Pallemearts, Mark, *Human Rights and the Environment* (Council of Europe Publishing, 2002).
de Klemn, Cyrille, *La conservation des milieux en dehors des aires protégées,* Sauveguarde de la nature n 56 Les éditions du Conseil de l'Europe, 1992.
De Sadeleer, Nicolas et al., *Access to Justice in Environmental Matters and the Role of NGOs, Empirical Findings and Legal Appraisal* (Europa Law Publishing, 2005).
De Sousa-Santos, Boaventura, *Democratizing Democracy* (Verso, 2006).

Dolzer, Rudolf and Schreuer, Christoph, (eds), *Principles of International Investment Law* (Oxford University Press, 2008).

Donders, Yvonne M., *Towards a Right to Cultural Identity?* (Intersentia, 2002).

Donnelly, Jack, 'Third Generation Rights', Catherine Brolmann et al. (eds), *Peoples and Minorities in International Law* (Martinus Nijhoff, 1993), 119–50.

Dupuy, Pierre-Marie, Francioni, Francesco, and Petersmann, Ernst-Ulrich (eds), *Human Rights in International Investment Law and Arbitration* (Oxford University Press, 2009).

Dupuy, Pierre-Marie, *Droit International Public* (Dalloz, 2006).

Dupuy, Pierre-Marie, 'Le concept de société civil internationale, identification et genèse', Habib Gherari, and Sandra Szurek (eds), *L'émergence de la société civile internationale vers la privatisation du droit international?* (Cedin, 2003).

Ebbesson, Jonas and Okowa, Pheobe, *Environmental Law and Justice in Context.* Cambridge (Cambridge University Press, 2009).

Ebbesson, Jonas, 'Information, Participation and Access to Justice: the Model of the Aarhus Convention' Background Paper No. 5, Joint UNEP-OHCR Expert Seminar on Human Rights and the Environment (UNEP, 2002).

Eide, Asbjorn, Krause, Catarina, and Rosas, Allan (eds), *Economic, Social and Cultural Rights—A Textbook* (Martinus Nijhoff, 2001).

Egoz, Shelley, Jala Makhzoumi, and Gloria Pungetti, *The Right to Landscape. Contesting Landscape and Human Rights* (Routledge, 2011).

Fairclough, Graham, 'New Heritage Frontiers', in *Heritage and Beyond* (Council of Europe Publishing, 200929–41.

Fairclough, Graham and Rippon, Stephen (eds), *Europe's Cultural Landscape: Archaeologists and the Management of Change* (EAC Occasional Paper, 2002).

Fairclough, Graham and Lambrick, Georges, *Yesterday's World, Tomorrow's Landscape—the English Heritage Historic Landscape Project 1992–94.* (English Heritage, 1999).

Falk, Richard A., *Human Rights Horizons. The Pursuit of Justice in a Globalized World* (Routledge, 2000).

Fitzmaurice, Malgosia, *Contemporary Issues in Environmental Law* (Elgar Publishing, 2009).

Fladmark, Jan M., *Heritage: Conservation, Interpretation* (Donhead, 1993).

Forrest, Craig, *International Law and the Protection of Cultural Heritage* (Routledge, 2010).

Forsberg, Tuomas, 'Beyond Sovereignty, Within Territory. Mapping the Space of Late-Modern (Geo)Politics', *Cooperation and Conflict*, 31 (1996), 355–86.

Foucault, Michel, 'Of Other Spaces', *Diacritics*, 16 (1) (1986) 22–7.

Fowler, Peter, 'World Heritage Cultural Landscapes 1992–2002,' *World Heritage Papers 6* (UNESCO World Heritage Centre, 2003).

Fowler, Peter, *Landscapes for the World: Conserving a Global Heritage* (Windgather Press, 2004).

Francioni, Francesco, 'The Human Dimension of International Cultural Heritage Law: An Introduction', *EJIL*, 22(1) (2011), 9–16.

Francioni, Francesco, 'Human Rights in an Environmental Horizon', *EJIL*, 21(1) (2010), 41–55.

Francioni, Francesco, 'Access to Justice, Denial of Justice and International Investment Law', *EJIL*, 20(3) (2009), 729–48.

Francioni, Francesco, 'Culture, Heritage and Human Rights: An Introduction', in Francesco Francioni and Martin Scheinin (eds), *Cultural Human Rights* (Martinus Nijhoff, 2008), 1–15.

Francioni, Francesco (ed.), *The 1972 World Heritage Convention: A Commentary* (Oxford University Press, 2008).

Francioni, Francesco (ed.), *Access to Justice as a Human Right* (Oxford University Press, 2007).

Francioni, Francesco, 'Svilluppo Sostenible e Principi di Diritto Internazionale dell' Ambiente', *Sustainable Development and International Law: The Way Forward*, EUI Working Papers, 28 (2007), 7–21

Francioni, Francesco and Lenzerini, Federico, 'The Destruction of the Buddhas of Bamiyan and International Law', *EJIL*, 14(4) (2003), 619–51.

Francioni, Francesco, 'Thirty Years On'. Is the World Heritage Convention Ready for the 21st Century?, *Italian Yearbook of International Law*, 12 (2002), 13–38.

Francioni, Francesco, 'The Madrid Protocol on the Protection of the Antarctic Environment', *TexILJ*, 28 (1993), 47–72.

Francioni, Francesco, 'World Cultural Heritage List and National Sovereignty', *Humanitäres Völkerrecht*, (1993), 195–98.

Francioni, Francesco, 'Resource Sharing in Antarctica: For Whose Benefit?', *EJIL*, 1 (1990), 258–68.

French, Duncan, *International Law and Policy of Sustainable Development* (Juris Publishing, 2005).

Freyfogle, Eric, 'Context and Accommodation in Modern Property Law', *Stanford Law Review*, 41 (1989), 1529–56.

Frigo, Manlio, 'Cultural Property v Cultural Heritage: A Battle of Concepts in International Law', *International Review of the Red Cross*, 86 (2004), 367–78.

Galera, Susana, *The EU's first Pillar—Constitutional Basis in Judicial Review: A Comparative Analysis inside the European Legal System* (Council of Europe Publishing, 2010).

García San Jose, Daniel, *Environmental Protection and the European Convention of Human Rights* (Council of Europe Publishing, 2005).

Garet, Ronald, 'Communality and Existence: The Rights of Groups', *South California Law Review*, 56 (1993), 1001–50.

Geertz, Clifford, *The Interpretation of Cultures: Selected Essays* (Basic Books, 1973),

Gearty, Conor, 'Do Human Rights Help or Hinder Environmental Protection?', *Journal of Human Rights and the Environment*, 1 (2010), 7–22.

Gestri, Marco, 'I concetti di patrimonio comune dell umanità e di risorse di interesse generale nel diritto internazionale', in Giovanna Colombini (ed.), *I beni pubblici tra regole di mercato e interessi generali. Profili di diritto interno e internazionale* (Jovene, 2009), 91–104.

Ghanea, Nazila and Xanthaki, Alexandra (eds), *Minorities, Peoples and Self-Determination* (Martinus Nijhoff, 2005).

Gilbert, Jérémie, *Indigenous Peoples' Land Rights under International Law. From Victims to Actors* (Transnational Publishers, 2006).

Gillespie, Alexander, *Protected Areas and International Environmental Law* (Martinus Nijhoff, 2007).

Gillman, Derek, *The Idea of Cultural Heritage* (Institute of Art and Law, 2006).

Giorgis, Sébastien, *Rural Landscapes in Europe: Principles for Creation and Management.* Council of Europe Planning and Management Series No.3, (Council of Europe, 1995).

Goldsmith, Jack L. and Posner, Eric A., *The Limits of International Law* (Oxford University Press, 2005).

Goodhart, Michael, *Human Rights Politics and Practice* (Oxford University Press, 2009).

Gordon, Robert W., 'Paradoxical Property', in John Brewer and Susan Staves (eds), *Early Modern Conceptions of Property* (Routledge, 1996), 95–110.

Graham, Nicole, *Lawscape. Property, Environment and Law* (Routledge, 2011).

Gray, K. *Elements of Land Law* (Butterworths, 1993).

Gray, Kevin and Susan Francis Gray, 'The Idea of Property in Land', in Susan Bright and John Dewar (eds), *Land Law: Themes and Perspectives* (Oxford University Press, 1998), 15–51.

Groening, Gert, 'The Landscape Must Become The Law—Or Should It?', *Landscape Research*, 32 (5)(2007), 595–612.

Groni, Christian, Committee on Economic, Social and Cultural Rights *Day of General Discussion on the Right to Take Part in Cultural Life,* (Article 15 (1)a of the Covenant), 9 May 2008. E/C.12/40/3.

Grotius, Hugo, *The Freedom of the Seas or the Right which belongs to the Dutch to Take Part in the East Indian Trade, A Dissertation by Hugo Grotius, translated with a revision of the Latin text of 1633 by Ralph Van Dem Am Magoffin, edited with an introductory note by James Brown Scott* (Oxford University Press, 1916).

Grove, Richard H., 'The Origins of Western Environmentalism', *Scientific American*, (July 1992) 42–7.

Guimbatan, Rachel, 'Managing our Changing World Heritage: The Philippines Rice Terraces Experience', IOP Conference Series: *Earth and Environmental Science*, 6 (2009), session 57.

Gündling, Lothar, 'Our Responsibility to Future Generations', *AJIL*, 84 (1990), 207–12.

Haber, Wolfgang, 'Concept, Origin and Meaning of "Landscape"', in Bernd Von Droste et al., *Cultural Landscapes of Universal Value.* Components of a Global Strategy (Gustav Fischer Verlag with UNESCO, 1995), 38–42.

Habermas, Jürgen, *Between Facts and Norms* (MIT Press, 1996).

Hardin, Garrett, 'The Tragedy of the Commons', *Science*, 162 (1968), 1243–8.

Hartshorne, Richard, *The Nature of Geography: A Critical Survey of Current Thought in Light of the Past* (Association of American Geographers, 1939).

Harvey, David, *The Condition of Post-Modernity* (Blackwell, 1989).
Hellen, Stacey, *Human Rights for the 21st Century: Sovereignty, Civil Society, Culture* (Stanford University Press, 2009).
Hewitt, Andy, 'Privatizing the Public: Three Rhetorics of Art's Public Good in "Third Way" Cultural Policy', *Art & the Public Sphere*, (January 2011), 19–36.
Hobbes, Thomas, *Leviathan*, in Richard Tuck (ed.) (Cambridge University Press, 1991).
Holder, Jane, 'Building Spatial Europe: An Environmental Justice Perspective', in Joanne Scott (ed.), *Environmental Protection—European Law and Governance* (Oxford University Press, 2009).
Hunt, Lynn, *The New Cultural History* (University of California Press, 1989).
Immel I., 'Paradoxes in Participation Rights for Civil Society in EU Environmental Policy', *ECPR Graduate Conference Dublin*, 30 August–1 September 2010.
Ingold, Timothy, 'The Temporality of the Landscape', *World Archaeology*, 25 (2) (1993), 152–74.
Inglis, Fred, 'Nation and Community: a Landscape and its Morality', *The Sociological Review*, 25 (1977), 489–513.
Iwanska, Barbara, 'Recent Developments in the Polish Environmental Protection Law', Avosetta Group Meeting, Ghent, 1–3 June 2007.
IUCN, *Landscape Conservation Law; Present trends and perspectives in International and Comparative Law*, IUCN Environmental Policy and Law Paper No.39 (Island Press, 2000).
Jackson, John Brinckerhoff, *A Sense of Place, A Sense of Time* (Yale University Press, 1994).
Jackson, John Brinckerhoff, 'The Vernacular Landscape', in E. C. Penning-Roswell and D. Lowenthal (eds), *Landscape Meaning and Values* (Allen & Unwin, 1986).
Jackson, Robert H. (ed.), *Sovereignty at the Millennium* (Blackwell, 1999).
Jacques, David, 'The Rise of Cultural Landscapes', *International Journal of Heritage Studies*, 1 (1995).
Jameson, Frederick, *The Cultural Turn: Selected Writings on the Postmodern* (Verso, 1998).
Jennings, Robert, 'Sovereignty and International Law', in Gerard Kreijen (ed.), *State, Sovereignty and International Governance* (Oxford University Press, 2004), 27–44.
Jensen, Ole B. and Richardson Tim, *Making European Space: Mobility, Power and Territorial Identity* (Routledge, 2004).
Jokilehto, Jukka, 'World Heritage. Observations on Decisions related to Cultural Heritage', *Journal of Cultural Heritage Management and Sustainable Development*, 1 (2011), 61–74.
Jones, Michael, 'Landscape Democracy and Participation in a European Perspective', in Jones, Michael and Marie (eds), *The European Landscape Convention: The Challenges of Public Participation* (Springer, 2011).
Jones, Michael, 'The European Landscape Convention and Questions of Public Participation,' *Landscape Research*, 32 (5) (2007), 613–33.
Jones, Michael, Howard, Peter, and Olwig, Kenneth (eds), 'Multiple Interfaces of the European Landscape Convention', *Norwegian Journal of Geography*, 61 (2007), 207–15.

Jones, Michael, 'Landscape, Law and Justice—Concepts and Issues', *Norwegian Journal of Geography*, 60 (2006), 1–14.

Jones, Michael, 'The Concept of Cultural Landscape: Discourses and Narratives', in Hannes Palang and Gary Fry (eds), *Landscape Interfaces. Cultural Heritage in Changing Landscapes*. Landscape Series (Kluwer Academic, 2003), 21–51.

Jones, Michael, 'Landscape, Law and Justice. Report', *Annual Report*, 2003, 39–62 (Centre for Advanced Study at the Norwegian Academy of Science and Letters, 2003).

Jones, Michael, 'The Elusive Reality of Landscape. Concepts and Approaches in Landscape Research', *Norsk Geografisk Tidsskrift*, 45 (1991), 229–44.

Jongman, Rob H.G., *The New Dimensions of the European Landscape* (Springer, 2004).

Jorgensen, Karsten and Clemetsen, Morten et al. (eds), *Mainstreaming Landscape through the European Landscape Convention* (Routledge, 2016), 119–128.

Kamminga, Menno T. and Schenin, Martin, *The Impact of Human Rights Law on General International Law* (Oxford University Press, 2009).

Keisteri, Tarja, 'The Study of Changes in Cultural Landscapes,' *Fennia- International Journal of Cultural Geography* 168 (2013).

Khan, L. Ali, *The Extinction of Nation-States. A World without Borders* (Kluwer Law International, 1996).

Kiss, Alexandre and Shelton, Dinah, *International Environmental Law* (Martinus Nijhoff, 2007).

Kiss, A., Shelton, D. and Ishibashi. K. (eds), *Economic Globalisation and Compliance with International Environmental Agreements* (Aspen Publishing, 2003).

Kooijmans, Pieter, Internationaal Publiekrecht in Vogelvlucht (2000), translation from Dutch by Marcel Brus in 'Bridging the Gap between state Sovereignty and International Governance: The Authority of Law', G. Kreijen (ed.), *State, Sovereignty and International Governance* (Oxford University Press, 2004), 359.

Kramer, Ludwig, 'Public Interest Litigation in Environmental Matters before European Courts', *Journal of Environmental Law*, (1996), 1–18.

Kramer, Ludwig, *Focus on Environmental Law*. 2nd edition. (Sweet & Maxwell, 1997)

Kreijen, Gerard (ed.), *State, Sovereignty and International Governance* (Oxford University Press, 2004).

Kuleshova, Marina, Cultural Landscapes in the World Heritage List, paper presented at the Regional Seminar for CIS countries '*Safeguarding the World Heritage in the Context of New Global Challenges*, 1–3 March 2011, Moscow.

Lafarge, François, 'Landscapes in International Law and European Law.' *Landscape as Heritage: Negotiating European Cultural Identity*. M. Sassatelli (ed.), EUI Working Paper No 2006/05.

Lamazzo, Giovanni Paolo, *Trattato dell'arte della pittura*, Libro VI, Vol. lxxi; Milan, 1584.

Last, Kathryn, 'Heritage and Identity: The Challenge of Landscapes to the Nature/ Culture Dichotomy', in Monica Sassatelli (ed.), *Landscape as Heritage: Negotiating European Cultural Identity*. EUI Working Paper No 2006/05.

Layton, R., Thomas, J., and Stone, P. G. (eds), *Destruction and Conservation of Cultural Property* (Routledge, 2001).

Leander, Birgitta, *Preliminary List of Cultural Rights* (Culture and Development Coordination Office, 1996).

Lefebvre, Henri, *The Production of Space* (Blackwell, 1991).

Lehtinen, Ari Aukusti , 'Tracing Environmental Justice—On the Associations of Folk, Justice and the Environment', in Tiina Peil and Michael Jones (eds), *Landscape, Law and Justice, Proceedings of a Conference* (Novus Forlag, 2003), 81–94.

Lenzerini, Federico, 'Article 12. Protection of Properties not Inscribed on the World Heritage List', in Francesco Francioni and Federico Lenzerini (eds), *The 1972 World Heritage Convention. A Commentary* (Oxford University Press, 2008), 201–18.

Lenzerini, Federico and Vrdoljak, Ana (eds), *International Law for Common Goods, Normative Perspectives on Human Rights, Culture and Nature* (Hart, 2014).

Levine, Michel, 'Taste, Judgment and Ethics: Philosophical Aspects of Discourse on Landscape, Law and Identity', in William Taylor (ed.), *The Geography of Law: Landscape, Identity and Regulation* (Hart, 2006), 33–48.

Levinson, Sanford, *Written in Stone: Public Monuments in Changing Societies* (Duke University Press, 1998).

Leuprecht, Peter, 'Minority Rights Revisited: New Glimpses of an Old Issue', in Philip Alston, *Peoples' Rights* (Oxford University Press, 2001).

Lisitzin, Katri and Stovel, Henry, 'Training Challenges in the Management of Heritage Territories and Landscapes', *World Heritage Papers* 7 (UNESCO World Heritage Centre, 2003).

Logan, William. 'Closing Pandora's Box: Human Rights Conundrums in Cultural Heritage Protection', in Helaine Silverman and D. Fairchild Ruggles (eds), *Cultural Heritage and Human Rights* (Springer, 2007), 33–52.

Lokan, Andrew, 'From Recognition to Reconciliation: The Functions of Aboriginal Rights Law', *Melbourne University Law Review*, 23 (1999), 65.

Lomazzo, Gian Paolo, *Trattato dell'arte della pittura*. Libro VI, Vol. lxii; Milan, 158.

Lowe, Vaughan, *International Law* (Clarendon, 2007).

Lowe, 'Sustainable Development and Unsustainable Arguments', in Alan Boyle and David Freestone (eds), *International Law and Sustainable Development* (Oxford University Press, 1999), 19–37.

Lowenthal, David and Olwig, Kenneth (eds), *The Nature of Cultural Heritage and the Culture of Natural Heritage: Northern Perspectives on a Contested Patrimony* (Routledge, 2006).

Lowenthal, David, *The Heritage Crusade and the Spoils of History* (Viking, 1997).

Lowenthal, David 'Cultural Landscapes', *The UNESCO Courier: A Window Open on the World*, 50 (9) (1997), 18–20.

Lowenthal, David, 'European and English Landscapes as National Symbols', in Hooson, David (ed.), *Geography and National Identity* (Blackwell, 1994), 15–38.

Lowenthal, David, 'Age and Artefact. Dilemmas of Appreciation', in Donald W. Meinig (ed.), *The Interpretation of Ordinary Landscapes* (Oxford University Press, 1979), 103–28.

Loucaides, Loukis G., *The European Convention on Human Rights* (Martinus Nijhoff, 2007).

Louka, Elli, *International Environmental Law: Fairness, Effectiveness, and World Order (*Cambridge University Press, 2006).

Lozny, Ludomir R. (ed.), *Landscapes under Pressure. Theory and Practice of Cultural Heritage Research and Preservation* (Springer, 2006).

Makzouni, Jala and Egoz, Shelley (eds), *The Right to Landscape: Contesting Landscape and Human Rights* (Ashgate, 2011).

Mansi, Antonio, *La tutela dei beni cultural e del paesaggio* (Cedam, 2004).

Malpas, Jeff E., *Place and Experience: A Philosophical Topography* (Cambridge University Press, 1999).

Marson, Anna, 'Land-Use Planning Scandals in Tuscany: Mismanagement or Underestimation of General Public Interests?', *Politische Italien Forschung Occasional Papers*, No. 09/2010.

Mastalir, Roger W., 'A Proposal for Protecting The 'Cultural' and 'Property' Aspects of Cultural Property under International Law', *Fordham International Law Journal*, 16 (1992–1993), 1033.

McKee, Alan, *The Public Sphere: An Introduction* (Cambridge University Press, 2005).

Mendes, Joana, *Rights of Participation in European Administrative Law. A Rights Based Approach to Participation in Rulemaking* (EUI Thesis, 2008).

Meinig, Donal W. (ed.), *The Interpretation of Ordinary Landscapes* (Oxford University Press, 1979).

Merryman, John H., 'Cultural Property Internationalism', *IJCP*, 12 (2005), 11–39.

Merryman, John H., 'Protection of the Cultural Heritage?', *American Journal of Comparative Law*, 38 (1990), 513–22.

Merryman, John H., 'Two Ways of Thinking about Cultural Property', *AJIL*, 80 (1986), 831–53.

Meskell, Lynn, 'UNESCO's World Heritage Convention at 40. Challenging the Economic and Political Order of International Conservation', *Current Anthropology*, 54 (4) (2013) 483–94.

Meskell, Lynn, 'The Rush to Inscribe: Reflections on the 35th Session of the World Heritage Committee, UNESCO Paris, 2011', *Journal of Field Archaeology*, 37 (2) (2012), 145–51.

Meskell, Lynn, 'World Heritage and WikiLeaks: Territory, Trade, and Temples on the Thai-Cambodian Border', *Current Anthropology*, 57 (1) (2016), 72–95.

Meyer, Marakot J., *Architectural Heritage and Polity Making in the European Union 1970s–1990s* (EUI Thesis, 2004).

Meyer-Bisch, Patrice (ed.), *Les Droits Culturels, une catégorie sous-développée de droits de l'homme, Actes du VIIIe Colloque interdisciplinaire sure les droits de l'homme* (Editions Universitaires Fribourg Suisse, 1993).

Mikesell, Marvin,'Landscape', in David L. Sills, *International Encyclopaedia of Social Sciences,* vol.8 (Collier & Macmillan, 1968), 575–80.

Milani, Raffaele, 'The Idea of Landscape and the Perspectives of a Common European Policy', in Monica Sassatelli (ed.), *Landscape as Heritage: Negotiating European Cultural Identity*, 2006. EUI Working Paper No 2006/05.

Mitchell, Don, *The Right to the City, Social Justice and the Fight for Public Space* (The Guilford Press, 2003).

Mitchell, Don, 'Introduction: Public Space and the City', *Urban Geography*, 17 (2) (1996), 127–31.

Mitchell, William J.T. (ed.), *Landscape and Power* (University of Chicago Press, 2002).

Molenaar, ErikJ. and Oude Elferink, Alex G., *The International Legal Regime of Area Beyond National Jurisdiction: Current and Future Developments* (Martinus Nijhoff, 2010).

Moore, Niamh and Whelan, Yyvonne (eds), *Heritage, Memory and the Politics of Identity* (Ashgate, 1997).

Muir, Richard, *Approaches to Landscape* (Macmillan, 1999).

Nafziger, James, and Scovazzi, Tullio, *Le patrimoine culturel de l'humanité* (Martinus Nijhoff, 2008).

Nahlik, Stanislaw E., 'La protection internationale des biens culturels en cas de conflit armé', *Recueil des Cours* (1968) vol. I.

Newman, Conor and Strohmayer, Ulf, *Uninhabited Ireland: Tara, the M3 and Public Spaces in Galway*. Arlen House: Galway, 2007.

Nora, Pierre, 'Between Memory and History: Les Lieux de Mémoire', *Representations*, 26 (1989), 7–25.

Nordstrom, Nina, *More Information—Better Environment? A study in International Law on Duties to Share and Rights to Access Environmental Information*, (EUI Thesis, Florence).

Nowlan, Jacqueline, 'Cultural Property and the Nuremberg War Crimes Trial', *Humanitaeres Voelkerrecht* 4 (1993), 221–23.

O'Brien, Richard, *Global Financial Integrations: The End of Geography* (Pinter, 1991).

Odinkalu, Chidi Anselm, 'Analysis of Paralysis or Paralysis by Analysis. Implementing Economic, Social and Cultural Rights under the African Charter on Human and Peoples' Rights', *Human Rights Quarterly*, 23 (2001), 327–69.

O'Keefe, Roger, 'World Cultural Heritage: Obligations to the International Community as a Whole?', *ICLQ*, 53 (1) (2004), 189–209.

O'Keefe, Roger, 'The Meaning of Cultural Property under the 1954 Hague Convention', *Netherlands International Law Review*, 46 (1) (1999) 26–56.

O'Keefe, Roger, 'The Right to Take Part in Cultural Life under Article 15 of the ICESCR', *ICLQ*, 47 (4) (1998), 904–23.

O'Keefe, Tadgh, 'Landscape and Memory: Historiography, Theory, Methodology', in Niamh Moore and Yvonne Whelan (eds), *Heritage, Memory and the Politics of Identity: New Perspectives on the Cultural Landscape* (Ashgate, 2007), 3–18.

Olwig, Kenneth, 'The Landscape of "Customary" Law Versus that of "Natural" Law', *Landscape Research*, 30 (2005), 299–320.

Olwig, Kenneth, 'Commons and Landscape', in Erling Berge and Lars Carlsson (eds), *Commons: Old and New: Proceedings from a Workshop* (Centre for Advanced Study, Oslo, 2003), 15–22.

Olwig, Kenneth, *Landscape Nature and the Body Politic: From Britain's Renaissance to America's New World* (University of Wisconsin Press, 2002).

Olwig, Kenneth, 'Recovering the Substantive Nature of Landscape', *Annals of the Association of American Geographers*, 86 (4) (1996), 630–53.

Onida, Marco, *Europe and the Environment. Essays in Honour of Ludwig Kramer* (Europa Law Publishing, 2004).

Orejas, Almudena and Ruiz de Arbol, Maria, *Landscapes as Cultural Heritage in the European Research* (Acción COST A27, 2004).

Ørebech, Peter et al. (eds), *The Role of Customary Law in Sustainable Development.* (Cambridge University Press, 2005).

O'Reilly, Niamh, 'Come One Come All? Public Participation in Environmental Law in Ireland: A Legal, Theoretical and Sociological Analysis', *Trinity C.L. Law Review*, 8 (2005), 73–105.

Ostrom, Elinor, *Governing the Commons, The Evolution of Institutions for Collective Action* (Cambridge University Press, 1990).

Ostrom, Elinor, et al. 'Revisiting the Commons: Local Lessons, Global Challenges', *Science*, 284 (1999), 278–82.

Otis, G. and A. Laurent, 'Indigenous Land Claims in Europe: The European Court of Human Rights and the Decolonization of Property', *Arctic Review on Law and Politics*, 4 (2) (2013), 156–80.

Palang, Hannes and Gary Fry (eds), *Landscape Interfaces. Cultural Heritage in Changing Landscapes*. Landscape Series (Kluwer Academic, 2003).

Pallemearts, Marc, 'Introduction: Human Rights and Environmental Protection', in Dejeant-Pons, Maguelonne and Pallemearts, Mark, *Human Rights and the Environment* (Council of Europe Publishing, 2002), 11–16.

Palombella, Gianluigi,*Reasons for Justice, Rights and Future Generations* (EUI Working Papers, Law 2007/0).

Pavlakos, George, 'Non-Individualism and Rights', in Koen De Feyter and George Pavlakos (eds), *The Tension between Group Rights and Human Rights. A Multidisciplinary Approach* (Hart, 2008), 147–71.

Pavoni, Riccardo, 'Environmental Rights, Sustainable Development, and Investor-State Case Law: A Critical Appraisal', in Pierre-Marie Dupuy, Francesco Francioni, and Ernst-Ulrich Petersmann (eds), *Human Rights in International Investment Law and Arbitration* (Oxford University Press, 2009), 525–56.

Pedroli, Bas et al. (eds), *Europe's Living Landscapes: Essays Exploring our Identity in the Countryside*, Landscape Europe (KNNV, 2007).

Pedroli, Bas and Goodman, Tessa (eds), *Landscape as a Project* (Melfi, 2010).

Peil, Tina and Mcihael Jones (eds), *Landscape, Law and Justice, Proceedings of a Conference* (Novus Forlag, 2003).

Pellet, Allain, '"Human Rightism" in International Law', *Italian Yearbook of International Law*, 3 (14) (2000).

Philips, Adrian, 'Landscape Conservation Law': Present Trends and Perspectives in International and Comparative Law', *Environmental Policy and Law* Paper No. 39, (IUCN, 2000).

Phillips, Adrian, 'Practical Considerations for the Implementation of the European Landscape Convention', IUCN, *Landscape Conservation Law: Present Trends and Perspectives in International and Comparative Law* (IUCN, 2000).

Pickard, Richard, *Policy and Law in Heritage Conservation* (Council of Europe Publishing, 2001).

Pozo, Vera, E., *An Inventory of EU Member States' Access to Justice in Environmental Matters* (Milieu Ltd, 2008).

Pressouyre, Léon, *The World Heritage Convention, Twenty Years Later* (UNESCO Publishing, 1996).

Prieur, Michel, *Pour un droit commun de l'environnement, Mélanges en l'honneur de Michel Prieur* (Dalloz, 2007).

Prieur, Michel, *Droit de l'Environnement* (Précis Dalloz, 2004).

Prieur, Michel, 'The Relationship between the Convention and other International Instruments, European Landscape Convention', *Council of Europe Review*, Council of Europe Publishing, *Naturopa*, 2002, No.98.

Prieur, Michel, 'Legal Provisions for Cultural Landscapes Protection in Europe', in *Cultural Landscapes: the Challenges of Conservation*, World Heritage Papers 7, World Heritage 2002 (UNESCO Publishing, 2002), 150–56.

Prieur, Michel, 'Le Paysage en Droit Compare et en Droit International', *Environmental Policy and Law*, 27 (4)(1997).

Priore, Riccardo, *No People, No Landscape: luci e ombre nel processo di attuazione in Italia* (Angeli, 2009).

Priore, Riccardo, Presentation at a study day on the European Landscape Convention on 18 January 2001, *Revue européenne de droit de l'environnement*, October 2003.

Priore, Riccardo, 'La Convention Européenne du Paysage', *Revue européenne de droit de l'environnement* (2000), No. 3, 285.

Prott, Lyndel and O'Keefe, Patrick, Cultural 'Heritage' or Cultural 'Property'?, *IJCP*, 1 (1) (1992), 307–20.

Prott, Lyndel, 'Cultural Rights as Peoples' Rights in International Law', in James Crawford (ed.), *10 Bulletin of the Australian Society of Legal Philosophy* (Clarendon Press, 1988), 93–106.

Prott, Lyndel, *Law and the Cultural Heritage.* Vol. 1 (Oxford University Press, 1984).

Prott, Lyndel, *Commentary on the UNIDROIT Convention* (Institute of Art and Law, 2007).

Quillacq, Patricia A., *Sources et manifestations du principe de participation publique en matière d'environnement.* (EUI Doctoral Thesis, 2007).

Raustiala, Kal, 'The "Participatory Revolution" in International Environmental Law', *Harvard Environmental Law Review*, 21 (1997), 537–45.

Rawls, John , *A Theory of Justice* (Harvard University Press (revised edition), 1999).

Rogers, Catheirne A. and Alford, Roger P. (eds), *The Future of Investment Arbitration* (Oxford University Press, 2009).

Rose, Carole M., 'Property as Wealth, Property as Propriety', in Chapman, John (ed.), *Nomos XXXIII: Contemporary Justice* (New York University Press, 1991), 223–47.

Rössler, Mechtild, World Heritage Cultural Landscapes: A UNESCO Flagship Programme 1992–2006, *Landscape Research* 31 (4) (2006), 333–53.

Rössler, Mechtild, 'World Heritage Cultural Landscapes in the European Region', in R. Kelly et al. *The Cultural Landscape. Planning for a Sustainable Partnership between People and Place* (ICOMOS-UK, 2001).

Roussin, Lucille A., 'Cultural Heritage and Identity', *Cardozo Journal of International and Comparative Law*, 11 (2) (2003), 707–10.

Ryall, Aine, *Effective Judicial Protection and the Environmental Impact Assessment Directive in Ireland (*EUI Doctoral Thesis, 2003).

Sadeleer, Nicolas de (ed.), *Access to Justice in Environmental Matters and the Role of NGOs. Empirical Findings and Legal Appraisal* (Europa Law Publishing, 2005).

Sands, Phillip, *Principles of International Environmental Law* (Cambridge University Press, 2003).

Sands, Phillip, 'The Environment, Community and International Law', *HarvILJ*, 30 (1989), 393.

Santoloci, Maurizio, Benedetto, Gaetano, *Edilizia, vincoli paesaggistici ed altri illeciti territoriali: tecnic di controllo ambientale* (Laurus Robuffo, 3rd edn, 2004).

Sassatelli, Monica, 'Landscape of Identity: The European Landscape Convention in the Construction of a European Identity', in Monica Sassatelli (ed.), *Landscape as Heritage: Negotiating European Cultural Identity*, EUI Working Paper No 2006/05.

Sax, Joseph, 'Heritage Preservation as Public Duty: The Abbé Grégoire and the Origins of an Idea', *Mich. L. Rev.*, 88 (1990).

Scazzosi, Lionella (ed.), *Reading the Landscape. International Comparison/Leggere il Paesaggio. Confronti internazionali* (Gangemi, 2002).

Scazzosi, Lionella, *Politiche e culture del paesaggio/ Landscape policies and cultures* (Gangemi, 2001).

Schall, Christian, 'Public Interest Litigation Concerning Environmental Matters before Human Rights Courts: A Promising Future Concept?', *Journal of Environmental Law*, 20 (3) (2008), 417–53.

Schama, Simon, *Landscape and Memory* (Knopf, 1995).

Scheinin, Martin, 'The Right to Enjoy a Distinct Culture: Indigenous and Competing uses of Land,' Theodore S. Orlin, Allan Rosas and Martin Scheinin (eds), *The Jurisprudence of Human Rights Law: A Comparative Interpretive Approach* (Institute for Human Rights, 2000).

Schrijver, Nico and Weiss, Friedl (eds), *International Law and Sustainable Development* (Martinus Nijhoff, 2004).

Sciso, Elena, 'Punta Perotti: ancora una condanna per una confisca da parte della Corte europea dei diritti dell'uomo', *Rivista di Diritto Internazionale*, vol.XCII (2009), 487–96.

Scott, Joanne, *Environmental Protection - European Law and Governance* (Oxford University Press, 2009).

Segger, Marie-Claire C. and Khalfan, Ashfaq, *Sustainable Development Law: Principles, Practices & Prospects* (Oxford University Press, 2004).

Segger, Marie-Claire C. and Weeramantry, C. G. (eds), *Sustainable Justice: Reconciling Economic, Social and Environmental Law* (Martinus Nijhoff Publishers, 2005).

Settis, Salvatore, *Paesaggio, Costituzione, Cemento. La bataglia per l'ambiente contro il degrado civile* (Enaudi, 2010).

Seipp, David J., 'The Concept of Property in the Early Common Law', *Law and History Review*, 12 (1) 29–91.

Shaw, Malcolm N., *International Law* (Cambridge University Press, 2009).

Sheldrake, Philip F., *Spaces for the Sacred: Place, Memory and Identity* (John Hopkins University Press, 2001).

Shelton, Dinah, Environmental Rights, in Philip Alston (ed.), *Peoples' Rights* (Oxford University Press, 2001).

Shelton, Dinah, 'Human Rights and the Environment, Past, Present and Future Linkages and the Value of a Declaration', High Level Expert meeting on the New Future of Human Rights and the Environment: Moving the Global Agenda Forward, Nairobi, 30 November–1 December 2009.

Schonberg, Søren, *Legitimate Expectations in Administrative Law* (Oxford University Press, 2000).

Sills, David L., *International Encyclopaedia of Social Sciences*, vol. 8 (Collier & Macmillan, 1968).

Simma, Bruno, 'International Human Rights and General International Law: A Comparative Analysis', *Collected Courses of the Academy of European Law 4* (Academy of European Law, 1993).

Sivakumaran, Sandesh, 'Impact on the Structure of International Obligations', in Menno T. Kamminga and Martin Scheinin (eds), *The Impact of Human Rights Law on General* (Oxford University Press, 2009).

Slavin, Michael, *The Book of Tara* (Wolfhound Press, 1996).

Smith, Laurajane, *The Uses of Heritage* (Routledge, 2006).

Sohn, Louis B., 'The Stockholm Declaration on the Human Environment', *Harv ILJ*, 14 (1973), 423 ff.

Ssenyonjo, Manisuli, *Economic, Social and Cultural Rights in International Law* (Hart Publishing, 2009).

Stamatopoulou, Elsa, *Cultural Rights in International Law: Article 27 of the Universal Declaration of Human Rights and Beyond* (Martinus Nijhoff, 2007).

Stanners, David and Bourdeau, Philippe, *Europe's Environment, The Dobris Assessment.* (European Environmental Agency, 1995).

Stavenhagen, Rodolfo, 'Cultural Rights: A Social Science Perspective', in Asbjorn Eide et al. (eds), *Economic, Social and Cultural Rights—A Textbook* (Martinus Nijhoff, 2001.

Stephens, Tim, *International Courts and Environmental Protection* (Cambridge University Press, 2009).

Stevenson, E., *Culture and Citizenship* (Sage, 2001).

Stewart, Pemala J. and Strathern, Andrew (eds), *Landscape, Heritage, and Conservation. Farming Issues in the European Union* (Carolina Academic Press, 2010).

Stewart, Pemala J. and Strathern, Andrew (eds), *Landscape, Memory and History, Anthropological Perspectives* (Pluto, 2003).

Stråth, Bo, 'A European Identity: The Historical Limits of a Concept', *European Journal of Social Theory*, 5 (4) 387– 401.

Strecker, Amy, 'The Law is at Fault? Landscape and Agency in International Law', in Tim Waterman and Ed Wall (eds), *Landscape and Agency* (Ashgate, 2017), 52–65.

Strecker, Amy, 'The Human Dimension to Landscape Protection in International Law', in Federico Lenzerini and Silvia Borelli (eds), *Cultural Heritage, Cultural Rights, Cultural Diversity: New Developments in International Law* (M. Nijhoff, 2012), 327–47.

Strecker, Amy, 'The "Right to Landscape" in International Law', in Jala Makhzoumi, Shelley Egoz, and Gloria Pungetti (eds), *The Right to Landscape: Contesting Landscape and Human Rights* (Ashgate, 2011), 57–71.

Sundseth, Kerstin, *Natura 2000. Protecting Europe's biodiversity* (Council of Europe Publishing, 2008).

Supanich, Gary, 'The Legal Basis of Intergenerational Responsibility: An Alternative View—The Sense of Intergenerational Identity', *Yearbook of International Environmental Law*, 3 (1) (1992), 94–107.

Symonides, Janusz, 'Cultural Rights: An Underdeveloped Category of Human Rights', *International Social Sciences Journal*, 50 (1998), 158.

Taylor, William, *The Geography of Law: Landscape, Identity and Regulation*. (Hart Publishing, 2006).

Thompson, Georges, 'La Communauté européenne et le paysage' *Revue juridique de l'environnement*, No. 4, (1993) 541–76.

Tolba, Mostafa K., *The Implications of the Common Concern of Mankind Concept on Global Environmental Issues,* Note of the Executive Director of UNEP to the Group of Legal Experts meeting, Malta, 13-15 December, 1990, available at: <http://www.juridicas.unam.mx/>.

Torsello, Mario L., *Il Codice dei Beni Culturali e del Paesaggio*, 1 Commento, 2004.

Treves, Tullio et al. (eds), *Civil Society, International Courts and Compliance Bodies* (Press, 2005).

Tuan, Yi-Fu, 'Thought and Landscape: The Eye and the Mind's Eye', in Donald W. Meinig (ed.), *The Interpretation of Ordinary Landscapes* (Oxford University Press, 1979), 89–102.

Tuan, Yi-Fu, 'Foreward', in Kenneth Olwig, *Landscape, Nature and the Body Politic: From Britain's Renaissance to America's New World* (University of Wisconsin Press, 2002), xix.

Turk, Alexander, *Judicial Review in EU Law* (Elgar Publishing, 2009).

Turner, Jane, *The Dictionary of Art* (Macmillan, Vol. 18).

Ucko, Peter J. and Layton, Robert (eds), T*he Archaeology and Anthropology of Landscape: Shaping your Landscape*. One World Archaeology 30 (papers from the 1994 World Archaeology Congress, New Delhi) (Routledge, 1999).

Underkuffler, Laura S., *The Idea of Property. Its Meaning and Power* (Oxford University Press, 2003).

Underkuffler, Laura S., 'On Property. An Essay', *Yale Law Journal*, 100 127, reprinted in Elizabeth Mensh and Alan Freeman (eds), *Property Law. International Library of Essays in Law and Legal Theory* (New York University Press, 1992).

Unerstall, Herwig, 'Public Participation in the Management and Establishment of the Natura 2000 Network: Legal Framework and Administrative Practices in Selected Member States', *Journal for Environmental Planning Law*, 5 (2008) 35–68.

UNESCO World Heritage Centre: Cultural Landscapes, The Challenges of Conservation. Proceedings of the Conference: Shared Legacy, Common Responsibility, 11–12 November 2002, Ferrara, Italy, *World Heritage Papers 7*, 2002.

Vadi, Valentina, 'Cultural Heritage and Investment Law: A Stormy Relationship', *IJCP*, 15 (2008), 1–24.

Vasak, Karel, 'Pour une troisième génération des droits de l'homme', in Cristophe Swinarski (ed.), *Essays on International Humanitarian Law and Red Cross Principles in Honour of Jean Pictet* (Martinus Nijhoff, 1984).

Von Droste, Bernd, Plachter Harald and Rössler Mechtild (eds), *Cultural Landscapes of Universal Value* (Gustav Fischer Verlag, 1995).

Von Droste, Bernd et al., *Linking Nature and Culture. Report on the Global Strategy, Natural and Cultural Heritage Expert Meeting, 25–29 March 1998*, Amsterdam, Netherlands.

Von Schorlemer, Sabine, 'Compliance with the World Heritage Convention: Reflections on the Elbe Valley and the Dresden Waldschlössen Bridge', *German Yearbook of International Law*, 51 (2008), 321–90.

Vrdoljak, Ana, 'Minorities, Cultural Rights and Intangible Heritage', *ESIL Research Forum on International Law Contemporary Issues.* Geneva 26–28, May 2005.

Wates, Jeremy, 'NGOs and the Aarhus Convention', in Tullio Treves et al. *Civil Society, International Courts and Compliance Bodies* (Asser Press, 2005),

Weeranmantry, Christopher G., Human Rights and Scientific and Technological Progress, in Janusz Symonides, *Human Rights: New Dimensions and Challenges* (Ashgate, 1998), 245–46.

Westra, L., *Environmental Justice and the Rights of Indigenous Peoples, International and Domestic Legal Perspectives* (Earthscan, 2008).

Wellens, Karen, 'Revisiting Solidarity as (Re) Emerging Constitutional Principle', in Rüdiger Wolfrum (ed.), *Solidarity: A Structural Principle of International Law* (Springer, 2010), 3–54.

Wellens, Karen and Komori Teruo, *Public Interest Rules of International Law. Towards Effective Implementation* (Ashgate, 2009).

Whiston Spirn, A., *The Language of Landscape* (Yale University Press, 1998).

Weiss, Thomas G. and Thakur, Ramesh, *The UN and Global Governance: An Idea and its Prospects* (Indiana University Press, 2010).

Wilhelm, M. 'L'Entendue des Droits a l'Identité a la Lumière des Droits Autochtones', in Meyer-Bisch, P. (ed.), *Les Droits Culturels, une catégorie sous-développée de droits de l'homme, Actes du VIIIe Colloque interdisciplinaire sure les droits de l'homme*, (Editions Universitaires Fribourg Suisse, 1993), 226 ff.

Williams, Raymond, *Problems in Materialism and Culture* (Verso, 1980).
Williams, Sue, The Desire to Protect and Preserve, UNESCO *Sources* No. 80/ June 1996.
Wolfrum, Rudiger and Kojima Chie (eds), *Solidarity: A Structural Principle of International Law* (Springer, 2009).
Wolfrum, Rudiger and Roben, Volker (eds), *Development of International Law in Treaty Making* (Springer, 2005).
Wylie, John, *Landscape* (Routledge, 2007).
Xanthaki, Alexandra, *Indigenous Rights and United Nations Standards: Self-Determination, Culture and Land* (Cambridge University Press, 2009).
Zacharias, Diana, *The International Regime for the Protection of the World Cultural and Natural Heritage* (Verlag, 2002).
Zemanek, Karl, 'New Trends in the Enforcement of Erga Omnes Obligations', 4 *Max Plank Y.B.* U.N.L. 1, 2000.
Zoido Naranjo, Florencio, *Paísaje y Ordenación del Territorio* (Junta de Andalucía-Fundación Duques de Soria, 2002).

Index